PROZESSE REFLEXIVEN ENTWERFENS
PROCESSES OF REFLEXIVE DESIGN

PROZESSE REFLEXIVEN ENTWERFENS
PROCESSES OF REFLEXIVE DESIGN

Margitta Buchert (ed.)

a_ku jovis

PROZESSE PROCESSES

TREIBENDE KRÄFTE
DRIVING FORCES

VERSCHRÄNKUNGEN
ENTANGLEMENTS

TRANSFORMATION
TRANSFORMATION

PREFACE

Margitta Buchert

Various facets of the genesis, transformation and interaction of design and research are presented in this book REFLEXIVE DESIGN PROCESSES. Perspectives that have already been accorded importance in 'classical' design-related research and furthermore constitute a recurring topic in current discourses and in practice are highlighted innovatively and previous discussions are extended productively. What type of processes and process characteristics can be differentiated against the background of various bodies of knowledge that cannot be fully grasped and different influences? How do creative processes and systemization work affect each other? Which design-related and which knowledge-generating possibilities of action come to the fore? How are specific forms of knowledge and their interactions generated, evaluated and transformed? The book presents a wide spectrum of approaches, descriptions and explorations of different types of processes and process characteristics within the dynamics of design and research. It shows what cognitive, structural and esthetic potential the thematization of processes holds and how this can be understood exemplarily and communicated in terms of the relevance of high-quality design of the human living environment.

The publication preceeded the 8th International DARA Symposium on Design and Research in Architecture and Landscape, which was held in April 2018 in Hannover-Herrenhausen. The ten thematically varied contributions by authors from practice, research and teaching bring together basic levels of understanding, illuminate various types of process and their properties, as well as outline possibilities and research potential. They present new impulse-giving perspectives on the combination of scientific

VORWORT

Margitta Buchert

Verschiedene Facetten der Genese, Transformation und Interaktion von Entwerfen und Forschen werden im vorliegenden Buch PROZESSE REFLEXIVEN ENTWERFENS aufgezeigt. Perspektiven, die bereits in ‚klassischen' Entwurfsforschungen Bedeutung erhielten und ebenso ein wiederkehrendes Thema in aktuellen Diskursen und in der Praxis bilden, werden innovativ akzentuiert und bisherige Diskussionen gewinnbringend erweitert. Welche Art von Prozessen und Prozesseigenschaften können vor dem Hintergrund nicht vollständig greifbarer verschiedenartiger Wissensbestände und unterschiedlicher Einflüsse differenziert werden? Wie wirken Systematisierungsarbeit und kreative Prozesse ineinander? Welche entwerferischen und welche wissenschaffenden Handlungsmöglichkeiten treten dabei in den Vordergrund? Wie werden spezifische Wissensformen und ihre Interaktionen generiert, evaluiert und transformiert? Dazu wird ein breites Spektrum der Erschließung, Beschreibung und Erprobung unterschiedlicher Typen von Prozessen und Prozesseigenschaften in den Dynamiken des Entwerfens und Forschens vorgeschlagen. Es wird aufgezeigt, auf welche kognitiven, strukturellen und ästhetischen Potentiale die Thematisierung von Prozessen hinweist und wie diese beispielhaft für die Relevanz qualitätsvoller Gestaltung des menschlichen Lebensumfelds verstanden und kommuniziert werden können.

Der Publikation ging das 8. Internationale DARA-Symposium zum Entwerfen und Forschen in Architektur und Landschaft voraus, das im April 2018 in Hannover-Herrenhausen stattfand. Die zehn Beiträge von Autorinnen und Autoren aus Praxis, Forschung und Lehre bündeln in thematisch vielfältigen Beiträgen grundlegende Verständnisebenen, beleuchten verschiedene Prozessarten und ihre Eigenschaften und skizzieren Möglichkeitsräume und Forschungspotentiale. Sie präsentieren neue impulsgebende Positionen zur Kombination wissenschaftlicher und praxisnaher Forschung. Vor dem Hintergrund der stetig wachsenden Relevanz von ebenso intensiv wie kontrovers geführten Diskursen zur Entwurfsforschung sowie zu Verbindungen von Entwerfen und Forschen in Architektur,

and practice-related design. In view of the increasing relevance of both intense and controversial discussions about design-related research, as well as the connections between design and research in architecture, landscape architecture and urban design, the relationship between design and research is probed in a way that is less the precise result of methodical derivations or systematic deductions and more of an integration and linking of various, even 'imperfect', methodological approaches. The contributions touch on exemplary as well as superordinate questions and reveal many interconnections. They have been compiled within the three framework subject areas of 'driving forces', 'entanglements' and 'transformation', thereby opening up the possibility of linking design and research and their relationships with various formation and knowledge-gaining activities. Furthermore, it also provides an opportunity to outline a new and reinforce the significance of architecture and planning culture qualities for the creative design of the human living environment. Of course, the scope of the questions and discourses in these contributions cannot be exhaustive, but some areas can therefore be expounded in greater detail. The approaches to PROCESSES of design and research emerge themselves as creative acts, whose interplay shows on how many levels insight production and knowledge genesis are conceptualized and can be carried out.

Special thanks go to the contributing authors for their varied texts and the pleasant cooperation. A big thank you also to the team at jovis Verlag for the reliable and high-quality cooperation, as well as Lynne Kolar-Thompson for the accomplished translation of the German texts into English, as well as Steffen Bösenberg for knowledgeable translations into German, and the a_ku-team, first and foremost Julian Benny Hung for the contribution to the development and implementation of the layout and graphics, Sarah Wehmeyer for the organization of the symposium and logistical tasks, as well as both and Steffen Bösenberg for a variety of editorial work. Not least, we would like to thank the Faculty for Architecture and Landscape and Leibniz University Hanover for supporting the symposium and the publication.

Landschaftsarchitektur und Städtebau wird hier das Spannungsverhältnis von Entwerfen und Forschen in einer Weise ergründet, die weniger präzises Ergebnis methodischer Ableitungen oder systematischer Deduktionen ist als vielmehr verschiedene, auch ‚unperfekte', methodische Annäherungen integriert und verbindet. Die Beiträge berühren exemplarische ebenso wie übergreifende Fragen und weisen untereinander zahlreiche Bezüge auf. Sie wurden zu den drei rahmenden Themenbereichen ‚Treibende Kräfte', ‚Verschränkungen' und ‚Transformation' zusammengestellt und damit die Möglichkeit geöffnet, Entwerfen und Forschen und ihre Relationen mit verschiedenen Entstehungs- und Erkenntnisgeschehen zu verbinden. Darüber hinaus kann so auch die Möglichkeit geöffnet werden, die Bedeutung architektur- und planungskultureller Qualitäten für die kreative Gestaltung des Lebensumfelds der Menschen neu zu konturieren und zu stärken. Selbstverständlich ist das Fragen- und Diskursfeld in diesen Beiträgen nicht erschöpfend zu erfassen, doch kann es damit in einigen Anteilen expliziert werden. Die Annäherungen an PROZESSE von Entwerfen und Forschen treten dabei selbst als kreative Akte hervor, die im Zusammenspiel aufzeigen, auf wie vielen Ebenen Erkenntnisproduktion und Wissensgenese konzeptualisiert werden und erfolgen kann.

An dieser Stelle sei insbesondere den mitwirkenden Autoren und Autorinnen herzlich gedankt für ihre vielseitigen Beiträge und die angenehme Zusammenarbeit. Ein großer Dank geht auch an das Team des jovis Verlags für die zuverlässige und qualitätsvolle Zusammenarbeit sowie an Lynne Kolar Thompson für die gelungene Übertragung deutscher Texte ins Englische sowie an Steffen Bösenberg für verständnisreiche Übersetzungen ins Deutsche. Ebenso gilt ein großer Dank dem a_ku-Team, an erster Stelle Julian Benny Hung, für die Mitentwicklung und Umsetzung von Layout und Grafik, an Sarah Wehmeyer für die Organisation des Symposiums sowie logistische Tätigkeiten sowie beiden und Steffen Bösenberg für diverse Lektoratsarbeiten. Nicht zuletzt sei ein Dank an die Fakultät für Architektur und Landschaft und die Leibniz Universität Hannover gerichtet für die Unterstützung des Symposiums und der Veröffentlichung.

CONCEIVING PROCESSES

Margitta Buchert

It is by all means customary to view designing, planning and research as a process, like any action. These actions comprise the intention, purpose, idea, initial decisions and concepts, consolidation, specification, recursive loops and realization, forming an almost banal fact and an inherent aspect. The associated connotations of the notion of 'process' or 'processual' comprise words such as procedure, development, progress, duration, becoming, transformation – all terms that incorporate time and change in a qualitative and active sense. This opens up sheer endless potential for questions about processes and process characteristics in connection with reflexive design. Even if insights on this subject can neither be reduced to individual schemata nor be fully grasped linguistically, there are more general superordinate aspects that allow approximations. These are the subject of focus on here within an outlined framework. The intention is to show with which reference points the focusing on processes can reveal a variety of ways of thinking as impulses, in order to present and stimulate innovative research methods from the field of design. The resulting bodies of knowledge are outlined not least to spur on the further research-related qualification and viable future spatial-physical design actions in the human living environment.

PROZESSE DENKEN

Margitta Buchert

Es ist durchaus vertraut, Entwerfen, Planen und Forschen wie jede Handlung als Prozess zu sehen. Intention, Absicht, Idee, erste Entscheidungen und Konzepte, Vertiefung, Konkretion und rekursive Schleifen bis hin zur Realisierung konstituieren diese Handlungen, bilden schlicht eine nahezu banale Gegebenheit und einen immanenten Anteil. Im Konnotationsfeld von ‚Prozess' bzw. ‚prozessual' finden sich Worte wie Verlauf, Entwicklung, Fortgang, Dauer, Werden, Wandel – allesamt Begriffe, die Zeit und Veränderung in einem qualitativen und aktiven Sinne einbeziehen. Damit öffnet sich ein schier unendliches Fragenpotential zu Prozessen und Prozesseigenschaften im Zusammenhang reflexiven Entwerfens. Auch wenn Erkenntnisse dazu weder auf einzelne Schemata reduziert noch sprachlich vollständig erfasst werden können, gibt es allgemeinere übergreifende Aspekte, die eine Annäherung erlauben. Ihnen wird hier in einer skizzenhaften Rahmung Aufmerksamkeit geschenkt. Die Intention ist es, darzulegen, mit welchen Ansatzpunkten die Fokussierung von Prozessen verschiedene Denkmöglichkeiten impulsgebend eröffnet, um innovative Forschungsweisen aus dem Entwurfsbereich aufzuzeigen und zu stimulieren. Die daraus erwachsenden Wissensbestände werden umrissen, um damit nicht zuletzt die weitere forschende Qualifizierung und zukunftsfähige räumlich-physische Gestaltungshandlungen im Lebensumfeld des Menschen anzufeuern.

DESIGN AND RESEARCH The focus on processes takes place within the superordinate context of 'Reflexive Design'. One of the basic motivations for this conceptual constellation was to sound out perspectives on how design and research can be combined for spatial considerations and how research can be viewed from a different perspective due to a better understanding of design. The concept of a threefold structure of research activities according to their focus and objective in research 'through, about or for' creative and artistic development was published 25 years ago at the London College of Art for the taxonomy of research in the arts and in design.[1] Since then, this triad has achieved a prominent status and has been partially modified and extended in the field of design-related research that has developed strongly in recent decades.[2] What possibilities present themselves if the focus is less on the search for closed categories and more on questions about the specific intelligence, capabilities and knowledge genesis of design and design-related research?[3] What impulses can then be generated for research practice and future design and what specific ways of experiencing and perceiving become evident in all their diversity? With 'Reflexive Design', a subject area has been generated as an open and flexible setting that provides the possibility, in the connection of design and research and their manifold relationships, to grasp forms of knowledge and methods of perception in an innovative manner.[4] In this context, reflexion is understood in such a way that it not only explores and shows how things are, but also speculates on how things could be, with the aim of triggering something that drives the practice of research and design forwards. The 'and' that is contained indirectly in the conceptual constellation – of reflexion/reflexivity and design as well as of design and research – emphatically promotes the possibility of not focusing on a specific determined relation, but of exploring the superordinate routes of a wide variety of relations and thereby providing a platform for what they create.[5]

E N T W E R F E N   U N D   F O R S C H E N   Die Thematisierung von Prozessen erfolgt im übergreifenden Fragenfeld von ‚Reflexivem Entwerfen'. Eine Grundmotivation für diese begriffliche Konstellation war es, Dimensionen auszuloten, wie Entwerfen und Forschen für räumliche Fragestellungen verbunden werden können und wie Forschen aus dem besseren Verständnis des Entwerfens aus einer anderen Perspektive betrachtet werden kann. Das Konzept einer Dreigliederung forschender Tätigkeiten nach ihrem Fokus und Ziel in Forschung ‚durch, über oder für' das entwerferische und künstlerische Schaffen wurde vor 25 Jahren am Londoner College of Art für die Taxonomie von Forschung in den Künsten und im Design publiziert.[1] Seitdem hat diese Trias einen prominenten Status erreicht und wurde in dem sich in den letzten Jahrzehnten stark entwickelnden Feld der Entwurfsforschung in Teilen variiert und erweitert.[2] Doch welche Möglichkeiten öffnen sich, wenn weniger die Suche nach geschlossenen Kategorien als vielmehr das Fragen nach der spezifischen Intelligenz, nach den Vermögen und der Wissensgenese von Entwerfen und Entwurfsforschung in den Vordergrund tritt?[3] Welche Impulse für die Forschungspraxis und zukünftiges Entwerfen können dann generiert und welche spezifischen Weisen von Erfahrung und Erkenntnis in ihrer Vielfalt sichtbar werden? Mit ‚Reflexivem Entwerfen' wurde ein Themenbereich als offenes und flexibles Setting generiert, mit dem in Verbindung von Entwerfen und Forschen und ihrer vielfältigen Relationen die Möglichkeit gesehen wird, Wissensformen und Erkenntnisweisen auf innovative Weise zu fassen.[4] Reflexion wird in diesem Zusammenhang so verstanden, dass sie nicht nur erkundet und aufzeigt, was ist, sondern auch spekuliert, was sein könnte, mit dem Ziel, etwas anzustoßen, das die Praxis vorantreibt, die Praxis des Forschens und des Entwerfens. Das ‚und', das in der Begriffskonstellation indirekt enthalten ist – von Reflexion/Reflexivität und Entwerfen sowie von Entwerfen und Forschen –, befördert nachdrücklich die Möglichkeit, nicht eine spezifische determinierte Relation im Blick zu haben, sondern die übergreifenden Routen verschiedenster Relationen zu erkunden und damit dem Raum zu geben, was sie hervorbringen.[5]

PROCESS SHAPE Given that designing and researching, as actions and events, naturally have a process character, it is possible to extract descriptions of and insights into processes from almost all studies relating to the research and exploration of design. So far there have only been tentative approaches to specifying how the special forms of production in design can be developed in conjunction with research processes. In relation to the logic of procedure, to systematic proceeding and to rationally determined design methods, reference is made to the 'Design Methods Movement' of the 1960s and 70s, as well as to more recent research on parametric and digital design.[6] Donald Schön's studies about the 'reflective practitioner' relating to understanding and communication levels in project developments and learning processes, or Nigel Cross's concepts of specific 'designerly ways of knowing', focused on phenomena such as creativity, reflection and implicit knowledge in connection with design processes.[7] They are among the studies that since the 1980s have increasingly shown the interplay of rational and intuitive levels and thus prompted further questions about the more concrete character of processes and process characteristics.[8] In the last two decades, it is especially transdisciplinary methodological tendencies that have provided impulses for design-related research, targeted towards practices and drawing interest to action procedures and behavior that had hitherto been disregarded, which are routinized and connected with implicit knowledge, including the ways of proceeding in the sciences themselves.[9] They flowed into different methodological approaches to research-related design in architecture that have been suggested in more recent times, such as the updating of the traditional view of visual and sculptural design tools or of historical and contemporary design and research methods.[10] The project 'Reflexive Design' is situated within this context, with the specific focus of exploring design knowledge for spatial considerations through examining the dense relationships between design and research and the relevance of reflexivity and reflexion as epistemic and creative generators in light of the theory and practice context. This position of 'Reflexive Design' is targeted mainly towards how the world could be. The question of the process structure can be understood as one of several knowledge-generating explorations in an ongoing search process. What is already known is refined and extended to illuminate further dimensions of reflexive design and to drive further exploration forwards. Overall it is therefore a process of increasing differentiation and structuring.

PROZESSGESTALT Da Entwerfen und Forschen als Handlungen und Geschehen selbstverständlich Prozesscharakter haben, können aus nahezu allen auf die Erforschung des Entwerfens bezogenen Studien Beschreibungen von und Erkenntnisse zu Prozessen extrahiert werden. Wie die besonderen Formen des Hervorbringens im Entwerfen mit Forschungsprozessen koevolutiv entwickelt werden können, blieb bislang nur in Ansätzen erfasst. Bezogen auf die Logik des Ablaufs, auf systematisches Vorgehen und rational gesteuerte Entwurfswege sei auf das ‚Design Methods Movement' der 1960er und 70er Jahre ebenso verwiesen wie auf neuere Forschungen zum parametrischen und digitalen Entwerfen.[6] Donald Schöns auf Verstehens- und Kommunikationsebenen in Projektentwicklungen und in Lernprozessen bezogene Studien zum ‚Reflective Practitioner' oder Nigel Cross' Konzepte zu spezifischen Wissensarten von Entwerfenden, zu ‚Designerly ways of knowing', thematisierten Phänomene wie Kreativität, Reflexion und implizites Wissen im Zusammenhang mit Entwurfsprozessen.[7] Sie zählen zu den Studien, die verstärkt seit den 1980er Jahren das Zusammenspiel von rationalen und intuitiven Ebenen aufzeigten und damit weitere Fragen zum konkreteren Charakter von Prozessen und Prozesseigenschaften anregten.[8] Impulsgebend für die Entwurfsforschung wirkten in den letzten beiden Jahrzehnten insbesondere disziplinübergreifende methodische Umschwünge, die auf Praktiken gerichtet sind und das Interesse auf Vorgänge des Handelns und Verhaltensakte richteten, die bislang unbeachtet blieben, die routinisiert und mit implizitem Wissen verbunden sind, inklusive der Handlungsweisen in den Wissenschaften selbst.[9] Sie flossen ein in unterschiedliche methodische Annäherungen an das Erforschen von Entwerfen in der Architektur, die in jüngerer Zeit vorgeschlagen wurden, wie die Aktualisierung des traditionsreichen Blicks auf die visuellen und plastischen Instrumente des Entwerfens oder auf historische und zeitgenössische Entwurfs- und Forschungsmethoden.[10] In diesem Zusammenhang situiert sich das Projekt ‚Reflexives Entwerfen' mit dem spezifischen Fokus, das Wissen des Entwerfens für räumliche Fragestellungen über die Thematisierung der dichten Relationen von Entwerfen und Forschen und die Relevanz von Reflexivität und Reflexion als epistemische und kreative Generatoren aus dem Theorie- und Praxiskontext heraus zu erforschen. Diese Position richtet sich hauptsächlich auf die Welt, wie sie sein könnte. Die Frage nach der Prozessgestalt kann dabei in einem anhaltenden Prozess der Suche als eine von mehreren wissensgenerierenden Erprobungen verstanden werden. Bereits Erkanntes wird verfeinert und erweitert, um weitere Dimensionen reflexiven Entwerfens zu erhellen und weitere Erkundung voranzutreiben. Es handelt sich somit übergreifend um einen Prozess zunehmender Differenzierung und Strukturierung.

'Those who do research do not know, but feel their way forwards, tinker, hesitate, keep their decisions in suspense.'

Michel Serres

„Wer forscht, weiß nicht, sondern tastet sich vorwärts, bastelt, zögert, hält seine Entscheidungen in der Schwebe."

Michel Serres

COMPLEX ORDER It is a challenge to empirically describe design and research and their relationships in architecture and landscape based on phenomena of processes and process characteristics. Design and research processes rarely have a permanent nature and involve numerous actions, even if they are methodologically directed or parametrically supported.[11] A light is cast, for example, on considerations of ordering methods, as well as of the beginning, the procedure and cultural contexts, of techniques for developing structures and rules of progression for ordering concepts, sorting or variant production and for decisions for which there are driving forces and in most cases defined objectives.[12] Apart from the conditions of the specific task and situation, which channel the procedures to certain degrees, subconscious and unreflective, habituated ways of perceiving, thinking and acting often intervene in the processes, which can be understood as a basic conception and as implicit knowledge, in individual practices.[13] In addition, design and research can be interwoven explicitly in a wide variety of ways, incorporating their very own tools and ways of proceeding, to bring forth new knowledge on the basis of actions, experiences, events and interpretations. Not least, attributed values must also be emphasized, which guide and accompany the processes and nuance the ways of proceeding, as well as the genesis of knowledge.[14] It is these that help to generate ordering frameworks in the multi-perspectivity. They reduce complexity before and during the iterative processes in design and research, even if this does not rule out the presence of other options.[15] It is the observation from a distance that takes on a special generative role in the process, in the individual design and research process, as well as in superordinate development processes, alongside trying out and doing, in the sense of an observation that is characterized by properties that combine esthetic, cognitive and reflexive aspects variously and refer to an undetermined framework of knowledge.[16] Reflexion, reflexivity and creative phases are closely interwoven in the processes of design and research in complex orders determined to varying extents. The search for specific properties, interactions and the relevance of process structures is therefore especially linked to dimensions of 'Reflexive Design'.

K O M P L E X E   O R D N U N G Entwerfen und Forschen und ihre Relationen in Architektur und Landschaft ausgehend von Phänomenen der Prozesse und Prozesseigenschaften empirisch zu beschreiben, ist eine Herausforderung. Entwurfs- wie auch Forschungsprozesse haben selten eine permanente Charakteristik und involvieren zahlreiche Aktionen, auch dann, wenn sie methodisch angeleitet oder parametrisch unterstützt werden.[11] In den Blick geraten dabei beispielsweise Fragen nach Ordnungsweisen, nach Anfang, Verlauf und kulturellen Kontexten, nach Techniken in der Ausbildung von Strukturen und Regeln des Fortschreitens für Anordnungen von Konzipieren, Sortieren oder Varianten-Produzieren und für Entscheidungen, für die es treibende Kräfte und in den überwiegenden Fällen bestimmte Ziele gibt.[12] Neben den Bedingungen der spezifischen Aufgabe und Situation, die Vorgehensweisen in gewissen Graden kanalisieren, greifen in den Prozessen oft unbewusste und unreflektierte habitualisierte Wahrnehmungs-, Denk- und Handlungsweisen, die als Grundkonzeption und als implizites Wissen verstanden werden können, in individuellen Praktiken ineinander.[13] Zudem können Entwerfen und Forschen unter Einbezug ureigener entwerferischer Instrumente und Vorgehensweisen explizit in unterschiedlichsten Weisen miteinander verschränkt werden, um aufgrund von Aktionen, Erfahrungen, Ereignissen und Interpretationen neues Wissen hervorzubringen. Nicht zuletzt sind auch Wertsetzungen hervorzuheben, welche die Prozesse leiten und begleiten und Vorgehensweisen wie auch die Genese des Wissens nuancieren.[14] Sie sind es, die ordnende Rahmungen in der Multiperspektivität miterzeugen. Sie reduzieren Komplexität vor und während der iterativen Prozesse im Entwerfen und Forschen, auch wenn dadurch das Vorhandensein anderer Optionen nicht ausgeschlossen wird.[15] Es ist das distanznehmende Betrachten, das im Prozess, im einzelnen Entwurfs- und Forschungsprozess wie auch bei übergreifenden Entwicklungsprozessen, neben dem Ausprobieren und Machen eine besondere generative Rolle einnimmt, im Sinne eines Betrachtens, das durch Eigenschaften charakterisiert ist, die Ästhetisches, Kognitives und Reflexives unterschiedlich vermischen und auf ein unbestimmtes Wissensgefüge verweisen.[16] Reflexion, Reflexivität und kreative Phasen sind in den Prozessen des Entwerfens und des Forschens in komplexen, unterschiedlich stark determinierten Ordnungen eng verwoben. So ist die Suche nach den spezifischen Eigenschaften, den Interaktionen und der Relevanz von Prozessgestalten in besonderer Weise verbunden mit Dimensionen ‚Reflexiven Entwerfens'.

DRIVING FORCES | ENTANGLEMENTS | TRANSFORMATION It is already evident from this preliminary description that a heterogenous collection of processes and accordingly also a multitude of process characteristics can be observed and can only be grasped tentatively in research. More specific and innovative understanding can be achieved through individual observations and precisely targeted questioning. For the purposes of more refined specification of ways of proceeding, events and knowledge gathering, conceptual frameworks have been suggested and specified as navigational guides for the levels of understanding of the contributions selected for this book: DRIVING FORCES, ENTANGLEMENTS and TRANSFORMATION.[17] These different aspects, in which the imagination, esthetics and practical handling are connected, with logic, analysis and systemization attempts coming to the fore alongside the specifics of integration, synthesis formation and speculation, each have their own characteristics and each display different means of observation, examination and knowledge genesis. They also reflect various discursive and contextual horizons and show certain parallels and overlaps to a larger or smaller degree. The conceptual field of DRIVING FORCES characterizes dimensions of the 'knowledge-ability' of process characteristics, as well as ways of thinking and acting that stimulate the approaches to and initiations of design processes and various phases of its unfolding in a targeted and regulatory manner. Driving forces are also involved in conditions of the situational context and in the development of the individual basic concept and stance, as well as in questions about how generic and specific processes are interwoven in the consolidating procedure. Where designers in architecture, landscape architecture and urban design interact exploratively with central design media, such as visual media or models, there is the possibility of a differentiated understanding of the dense relationships between design and research in ENTANGLEMENTS of varying types. These can be viewed not only as actions and (re)presentations in the context of design projects, but at the same time as segments of researching processes in which these were found and whose epistemic dimensions of 'making visible' go beyond the individual project. Finally, TRANSFORMATION refers to the wider spectrum in the historical course of events and to the intention of achieving transformational effectiveness with the concepts and projects by means of processes of modification and alternative construction. Exemplary approaches to explorative and experimental practice can contribute here to enriching knowledge within the horizon of the living environment about how dense relationships between design and research can be newly constituted.

TREIBENDE KRÄFTE I VERSCHRÄNKUNGEN I TRANSFORMATION Aus dieser vorläufigen Beschreibung kann bereits deutlich werden, dass eine heterogene Sammlung von Prozessen und dementsprechend auch eine Vielzahl von Prozesseigenschaften zu beobachten und daher forschend nur näherungsweise zu erfassen sind. Spezifischere und innovative Verständnisse können über Einzelbeobachtungen und präziser zugeschnittene Fragestellungen erlangt werden. Zur Orientierung und feineren Bestimmung von Vorgehensweisen, Ereignissen und Erkenntnisgeschehen wurden für die Verständnisebenen der für dieses Buch ausgewählten Beiträge begriffliche Fassungen als Navigationshilfen vorgeschlagen und charakterisiert: TREIBENDE KRÄFTE, VERSCHRÄNKUNGEN und TRANSFORMATION.[17] Diese verschiedenen Ebenen, in denen Imagination, Ästhetik und praktisches Handeln verknüpft sind und damit neben Logik, Analyse und Systematisierungsversuchen Spezifika von Integration, Synthesebildung und Spekulation hervortreten, haben je eigene Charakteristiken und zeigen je verschiedene Mittel der Beobachtung, Untersuchung und Wissensgenese. Sie spiegeln zudem diverse diskursive und kontextuelle Horizonte und weisen ebenfalls, mehr oder weniger deutlich hervortretend, einige Parallelen und Überschneidungen auf. Mit dem begrifflichen Feld TREIBENDE KRÄFTE werden Dimensionen des ‚Wissen-Könnens' von Prozesseigenschaften charakterisiert wie Denk- und Handlungsweisen, die Annäherungen und den Einstieg in Entwurfsprozesse und verschiedene Phasen seines Verlaufs gezielt stimulieren und ihn regulieren können. Ebenfalls sind treibende Kräfte in Bedingungen des situativen Kontexts und in der Entwicklung der individuellen Grundkonzeption und Haltung einbezogen und im weiteren Fragen danach, wie generische und spezifische Prozesse im konkretisierenden Vorgehen ineinandergreifen. Dort, wo Entwerfende in Architektur, Landschaftsarchitektur und Städtebau mit zentralen Medien der Entwurfstätigkeit forschend interagieren wie bildlichen Medien oder Modellen, öffnet sich ein Feld zum differenzierteren Verständnis dichter Relationen von Entwerfen und Forschen in VERSCHRÄNKUNGEN unterschiedlicher Art. Diese können nicht nur als Aktionen und (Re-)Präsentationen im Rahmen entwerferischer Projekte gesehen werden, vielmehr zugleich auch als Segmente forschender Prozesse, in denen zu ihnen gefunden wurde und deren epistemische Dimensionen des ‚Sichtbarmachens' über das Einzelprojekt hinausweisen. TRANSFORMATION schließlich verweist auf den größeren Spannungsbogen im historischen Verlauf und ebenso auf die Intention, mit den Konzepten und Projekten transformatorische Wirksamkeit zu erreichen über Prozesse der Modifikation und alternativen Konstruktion. Exemplarische Annäherungen explorativer und experimenteller Praxis können hier dazu beitragen, im Horizont der Lebenswelt das Wissen darüber zu bereichern, wie dichte Relationen von Entwerfen und Forschen neu konstituiert werden können.

METAMORPHOSES OF COGNITION The differentiation approaches gained through the comparative discourse analysis from the individual researches also prove in further comparisons to be relatively stable. Even if this draws attention to a network of artefacts that incorporates hybrid actors, design and research processes in the context of 'Reflexive Design' do not take place without the individual people, as part of specific social, cultural and historical contexts and featuring imagination and non-cognitive aspects that contribute to shaping processes and process properties.[18] Despite many and welcome techno-social developments, one cannot speak of a methodologically generalizable field of knowledge. One must therefore steer a middle course between generalizable knowledge and that which is individual and at the same time culturally defined. Iterations of indetermination and new clarity also remain. Finally, the new knowledge gained also presents new possibilities of recognizing new gaps in knowledge, thereby encouraging further research. Thinking about processes stimulates metamorphoses of cognition and remains complex, challenging and stimulating.

METAMORPHOSEN DES ERKENNENS Die über die vergleichende Diskursanalyse aus den Einzelforschungen gewonnenen Differenzierungsansätze erweisen sich auch im weiteren Vergleich als relativ stabil. Auch wenn damit der Blick auf ein Netzwerk von Artefakten gelenkt wird, die hybride Akteure einbeziehen, finden Prozesse von Entwerfen und Forschen im Kontext ‚Reflexiven Entwerfens' nicht ohne die individuellen Menschen statt, eingebunden in spezifische soziale, kulturelle und historische Kontexte und ausgestattet mit Imagination und mit nicht-kognitiven Eigenschaften, die Prozesse und Prozesseigenschaften mitgestalten.[18] Trotz zahlreicher und begrüßenswerter technosozialer Entwicklungen kann von einem methodologisch generalisierbaren Erkenntnissubjekt nicht gesprochen werden. Es bleibt bei einem Mittelweg zwischen verallgemeinerbaren Erkenntnissen und individuellen und zugleich kulturell geprägten. Und es bleibt bei Iterationen von Unbestimmtheit und neuer Klarheit. Letztlich eröffnet das gewonnene neue Wissen auch Möglichkeiten, neues Nichtwissen zu erkennen und fördert dadurch weitere Forschung. Prozesse zu denken stimuliert Metamorphosen des Erkennens, bleibt komplex, herausfordernd und anfachend.

1 Zur Dreigliederung vgl. | On the tripartite cf. Christopher Frayling, Research in art and design, in: Royal College of Art Research Papers 1 (1993/94), London: Royal College of Art 1993, 1-5, passim und | and 5 **2** Zu Varianten und Erweiterungen vgl. beispielsweise | On variations and extensions cf. e.g. Ken Friedman, Theory construction in design research. Criteria, approaches and methods, in: Design studies 24(2003)/6, 507-522; Rosan Chow, What should be done with the different versions of research-through-design?, in: Gesche Joost/Kora Kimpel/Claudia Mareis, Entwerfen Wissen Produzieren. Designforschung im Anwendungskontext, Bielefeld: Transcript 2010, 145-158; Wolfgang Jonas, Exploring the swampy ground, in: Simon Grand/id. (eds.), Mapping design research, Birkhäuser: Basel 2012, 11-41 **3** Vgl. hierzu auch | Cf. on this subject David Leatherborow, The project of design research, in: Michael U. Hensel (ed.), Design innovation for the built environment. Research by design an the renovation of practice, London: Routledge 2012, 5-13,12 **4** Vgl. | Cf. Margitta Buchert, Reflexives Entwerfen. Topologien eines Forschungsfelds/Reflexive design. Topologies of a research field, in: id. (ed.), Reflexives Entwerfen. Reflexive design, Berlin: Jovis 2014, 24-49 **5** Zum Potential des ‚und' vgl. auch | On the potential of the 'and' cf. also Gilles Deleuze/Claude Parent, Dialogues, Paris: Flammarion 1996, 68-69 **6** Vgl. | Cf. Jesko Fezer, A non-sentimental argument. Die Krise des Design Methods Movement 1962–1972, in: Daniel Gethmann/Susanne Hauser (eds.), Kulturtechnik Entwerfen. Praktiken, Konzepte, Medien in Architektur und Design Science, Bielefeld: Transcript 2009, 287-304, 291-291; Vera Bühlmann/Ludger Hovestadt, EigenArchitecture. Computability as literacy, Wien: Ambra 2013, passim **7** Donald Schön, The reflective practitioner. How professionals think in action (1983), 3. ed. Aldershot: Ashgate 2003, 128-203; hierzu und zum Folgenden auch | on that and the following cf. also Buchert 2014 op. cit. (Anm. 4 | note 4), 26-33 **8** Vgl. hierzu übergreifend | Cf. on that comprehensively Claudia Mareis, Design als Wissenskultur. Interferenzen zwischen Design und Wissensdiskursen seit 1960, id. et al 2010 op. cit. (Anm. 2 | note 2), 285-388 **9** In diesen Ausführungen werden zwei Tendenzen zusammengefasst, die in Theoriediskursen auch als Performative turn und als Practice turn bezeichnet werden. Vgl. dazu | In these notions two tendencies are summarized which in theoretical discourse are called performative and practice turn. | Cf. Erika Fischer-Lichte, Ästhetik des Performativen, Frankfurt/Main: Suhrkamp 2004; Theodore Schatzki/Karin Knorr Cetina/Eike von Savigny (eds.), The practice turn in contemporary theory, London et al.: Routledge 2005; Krista Sykes, Introduction, in: id. (ed.), Constructing a new agenda. Architectural theory 1993–2009, New York: Princeton Architectural Press 2010, 14-29, 16-23 sowie | as well as Michel Foucault, Archäologie des Wissens, Frankfurt/Main: Suhrkamp 1981, 14-15; Hans-Jörg Rheinberger: Experimentalsysteme und epistemische Dinge. Göttingen: 2001, passim und | and 24; Andrea Belliger/David J. Krieger (eds.), ANThology. Ein einführendes Handbuch zur Akteur-Netzwerk-Theorie, Bielefeld: Transcript 2000, passim und | and 13-45

10 Vgl. z.B. | Cf. e.g. Daniel Gethmann/Susanne Hauser (eds.), Kulturtechnik Entwerfen, Bieldfeld: Transcript 2009; Helga Blocksdorf/Ute Frank/Marius Mensing/Anca Timofticiuc (eds.), Eklat. Entwerfen und Konstruieren in Lehre, Anwendung und Theorie, Berlin: TU 2011; Sabine Ammon/Eva-Maria Froschauer (eds.), Wissenschaft Entwerfen, Paderborn: Wilhelm Fink 2013; Jürgen Weidinger, Entwurfsbasiert forschen, Berlin: TU 2014; Gabriela Goldsmith, Linkography. Unfolding the design process, Cambridge, Mass.: MIT Press 2014; Philip Plowright, Revealing architectural design. Methods, frameworks, tools, London et al.: Routledge 2015; Jürgen Weidinger, Designing knowledge, Berlin: TU 2015; Hannah Groninger/Roger Häußling/Claudia Mareis/Thomas H. Schmitz (eds.), Manifestationen im Entwurf. Design, Architektur, Ingenieurwesen, Bielefeld: Transcript 2016; Carolin Stapenhorst, Concept. A dialogical instrument in architectural design, Berlin: Jovis 2016; Angelika Schnell/Eva Sommeregger/Waltraud Indrist, Entwerfen erforschen, Basel: Birkhäuser 2016 **11** Vgl. z.B. | cf. e.g. Hans-Jörg Rheinberger, Über die Kunst, das Unbekannte zu erforschen, in: Andrea Sabisch/Karl-Josef Paczini/Daniel Tyradellis (ed.), Das Unverfügbare. Wunder, Wissen, Bildung, Zürich: Diaphanes 2013, 143-149; Nathalie Bredella, Bildgebungsverfahren und computerbasierte Architektur. Zur Operativität und Materialität digitaler Modellierungen im Entwurf, in: Sabine Ammon/Inge Hinterwaldner (eds.), Bildlichkeit im Zeitalter der Modellierung, Paderborn: Wilhelm Fink 2017, 346-367 **12** Vgl. hierzu auch | Cf. on this subject also Donald A. Schön, The reflective practitioner. How professionals think in action, 3rd ed. Aldershot: Ashgate 2003, 48 und | and 103; Nigel Cross, Designerly ways of knowing, London: Springer 2006, 147-149; Bryan Lawson, How designers think in action. The design process demystified, 4. ed. Oxford: Elsevier 2006, 292-293 **13** Zu Habitus vgl. | On habitus see Pierre Bourdieu, Entwurf einer Theorie der Praxis – auf der ethnologischen Grundlage der kabylischen Gesellschaft, Frankfurt/Main: Suhrkamp 1976, 139-202, 169; zu Grundkonzeption und implizitem Wissen vgl. | On basic conception and tacit knowledge see Margitta Buchert, op. cit (Anm. | note 4), 24-49, 29-33 **14** Vgl. hierzu auch | Cf. on this subject also Ivar Holm, Ideas and beliefs in architecture and industrial design. How attitudes, orientations, and underlying assumptions shape the built environment, Oslo: AHO 2006, 68 und/and 219-367 **15** Vgl. hierzu auch | Cf. on that also Robert M. Entmann, Framing: Toward a clarification of a fractured paradigm, in: Journal of Communication (1993)/3, 51-58; Kees Dorst, Understanding design, Amsterdam: BIS 2006, 130-132 **16** Vgl. | Cf. Michel de Certeau, Kunst des Handelns, Berlin: Merve 1988, 148; Franz Breuer, Reflexive grounded theory. Eine Einführung in die Forschungspraxis, Wiesbaden: VS 2009, 29-30 **17** Vgl. weiter hinten in diesem Buch | see later in this book 33-39, 97-103, 163-169 **18** Vgl. dagegen | Cf. in contrast Andrea Belliger/David J. Krieger, Einführung, in: ids. (eds.), ANThology. Ein einführendes Handbuch zur Akteur-Netzwerk-Theorie, Bielefeld: Transcript 2000, passim und | and 13-45, 18

„Manchmal ist es weder fachliches Können noch Wissen per se, das wichtig ist, sondern eine Art des Sehens und Wahrnehmens, die ein wesentliches Vermögen in einer Handlung sein kann." | 'Sometimes it is neither skill nor knowledge per se that is important but a way of seeing or perceiving that may be the crucial ability in an activity.'

Bryan Lawson

TREIBENDE KRÄFTE
DRIVING FORCES

Can concrete knowledge about design processes become accessible if 'driving forces' for special phases, moments and sequences come to the fore as a research subject? The project develops, as a rule, within the context of socio-cultural, technical, economic and legal conditions and possibilities. As a reaction to the specific situation of the location and the task, the design procedure unfolds in iterative processes of complex and mixed order genesis, comprising materials, tools and media and against the background of experiences, observations and knowledge.[1] Increasing expertise is added over the course of time and development. A variety of research attention has been dedicated to these aspects in recent decades, but fundamental questions on the subject have by no means been exhaustively clarified yet.[2] In what way, for example, can entities of experience be grasped that exemplify still little-known dimensions of 'knowledge-ability' and make process characteristics comprehensible and in part also generalizable and transferable?

The subtle observation of concrete practice with its performative character becomes a focal point if one thematizes the forces that set and keep something in motion or motivations for and triggers of design and research acts.[3] The challenge for the research activity then lies in the recognition, description and explanation of a respective knowledge ensemble, whereby it is also shown how the concrete can become the driving moment of abstraction.[4] This involves knowledge about the shaping, orientation and directing of design and research processes. The ability to continue the procedural knowledge formations can be provided by a high evidence level of the abstract general in the concrete specific. Furthermore, the prompts stimulating active steps on a conceptual level comprise the freedom for specific interpretation and refinement. They can be experienced multiple times, albeit with a different nuancing each time.

Kann konkretes Wissen über Entwurfsprozesse greifbar werden, wenn ‚treibende Kräfte' für spezielle Phasen, Momente und Sequenzen als Forschungsfrage in den Vordergrund treten? Das Projekt entwickelt sich in der Regel im Rahmen sozio-kultureller, technischer, ökonomischer und auch gesetzlicher Bedingungen und Möglichkeiten. In Reaktion auf die spezifische Situation des Ortes und der Aufgabe entfaltet sich der Entwurfsverlauf in iterativen Prozessen komplexer und gemischter Ordnungsgenese unter Einbezug von Materialien, Instrumenten und Medien und vor dem Hintergrund von Erfahrungen, Beobachtungen und Wissen.[1] Die zunehmende Expertise tritt im Verlauf der Zeit und Entwicklung hinzu. Vielfältige forschende Aufmerksamkeit wurde in den letzten Dekaden diesen Aspekten gewidmet, doch konnten grundlegende Fragen dazu noch lange nicht erschöpfend geklärt werden.[2] In welcher Weise beispielsweise können Gestalten des Erfahrens erfasst werden, die noch wenig bekannte Dimensionen des ‚Wissen-Könnens' veranschaulichen und Prozesseigenschaften nachvollziehbar und in Teilen auch verallgemeinerbar und transferfähig machen?

Die subtile Beobachtung der konkreten Praxis in ihrem performativen Charakter rückt ins Blickfeld, wenn die Kräfte, die etwas in Bewegung setzen und halten, oder Motivationen für und Auslöser von Entwurfs- und Forschungsakten thematisiert werden.[3] Die Herausforderung für das Forschungshandeln liegt dann im Erkennen, Beschreiben und Erklären eines entsprechenden Wissensensembles, wobei auch hervortritt, wie das Konkrete zum treibenden Moment der Abstraktion werden kann.[4] Dabei geht es um Erkenntnisse zur Gestaltung, Orientierung und Lenkung von Prozessen des Entwerfens und des Forschens. Die Fortsetzbarkeit der prozeduralen Wissensformationen kann durch einen hohen Anschauungswert des abstrakten Allgemeinen im konkreten Besonderen gegeben sein. Im Weiteren beinhalten die auf einer begreifenden Ebene stimulierenden Darbietungen zu Handlungsschritten die Freiheit zur je spezifischen Interpretation und Verfeinerung. Sie können mehrmals erfahren werden, wenn auch mit je unterschiedlicher Nuancierung.

For the mostly difficult initiation of the design phase or also in comparable micro situations during the design process, Hilde Léon suggests – comparable to heuristic models – the sharpening of perception through attention to appearances, design forms and presences. She shows how, through such perception processes and experiences, one can promote not only important and fundamental steps for the design work, relating to the location and task, but also potential and driving forces for bringing forth creative ideas for complex ordering processes. In view of experiences that can be gained from the sensory and meaningful perception of works of fine art, especially from the evoked other and unfamiliar world perception, she shows possibilities of breaking out of trusted schemata and blockades in complex situations and paving the way for solutions. The pointed emphasis on fundamental perception potential and levels of action serves the purpose of both the research approach and stimulation for the design and research activity.

The timeframe that often acts as a driving force when carrying out a design activity, which urges decision-making, is the focus of the contribution by Katja Benfer and Cyrus Zahiri. Through self-reflexive diagnostic descriptions of their practice, the anatomy of routine is outlined and analyzed. Intermediate phases and periods of activity in the design procedure are characterized as symptomatic formations of time experiences and combined with the presentation of strategies that are used to stop part of a process and save time. They also harbor creative potential. The approaches to descriptive methods for understanding the handling of these situations have an initiating effect for outlining differences in greater detail in further steps and through comparison. They thus enrich the basic knowledge for design actions, as well as open further research perspectives.

Für den meist schwierigen Einstieg in die Entwurfsphase oder auch in vergleichbare Mikrosituationen im Entwurfsgeschehen schlägt Hilde Léon, heuristischen Modellen vergleichbar, die Schärfung der Wahrnehmung durch Aufmerksamkeit für Erscheinungen, Gestaltungsformen und Präsenzen vor. Sie zeigt auf, wie durch solche Wahrnehmungsprozesse und Erfahrungen nicht nur wichtige und grundlegende Schritte für die Entwurfsarbeit, bezogen auf Ort und Aufgabe, befördert werden können, sondern auch Potentiale und Triebkräfte zum Hervorbringen kreativer Ideen für komplexe Ordnungsprozesse. Im Blick auf Erfahrungen, die aus der sinnlich-sinnhaften Wahrnehmung von Werken der bildenden Künste, insbesondere aus der jeweils evozierten anderen, unvertrauten Weltwahrnehmung, gewonnen werden können, zeigt sie Möglichkeiten auf, um in komplexen Situationen aus bekannten Schemata und Blockaden herauszukommen und Lösungswege zu eröffnen. Die Zuspitzung auf grundlegende Wahrnehmungspotentiale und Handlungsebenen dient gleichermaßen der forschenden Erschließung und der Stimulation für das entwerfende und auch forschende Handeln.

Den im Vollzug des Entwurfshandelns oftmals als treibende Kraft wirkenden Zeitrahmen, der zu Entscheidungsfindungen drängt, thematisiert der Beitrag von Katja Benfer und Cyrus Zahiri. In selbstreflexiven diagnostischen Beschreibungen ihrer Praxis wird die Anatomie der Routine erfasst und analysiert. Zwischenphasen und Momente des Handelns im Entwurfsverlauf werden als symptomatische Formationen des Zeit-Erfahrens charakterisiert und verbunden mit dem Aufzeigen von Strategien, die eingesetzt werden, um einen Prozessabschnitt zu stoppen und Zeit einzusparen. Sie beinhalten zugleich kreatives Potential. Die vorgenommenen Annäherungen an Beschreibungsarten zum Verstehen des Umgangs mit diesen Situationen wirken initiierend dafür, in weiteren Schritten und im Vergleich Differenzen stärker zu konturieren. So bereichern sie das Grundwissen für Entwurfshandeln ebenso wie sie weitere Forschungsperspektiven öffnen.

Another process structure is presented by the contribution by Caroline Voet, with a focus on her own research biography. With an analytical intention, it presents how the experience of design-based research was constituted in individual sequences and the gained thematic orientations developed over a longer period for the basic conception of her own professional practice. Furthermore, it illuminates exemplarily how research avenues and fundamental knowledge act as generic forces in the conception and concrete constructive-technical and creative formulation of specific designs.[5] There are also illuminating references to the relevance of institutions, persons and theoretical concepts, as well as to the basic variability of areas of knowledge and their interpretation over the course of historical change. This is emphasized significantly here based on the example of process characteristics of parametric design with digital tools. Through their combination with the exploratory search for artisanal and humanistic values, emerging from the resistance against one-sidedness, the concept of tectonics is taken up as a promising approach to a qualitatively extended spatial syntax. At the same time, a segment of the collective portrait of the discipline around 2015 is outlined, especially how generic and specific processes can be linked.

Eine andere Prozessgestalt präsentiert der Beitrag von Caroline Voet mit dem Schwerpunkt der eigenen Forschungsbiografie. In analysierender Absicht wird dargeboten, wie sich in einzelnen Sequenzen das Erfahren entwurfsbasierten Forschens konstituierte und die gewonnenen thematischen Ausrichtungen über einen längeren Zeitraum zur Grundkonzeption der eigenen professionellen Praxis entwickelten. Darüber hinaus wird exemplarisch deutlich, wie Forschungswege und grundlegende Erkenntnisse in der Konzeption und konkreten konstruktiv-technischen und gestalterischen Formulierung spezifischer Entwürfe als generische Kräfte wirken.[5] Erhellend wirken zudem die Hinweise auf die Relevanz von Institutionen, Personen und theoretischen Konzepten sowie auf die grundlegende Veränderlichkeit von Wissensbereichen und ihrer Interpretation im historischen Wandel. Dies tritt hier signifikant am Beispiel von Prozesseigenschaften parametrischen Entwerfens mit digitalen Werkzeugen hervor. Durch ihre Kopplung mit dem aus dem Widerstand gegen Vereinseitigungen erwachsenen forschenden Suchen nach handwerklichen und humanistischen Werten wird über das Konzept der Tektonik eine vielversprechende Annäherung an eine qualitativ erweiterte räumliche Syntax vorgeschlagen. Gleichzeitig wird damit ein Segment des kollektiven Porträts der Disziplin um 2015 skizziert, insbesondere wie generische und spezifische Prozesse verbunden sein können. MB

1 Vgl. z.B. | Cf. e.g. Bryan Lawson, What designers know, Amsterdam et al.: Elsevier 2004 **2** Vgl. z.B. | Cf. e.g. Ken Friedman/Erik Stolterman, Series Foreword, in: Gabriela Goldsmith, Linkography. Unfolding the design process, Cambridge, Mass.: MIT Press 2014, 9-13; Philip Plowright, Revealing architectural design. Methods, frameworks, tools, London et al.: Routledge 2015, passim und | and 185-202 **3** Zu performativen Forschungsprozessen in der Lehre vgl. auch | On performative processes of research in the field of teaching see also Angelika Schnell/Waltraud Indrist/Ruth Sommeregger, Entwerfen erforschen. Der ‚performative turn' im Architekturstudium, Basel: Birkhäuser 2016, passim **4** Vgl. hierzu auch | Cf. on this subject also Hans-Jörg Rheinberger in Referenz auf Gaston Bachelards Wissenschaftstheorien | in reference to Gaston Bachelards theories on science: Hans-Jörg Rheinberger, Iterationen, Berlin: Merve: 2005, **5** Vgl. hierzu auch | Cf. on this subject also Kees Dorst/Bryan Lawson, Design expertise, Oxford et al.: Elesvier 2009, 70-77

BEFORE STARTING

Strategies for designing

Hilde Léon

The secret of becoming, the impulse for doing and the process from something non-existent via an idea to a product are fascinating. It is therefore appealing to trace the creative process of an artifact. How many appropriated and biographical elements, what degree of social attitude and historical background, what extent of what is learned and how much talent determine a work? An entire branch of creativity research is built on this, pursued by scientists, art historians and architecture theorists. Behavioral scientists are involved with it, as well as neurologists who research which parts of the brain, the left or right side, are activated to what degree.[1]

It is exciting, like looking into the notebook of a poet, to illuminate the world behind the doing, even if it cannot be explained by strict rules and clear formats. The artists as 'doers' are not only working according to an unspecified gut instinct, they are following an inner thread that is reflected more or less openly. This inner thread, as referred to vaguely here, is reinforced by an impulse of thinking and being, which is fed in turn by reflection about the world and individual experience, sometimes personal traumas. Each specific constellation has its own rules that one subordinates oneself to, sounds out and pushes the boundaries of.

VOR DEM BEGINN

Strategien zum Entwerfen

Hilde Léon

Das Geheimnis des Werdens, der Impuls für ein Machen und der Prozess von etwas nicht Vorhandenem über eine Idee zu einem Produkt, sind faszinierend. Deswegen ist es reizvoll, dem kreativen Prozess eines Artefakts auf die Spur zu kommen. Wie viel Angeeignetes und Biografisches, wie viel gesellschaftliche Haltung und historischer Hintergrund, wie viel Erlerntes und wie viel Begabung bestimmen ein Werk? Darauf baut ein ganzer Zweig der Kreativitätsforschung auf. Dem sind Wissenschaftler, Kunsthistoriker und Architekturtheoretiker auf der Spur. Das beschäftigt Verhaltensforscher ebenso wie Neurologen, die im Spin erforschen, welche Gehirnareale, die linke oder die rechte Seite, in welchem Maße aktiviert werden.[1]

Die Welt hinter dem Machen zu beleuchten, auch wenn es nicht mit strengen Regeln und klaren Formaten erklärbar ist, ist so aufregend wie in das Notizbuch eines Dichters zu schauen. Die Künstler als ‚Macher' arbeiten nicht nur mit unbestimmbarem Bauchgefühl. Sie verfolgen einen inneren Faden, der mehr oder weniger offen reflektiert wird. Dieser innere Faden, wie er hier vage bezeichnet werden soll, wird gestärkt aus einem Impuls des Denkens und Seins, der wiederum gespeist wird aus der Reflexion über die Welt und die individuelle Erfahrung, mitunter auch eigener Traumata. Jede spezifische Konstellation hat eine eigene Gesetzmäßigkeit, der man sich unterwirft, die man auslotet, die man sprengt.

In architecture, the task is usually set externally and specifies the framework that the designer must explore and perhaps go beyond. The needs, the norms and regulations, the conditions, the requirements are imposed from the outside.

Architecture is built on the past, is subject to a social code and is directly bound up with technological development. Architecture is also serving. At the same time, the conditions are not fixed and unchangeable. They must be questioned, and tasks can also be invented and newly developed. University is the right place for this. Practice is not reproduced here, instead it is explored and experienced in the first instance. In the process, apparent certainties can be stretched or turned upside down within a certain realm of possibility. At the same time, both at university and in practice, something extra is required that goes beyond the scope of the necessary. Only then does a concept and especially what is built have a chance to become architecture. In relation to this, it was postulated recently by the curators of the Architecture Biennale in Venice: "What distinguishes good architecture is a spatial generosity and the wish to give something back to the society and place where one is working [...] Architecture has the ability to improve a place."[2] In a kind of self-reflection, it is about the question of how one – at least rudimentarily – reaches the point where architecture can take on a special character, one that is appropriate for the task and the location and receives a certain aura within its social context. Even if a diverse vagueness comes into it, it presents the opportunity to interpret one's own approaches and to subject oneself to the attempt to explain the world behind the doing.

PROCESSES This is where the process comes into play. A temporal aspect is already inherent in the word process. A product is namely not suddenly just there, without a process, but is the result of becoming. Today process is referred to by natural and social sciences as a 'directed unfolding of an event', in other words an occurrence that provides information about a period of time, which is observed and analyzed.[3] It is also important to observe and analyze in architecture, as it is relevant for the process of generating ideas. At the end of a legal process there is also a product, namely the verdict. Over the course of the process it matures and develops according to aspects that are brought in from the outside and must be judged according to legal criteria: without a charge, no trial.[4] This comes even closer to the process of designing in architecture.

Even if a task, a requirement, a necessity is imposed on the architect in most cases, it does not preclude the possibility of exploring it oneself. The 'task' is not prescribed by the client and handed over to the contractor, in other words split into client and

In der Architektur wird die Aufgabe in der Regel von außen gestellt und gibt den Rahmen vor, den der Entwerfende ausloten und möglicherweise überschreiten muss. Die Notwendigkeit, die Normen und Gesetze, die Bedingungen, die Bedürfnisse werden von außen herangetragen.

Architektur baut auf Vergangenheit auf, ist gesellschaftlichem Kodex unterworfen, ist unmittelbar mit technologischer Entwicklung verbunden. Architektur ist zudem dienend. Gleichzeitig sind die Bedingungen nicht fix und unveränderlich. Sie müssen hinterfragt werden, und Aufgaben können auch erfunden und neu entwickelt werden. Und dafür ist die Hochschule der richtige Ort. Praxis wird hier nicht reproduziert; sie wird vielmehr ausgelotet und überhaupt erst erfahren. Dabei können scheinbare Gewissheiten in einem Möglichkeitsraum erweitert oder auf den Kopf gestellt werden. Gleichzeitig braucht es in der Hochschule und ebenso in der Praxis genau ein Mehr, das über das Maß des Notwendigen hinausgeht. Erst dann hat ein Konzept und erst recht das Gebaute die Chance, Architektur zu werden. So wurde beispielsweise kürzlich von den Kuratorinnen der Architekturbiennale in Venedig postuliert: „Was gute Architektur auszeichnet, ist eine räumliche Großzügigkeit und das Bedürfnis, der Gesellschaft und dem Ort, an dem man arbeitet, etwas zurückzugeben [...] Architektur hat die Fähigkeit, einen Ort zu verbessern."[2] In einer Art Selbstreflexion geht es hier um die Frage, wie man – mindestens ansatzweise – dorthin kommt, dass Architektur einen besonderen Charakter bekommen kann, einen Charakter, der für die Aufgabe und den Ort angemessen ist und eine besondere Aura in seinem sozialen Kontext erhält. Auch wenn dabei diverse Vagheit ins Spiel kommt, bietet sich die Chance, die eigenen Ansätze selbst zu interpretieren und sich selbst dem Versuch auszusetzen, die Welt hinter dem Machen zu erklären.

P R O Z E S S E Hier kommt der Prozess ins Spiel. Schon im Wort Prozess ist ein zeitlicher Aspekt vorherrschend. Es ist eben nicht plötzlich ein Produkt da, es ist also nicht prozesslos, sondern es ist ein Werden. Von den Natur- und Sozialwissenschaften wird Prozess heute als ein ‚gerichteter Ablauf eines Geschehens' bezeichnet, also ein Geschehen, das Auskunft über einen Zeitraum gibt, der beobachtet und analysiert werden will.[3] In der Architektur gilt es ebenfalls zu beobachten und zu analysieren. Dies ist relevant für den Prozess der Ideenfindung. Auch beim juristischen Prozess steht am Ende ein Produkt, nämlich das Urteil. Im Laufe des Prozesses reift und entwickelt es sich über Aspekte, die von außen herangetragen werden und nach Kriterien des Rechts beurteilt werden müssen: ohne Anklage, kein Prozess.[4] Hier kommen wir dem Prozess des Entwerfens von Architektur noch näher.

1-2 | Stephan Huber: Shining, 2003

architect, instead it is more of a coming together and it is the task itself that is shifted if necessary. Without a question there is no answer in architecture, just as in a trial no sentence is required without a charge.

DISTRUSTING APPEARANCES This is why one of the first steps is to understand the task. It is not primarily about taking on what is on the program or the dimensions required, but about sounding out what potential this task harbors. Of course, one should take the program seriously, as it comprises the budget, specifications and many dependent factors, and at the same time any questioning is initially built on what is known. However, in addition there are many levels behind it and unwritten lines in between. For if what is familiar is merely repeated, it leads to a dead end of poor-quality architecture. Contrary to this, it is often argued that one should not reinvent the wheel every time. However, resorting to this phrase has more to do with resistance and invalidation. It can only become a convincing argument if one fears getting lost in detail or wasting time with the trivial, instead of keeping a focus on the essential. However, what constitutes the essential is influenced by one's own attitude and each person must decide for themselves. Ideally one could try to approach a task as if one had never heard of it before, as if it were entirely new. Experience can be a hindrance, one knows too much and then skips over many steps in the process of becoming. It is not worth setting a task if one believes one knows the outcome from the outset.[5]

We should make use of this open, largely unbiased point of view beyond the obvious to create potential for ideas. It is surely a good tactic to be suspicious of the familiar and to distrust the obvious. This calls to mind a work of art by Stephan Huber, a series of photographic images (fig. 1 and 2).[6] On the first picture of the series one can see a residential house, a detached single-family house with a pitched roof, gable, terrace and balcony – rather commonplace, familiar and inconspicuous. It is only at a second glance that one notices the setting. The following description clearly characterizes the properties

Auch wenn in den meisten Fällen eine Aufgabe, ein Bedürfnis, eine Notwendigkeit an den Architekten herangetragen wird, schließt das nicht die Möglichkeit aus, sich selbst die Fragestellung zu suchen. Dabei wird ‚Aufgabe' nicht vom Auftraggeber vorgegeben und dem Auftragnehmer übergeben, also in Bauherr und Architekt gesplittet, vielmehr ist es eine Personalunion und verschiebt allenfalls die Fragestellung selbst. Ohne eine Frage gibt es in der Architektur keine Antwort, wie in einem Prozess eben ohne Anklage kein Richterspruch verlangt ist und eben kein Prozess vorausgeht.

DEM ANSCHEIN MISSTRAUEN Deswegen ist es einer der ersten Schritte, die Aufgabe zu verstehen. Dabei geht es nicht vorrangig darum, aufzunehmen, was im Programm steht und an Dimensionen gefordert wird, sondern auszuloten, was diese Aufgabe für ein Potential bereithält. Natürlich sollte man das Programm ernst nehmen, da es mit Budget, mit Vorgaben und mit vielen Abhängigkeiten zu tun hat, und gleichzeitig baut jede Fragestellung zunächst auf dem auf, was bekannt ist. Aber es gibt zusätzlich mehrere Ebenen dahinter und die ungeschriebenen Zeilen dazwischen. Denn wenn Bekanntes nur repetiert wird, führt es in eine Sackgasse von qualitätsarmer Architektur. Demgegenüber wird oft argumentiert, dass man das Rad nicht jedes Mal neu erfinden solle. Doch sich auf diese Phrase zu berufen, hat mehr mit Abwehr und Abwertung zu tun. Das kann nur dann zum überzeugenden Argument werden, wenn man fürchtet, sich im Detail zu verlieren oder sich mit Nichtigem abzugeben, statt eine Konzentration auf das Wesentliche zu behalten. Doch was das Wesentliche ist, wird von der eigenen Haltung beeinflusst und muss von jeder Person selbst bestimmt werden. Idealerweise könnte man versuchen, sich einer Aufgabe so zu stellen, als hätte man zuvor nie davon gehört, als wäre sie vollkommen neu. Die Erfahrung kann da geradezu ein Hindernis sein, man weiß zu viel und überspringt dann gleich viele Schritte im Prozess des Werdens. Eine Aufgabe ist nicht wert, gestellt zu werden, wenn man das Ergebnis schon von vornherein zu kennen meint.[5]

Wir sollten diesen offenen, möglichst unvoreingenommenen Blick hinter dem Offensichtlichen nutzen, um Potentiale für Ideen zu kreieren. Das Bekannte zu beargwöhnen und dem Offensichtlichen zu misstrauen, ist sicherlich eine gute Taktik. In diesem Zusammenhang steht mir ein Kunstwerk von Stephan Huber, eine Serie von fotografischen Ansichten vor Auge (Abb. 1 und 2).[6] Auf dem ersten Bild der Serie ist ein Wohnhaus zu sehen, ein allein stehendes Einfamilienhaus mit Satteldach, Gauben, Terrasse und Balkon, ziemlich banal, bekannt und unauffällig. Erst auf dem zweiten Blick fällt der Blick auf die Umgebung. Die nachfolgende Beschreibung charakterisiert die Eigenschaften, die dabei wahrgenommen werden können, klar: „Das Haus in der Eiswüste ist ein deutlicher Verweis auf das völlig eingeschneite und somit von der Außenwelt abgeschnittene Overlook-Hotel in Stanley Kubricks Film ‚Shining'. Alleine schon dadurch, dass Huber der

that can be perceived: "The house in the ice desert is a clear reference to the Overlook Hotel in Stanley Kubrick's movie The Shining that is completely snowed in and therefore completely cut off from the outside world. Even just due to the fact that Huber gives the photo series the movie title, the homely-looking house does not appear as an alternative to the icy surrounding atmosphere that destroys humanity, but rather as a trap. As the picture sequence unfolds, the viewer recognizes the stage illusion of what is happening. Image by image, the scenography crumbles. Dry ice fog, plastered polystyrene icebergs and the house become recognizable as a model-like stage construction that makes no pretense to deception, but draws its effect from the moment of unveiling, the offensive presentation of the constructed as a construct. Huber loves these kinds of ambiguities.[7] The experience of the artistic work can be an impulse for generative micro-strategies for initiating design ideas. This work of art clearly and radically conveys the potential attitude of mistrusting initial appearances. Not allowing oneself to be swayed by the first appearance, by the familiar and safe, but taking a close look and allowing an insight behind the scenes, as well as illuminating the program variously and venturing a critical look beyond the surface, are possible ways to acquire ideas. For all tasks, the question that presents itself, is what is really important and how can I express it within my concept.

THE EXISTING AS A CATALYST Architecture is never self-contained, as there is always something that is already there. There is always a context with all its historical layers. However commonplace it may appear, it still offers potential for ideas. One might imagine a context-free environment as the open sea or a flat meadow. However, both harbor potential, whether it is the colors of the sea at different times of day, the constant movement of the water, or the endlessly wide horizon. Engaging with the location, searching for hidden qualities, is a further source of ideas. The art of reshaping is the relationship between what is available and the possibilities.

It is precisely because of this that the project in the Duisburg inland port by Dani Karavan from the year 1999 provides so many impulses (fig. 3 and 4).[8] Remains of the former development (industrial halls) were preserved here to use them as event locations or viewing towers. Ground plan lines of the demolished buildings were represented abstractly with white concrete strips. The central path was composed like a mosaic out of the rubble and a triangular hill and a rockery were formed out of the demolition remains. In addition, various water features have been created and planting was included, for example mountain pines on the viewing tower and honeyshucks in one of the former halls. Crop and sunflower fields and old scales in the middle of the park are reminiscent of the former usage of the area as a crop trading facility ("breadbasket of the Ruhr region").

3-4 | Dani Karavan: Garten der Erinnerung | Garden of Memories, 2018

Fotofolge den Filmtitel gibt, erscheint das heimelig wirkende Haus nicht als Alternative zu der menschenvernichtenden eisigen Umgebungs-Atmosphäre, sondern eher als Falle. Im Ablauf der Bildfolge erkennt der Betrachter die Bühnenillusion des Geschehens. Bild für Bild bröckelt die Inszenierung, werden Trockeneisnebel, gipsbekleisterte Styropor-Eisberge und Haus als modellhafte Bühnenkonstruktion kenntlich, die überhaupt keinen Wert auf perfekte Täuschung legt, sondern ihren Mehrwert gerade aus dem Moment der Ent-Täuschung, der offensiven Vorführung des Konstruierten als Konstrukt zieht. Huber liebt Doppelbödigkeiten dieser Art.[7] Die Erfahrung des künstlerischen Werks kann Impuls sein für generative Mikrostrategien zur Initiierung von Entwurfsideen. Dieses Kunstwerk vermittelt anschaulich und radikal die Haltungsoption, dem ersten Anschein zu misstrauen. Sich nicht leiten lassen vom ersten Blick, vom Bekannten und Sicheren, sondern genau hinzuschauen und den Blick dahinter zuzulassen sowie das Programm vielfältig zu beleuchten und den kritischen Blick dahinter zu wagen, sind Möglichkeiten, um sich Ideen zu erobern. Dabei steht bei allen Aufgaben die Frage im Raum, was ist wirklich wichtig und wie kann ich das in meinem Konzept ausdrücken.

DAS VORHANDENE ALS KATALYSATOR Architektur ist nie selbstbezogen, denn es gibt immer etwas, was schon da ist. Es gibt immer einen Kontext mit all seinen historischen Schichten. Erscheinen sie auch noch so banal, so bieten sie dennoch ein Potential für Ideen. Bei der Vorstellung eines kontextfreien Umfeldes fällt einem vielleicht das offene Meer oder eine platte Wiese ein. Aber beide haben Potentiale, seien es die Farben des Meeres zu unterschiedlichen Tageszeiten, seien es die stete Bewegung des Wassers oder der unendlich weite Horizont. Sich-Einlassen auf den Ort, nach versteckten Qualitäten zu suchen, ist ein weiterer Fundus für Ideen. Die Kunst des Überformens ist die Beziehung von dem Vorhandenen zu den Möglichkeiten.

Gerade deswegen ist das Projekt im Binnenhafen Duisburg von Dani Karavan aus dem Jahr 1999 so impulsgebend (Abb. 3 und 4).[8] Überreste der ehemaligen Bebauung (Industriehallen) wurden hier erhalten, um sie als Veranstaltungsorte oder Aussichtstürme zu nutzen.

5 | Qin Yufen: Untitled, 2018

Especially the title of the park as a 'Garden of Memories', very close to the new synagog of Duisburg, indicates that the idea very evidently drew on what already existed. Even if this work by Dani Karavan appears too loaded and too obvious linguistically, it impresses with its design presence in this location. It is an impressive example of what potential the location and the task harbor for the generation of ideas. One must tap into this source.

A NEW VIEW OF THE FAMILIAR Designing architecture is often understood as a search for new forms. This makes sense but is often misleading. The new form emerges at the end of a process and not at the beginning. Furthermore, the new – which can be closely associated with a moment of surprise – is gained from the turning around of accustomed and familiar perspectives. The new gains its meaning by setting itself in relation to the familiar and placing it in a new context. It can lead to new qualities, to contradicting the generally expected, to countering conventional with a deeper understanding of the respective situations, as well as to triggering new sensory stimuli. What may appear very odd or even far-fetched can evoke new perspectives for the design, as well as a new attitude towards life.

The artist Qin Yufen pursues this with a wide range of approaches (fig. 5-6).[9] It surrounds the themes of her artistic work. Her preferred medium is mostly large-scale spatial installations with familiar, often simple everyday daily items. These include clothes horses, barbed wire, bamboo, fabrics.

The work I am alluding to here has been shown in various surroundings, giving the installation a constantly changing spatial impression. The respective space is densely filled in an unorderly manner with identical unfolded white clothes horses, which are available cheaply from hardware stores. White and slightly transparent cloths of the same size

6 | Qin Yufen: Yu Tang Chun (Frühling in der Jadehalle | Spring in the Jade Hall), 1994

Mit weißen Betonbändern wurden Grundrisslinien der abgerissenen Gebäude abstrahiert dargestellt. Aus dem Trümmerschutt wurden der zentrale Weg mosaikartig zusammengesetzt, und aus den Abbruchresten ein dreieckiger Hügel und ein Steingarten gebildet. Zudem sind verschiedene Wasserflächen herausgearbeitet. Auch Bepflanzung wurde einbezogen, beispielsweise wurden Bergkiefern auf dem Aussichtsturm und Gleditschien in einer der früheren Hallen angepflanzt. Durch Getreide- und Sonnenblumenfelder und eine alte Waage in der Mitte des Parks wurde zudem an die ehemalige Nutzung des Bereiches als Getreideumschlagplatz („Brotkorb des Ruhrgebietes") erinnert. Insbesondere der Titel des Parks als ‚Garten der Erinnerung' in unmittelbarer Nähe zur neuen Synagoge von Duisburg weist darauf hin, dass die Idee offensichtlich aus dem Vorhandenen gespeist wurde. Auch wenn dieses Werk von Dani Karavan im Überbau zu aufgeladen und sprachlich zu augenscheinlich erscheint, überzeugt es in seiner gestalterischen Präsenz an diesem Ort. Es ist ein eindrückliches Beispiel dafür, welches Potential für eine Ideenfindung im Ort und in der Aufgabe stecken. Man muss diesen Fundus für sich heben.

BEKANNTES NEU SEHEN Entwerfen von Architektur wird häufig als eine Suche nach neuen Formen verstanden. Das ist verständlich und doch oftmals irreführend. Die neue Form steht am Ende eines Prozesses und nicht am Anfang. Und: Das Neue, das naheliegend mit einem Überraschungsmoment verbunden sein kann, wird aus der Umkehrung gewohnter und bekannter Sichtweisen gewonnen. Das Neue erhält seine Bedeutung durch das Sich-ins-Verhältnis-Setzen zum Bekannten und dadurch, dieses in einen neuen Kontext zu rücken. Zu neuen Qualitäten kann es führen, dem allgemein Erwarteten zu widersprechen, dem üblichen Verständnis ein tieferes Verständnis der betreffenden Situationen entgegenzustellen und neue sinnliche Reize auszulösen. Was sehr merkwürdig, ganz und gar abwegig erscheinen mag, kann neue Sichtweisen für den Entwurf und im Weiteren auch ein neues Lebensgefühl evozieren.

are fixed onto each rail with wooden pegs. Due to the individual elements his installation appears simple, delicate and fragile, but nevertheless powerful as a grouped mass. Regardless of other possible layers of the work of art, such as socially related or political layers of meaning, the spatial effect is striking. Sometimes as a viewer one does not really want to know all the details. The reception of a work must not necessarily concord with the intention. It is precisely that makes a work an open work of art.[10] The esthetic charm lies in the layering of lines and cloths, in the reflection and in the visual axes, as well as in the varied shadows cast by this multilayered white installation. One does not perceive the clothes horses primarily as such. The appeal also lies in the contradiction between the banality of the objects and the elegant effect of the installation in its respective surroundings. In the first instance, one thinks one understands the installation, but it is only after a longer viewing that its emotional effect unfolds. There are many further examples of the effective power of the familiar when transformed through a new perspective and presentation. Searching for the new in the familiar is a strategy in which deeper layers and qualities are presented clearly and drastically through contrast or contradiction, to enable new experiences and generate impulses.

FIRST PLAY, THEN THINK Things do not just happen rationally in the process of designing, it is also a process of trial and error, meaning a tentativeness, a trying out, sometimes giving coincidence a chance. Surrendering oneself to the playful moment and the subconscious is helpful for exploring an idea.

Only over the further course of the process is it possible to sit back and analyze what has happened and how it can be developed further. Dialog with others can also serve this purpose. Not only between a teacher and a student, but among each other. By having to put my idea into words, by sketching whilst talking – the legendary doodling on the beer mat – I clarify my idea.[11] However, others also read something into what is being presented that one may not even have noticed up until this stage of the process. Furthermore, does one not ask precisely those whose attitude might potentially be most similar to one's own approach? Yes, one enquires in order to receive confirmation, to affirm one's position, even if one is not always aware of this.

We are familiar with this playful and subconscious moment from doodling while telephoning, or also from artistic works. An example of how lightness and light playfulness can become an artistic spatial concept is presented by works by the two Swiss artists Gerda Steiner and Jörg Lenzlinger (fig. 7).[12] Their installation at the Art Biennale in Venice 2003 filled the space of the San Staë church from the 17th century with delicate crafted and simply found objects, which exuded a special effect especially from the suggested

Dem geht die Künstlerin Qin Yufen mit sehr unterschiedlichen Ansätzen nach (Abb. 5-6).[9] Sie umkreist die Themen in ihrem künstlerischen Schaffen. Ihr bevorzugtes Medium sind meist großdimensionierte Rauminstallationen mit bekannten, oft einfachen alltäglichen Gebrauchsgegenständen. Dazu zählen Wäscheständer, Stacheldraht, Bambus, Stoffe.

Das Werk, auf das ich hier anspiele, wurde in verschiedenen Umgebungen gezeigt, wodurch sich die Installation in ihrem Raumeindruck immer wieder verändert hat. Der jeweilige Raum wurde mit gleichen ausgeklappten weißen Wäscheständern, die im Baumarkt für wenig Geld zu bekommen sind, ungeordnet dicht an dicht gefüllt. Weiße, gleich große und leicht transparente Reispapiere sind mit Holzklammern auf jeweils einer Schiene befestigt. Einfach, filigran, fragil wirkt diese Installation durch die einzelnen Kompartimente und dennoch in der gruppierten Masse kraftvoll. Ungeachtet anderer Ebenen des Kunstwerks, beispielsweise gesellschaftsbezogener oder politischer Bedeutungsschichten, ist die räumliche Wirkung frappierend. Manchmal will man es als Betrachter auch gar nicht so genau wissen. Die Rezeption eines Werkes muss nicht mit der Intention übereinstimmen. Das genau macht ein Werk zu einem offenen Kunstwerk.[10] Der ästhetische Reiz liegt in der Überlagerung von Gestänge und Tüchern, in der Reflektion und in dem Durchblicken sowie im vielfältigen Schattenwurf dieser vielschichtigen weißen Installation. Die Wäscheständer nimmt man als solche nicht primär wahr. Der Reiz liegt zudem im Widerspruch der Banalität der Objekte zu der auch eleganten Wirkung der Installation in ihrer jeweiligen Umgebung. Im ersten Augenblick meint man die Installation zu verstehen, aber erst bei längerer Betrachtung entfaltet sich ihre emotionale Wirkung. Es gibt eine Vielzahl weiterer Beispiele für die Wirkkraft des Bekannten in der Umwertung durch eine neue Sicht und Darstellung. Das Neue im Bekannten suchen ist eine Strategie, bei der tiefergehende Schichten und Qualitäten durch Kontrast oder Widerspruch deutlich und drastisch dargestellt werden, um neue Erfahrungen zu ermöglichen und Impulse zu generieren.

ERST SPIELEN, DANN DENKEN Im Prozess des Entwerfens geht es nicht nur rational zu, es ist auch ein ‚Trial-and-Error', womit ein Sich-Annähern, ein Ausprobieren gemeint ist und bisweilen erhält der Zufall eine Chance. Sich dem spielerischen Moment hingeben, sich dem Unbewussten ausliefern, ist hilfreich, um einer Idee auf die Spur zu kommen.

Erst im weiteren Verlauf des Prozesses ist es möglich, sich zurückzulehnen und zu analysieren, was nun passiert ist und wie man es weiterentwickeln kann. Dazu kann auch der Dialog mit einem Gegenüber dienen. Nicht nur vom Lehrenden zum Studierenden, sondern untereinander. Indem ich meine Idee in Worte fassen muss, indem ich beim Reden skizziere – die legendäre Zeichnung auf dem Bierdeckel – kläre ich meine Idee.[11] Aber der

7 | Gerda Steiner, Jörg Lenzlinger: Fallender Garten | Falling Garden, Biennale Venedig | Venice, 2003

horizontal perspective.[13] The church as a space could be felt especially intensely. With the soft white floor and the horizontal lying surface for the exhausted visitors of the Biennale, a quite 'heavenly effect' unfolded in this cool room. The two artists' way of working and their choice of materials are similar in various works and the spiritual link to Venetian history, as well as to biodiversity, may be the initial trigger of the work, but the strong sensory effect is especially the result of the combination of the baroque room and the playful and ironic variety of the delicate objects. Here it is not necessary the new either, but the novel composition of the familiar. It gains its power and expression from the plethoric accumulation. The impressive effect is perhaps also the result of the striking contrast between the dense and exuberant baroque space with its monumental works of art on the one hand and the delicateness of the minimized 'flying' objects on the other. This provides a stimulation to see both in a new way, the heavy and the light.

Playing enables searching without a purpose or aim, but nevertheless with high concentration and seriousness, creating a situation as can be observed among children in a concentrated moment. One must devote oneself to the task without imposing the stress of the workable on oneself. Simply make a start, with continuity.

AS SIMPLE AS POSSIBLE, BUT NOT SIMPLER Less is more! Mies von der Rohe is quoted repeatedly at every opportunity, even though it is not an actual statement of his, but instead describes his understanding of design. "As simple as possible, but not simpler!" The comedian Karl Valentin also apparently said this. Both contain similar elements, and neither are an instruction. However, the self-questioning that must remain to express an idea is a helpful starting point. First of all, there is a sounding

andere liest auch etwas in dem Präsentierten, was einem bis zu diesem Prozessschritt noch gar nicht aufgefallen sein mag. Befragt man im Übrigen nicht genau denjenigen, dessen Haltung dem eigenen Ansatz potentiell ähneln könnte? Ja, man fragt, um bestätigt zu werden, um seine Haltung zu festigen, auch wenn man sich dessen nicht immer bewusst ist.

Dieses spielerische und unbewusste Moment kennen wir vom Skizzieren beim Telefonieren, oder auch von künstlerischen Arbeiten. Ein Beispiel dafür, wie Leichtigkeit und leichte Verspieltheit zum künstlerischen Raumkonzept werden können, vermitteln Arbeiten der beiden Schweizer Künstler Gerda Steiner und Jörg Lenzlinger (Abb. 7).[12] Ihre Installation bei der Kunstbiennale in Venedig 2003 füllte den Raum der Kirche San Stae aus dem 17. Jahrhundert mit zarten gebastelten und einfach gefundenen Objekten, die insbesondere aus der vorgeschlagenen horizontalen Perspektive eine besondere Wirkung entfalteten.[13] Die Kirche als Raum wurde in besonders intensiver Weise spürbar. Mit dem weichen weißen Boden und der horizontalen Liegefläche für die erschöpften Besucher der Biennale entfaltete sich in diesem kühlen Raum eine geradezu ‚himmlische Wirkung'. Die Arbeitsweise des Künstlerpaars und ihre Materialwahl ähneln sich in verschiedenen Werken, und der geistige Überbau zur venezianischen Geschichte und auch zur Artenvielfalt mag die Initialzündung des Werkes sein, aber die starke sinnlich geprägte Wirkung entstand vor allem aus der Verbindung von barockem Raum und der spielerischen wie auch ironischen Vielfalt der zarten Objekte. Auch hier ist es nicht unbedingt das Neue, sondern auch hier wird Bekanntes neu zusammengesetzt. In einer vervielfachten Ansammlung entwickelt es seine Kraft und seinen Ausdruck. Die eindrückliche Wirkung entsteht vielleicht auch aus dem frappierenden Kontrast des dichten überbordenden barocken Raumes mit seinen monumentalen Kunstwerken auf der einen Seite und der Zartheit der minimierten ‚fliegenden' Objekte auf der anderen Seite. Das stimuliert dazu beides, das Schwere und das Leichte, neu zu sehen.

Das Spielen ermöglicht sinn- und zielfreies Suchen, aber dennoch mit hoher Konzentration und Ernsthaftigkeit und erzeugt eine Situation, wie man sie bei Kindern in einem konzentrierten Moment beobachten kann. Man muss sich der Aufgabe hingeben, ohne sich selbst den Stress des Verwertbaren aufzuerlegen. Einfach anfangen und zwar mit Kontinuität.

SO EINFACH WIE MÖGLICH, NUR NICHT EINFACHER Less is more! wird Mies van der Rohe immer wieder und bei jeder Gelegenheit zitiert, auch wenn Albert Einstein das Zitat zugeschrieben wird. Auch wenn es sich also nicht um eine tatsächliche Aussage von ihm handelt, beschreibt es doch sein Entwurfsverständnis. „So einfach wie möglich, nur nicht einfacher!" soll auch der Komiker Karl Valentin gesagt haben. Beides beinhaltet Ähnliches und beides ist keine Anleitung. Aber die Selbstbefragung, was bleiben muss, um eine Idee auszudrücken, ist ein hilfreicher Ansatz. Dabei wird erst geprüft, ob die vielen Ideen überhaupt zusammenpassen und ob die präferierte Idee Konsistenz hat. Eine gute Idee besitzt auch ein Eigenleben, ist eben nicht nur die

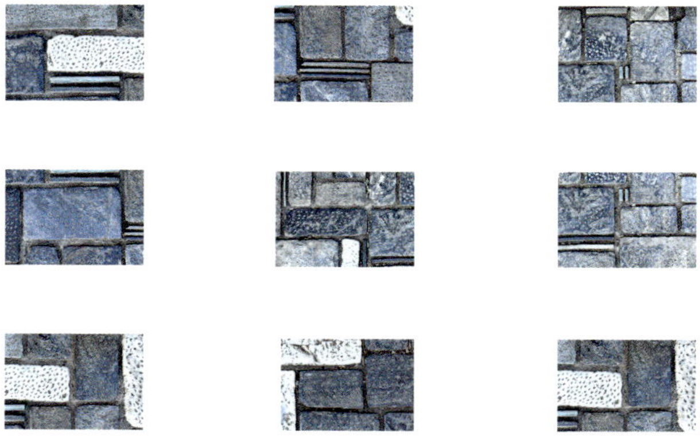

8 | Stone floor on the way to the Akropolis

out of whether the many ideas even fit together and whether the preferred idea has any substance. A good idea also has a certain autonomy and is not just the consequence of one condition or another. As already mentioned: it is only over the further course of the process that the concept is honed and reflected on repeatedly, also to substantiate and secure one's own decisions born out of the endless possibilities. All decisions – and there is a seemingly endless number at the different stages of the development process – must be tested in relation to the conceptual idea. Not schematically, but nevertheless seriously.

FINDING ANALOGIES Of course, it is not enough to sit down and wait for something to show up. One must initiate the process. It can be helpful in this respect to chart possibilities, to designate, to find concepts, to test volumes. What cannot be expressed is difficult to think about. Thinking in pictures and looking for analogies enable an approach to the respective theme.

For example, with the geometric pictures by Sean Scully with their endless variations of rectangular surfaces and colors, one apparently cannot find any relation to a potential reality. He himself, however, shows his analogies with photography from his real surroundings: for example barns, country houses, fences. All examples show colorful rectangles. One can tentatively follow how the artist focused on this. It then appears as if the world can be composed of rectangles of differing sizes (fig. 8).[14] With this relation to reality, his work appears evident, but at the same time he nevertheless liberates himself from the visible reality with the endless surprises and extensive possibilities of his work.

The strategies described here are not an answer for design tasks, but they are aids and tools. They sharpen the senses. In both a targeted and casual manner, they allow one to move step by step from the task to the concept.

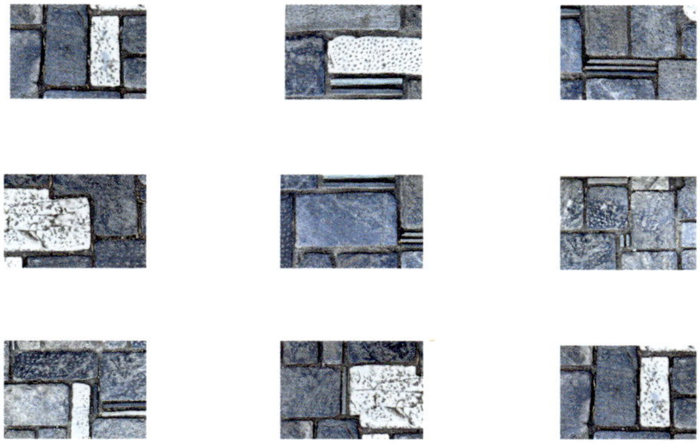

8 | Steinboden auf dem Weg zur Akropolis

Folge von dieser und jener Bedingung. Wie bereits gesagt: Erst im weiteren Verlauf des Prozesses wird das Konzept geschärft und immer wieder reflektiert, auch, um aus den unendlichen Möglichkeiten die eigenen Entscheidungen abzufedern und zu sichern. Alle Entscheidungen – und das sind auf den verschiedenen Ebenen des Entwicklungsprozesses scheinbar unendlich viele – müssen auf der Folie der Konzeptidee geprüft werden. Nicht schematisch, aber dennoch ernsthaft.

ANALOGIEN FINDEN Es reicht natürlich nicht, sich hinzusetzen und zu warten, dass etwas kommt. Man muss den Prozess in Gang setzen. Dabei kann es hilfreich sein, Möglichkeiten aufzuzeichnen, zu benennen, Begriffe zu finden, Volumina zu testen. Was man nicht ausdrücken kann, ist schwer zu denken. In Bildern zu denken, Analogien zu suchen, ermöglicht eine Annäherung an das jeweilige Thema.

So findet man beispielsweise bei den geometrischen Bildern von Sean Scully mit ihren unendlichen Variationen von rechteckigen Flächen und Farben vermeintlich keinen Bezug zu einer möglichen Realität. Er selbst jedoch zeigt seine Analogien mit Fotografien aus seiner realen Umgebung: Scheunen, Landhäuser, Zäune beispielsweise. Alle Beispiele zeigen farbige Rechtecke. Man kann ansatzweise nachvollziehen, wie der Künstler sich darauf fokussiert hat. Es hat dann den Anschein, als ließe sich die Welt aus verschieden großen Rechtecken zusammensetzen (Abb. 8).[14] Mit diesem Realitätsbezug erscheint sein Werk offensichtlich und dennoch befreit er sich gleichzeitig von der sichtbaren Realität mit den unendlichen Überraschungen und ausgedehnten Möglichkeiten seines Werkes.

Die hier beschriebenen Strategien sind keine Antwort für entwurfliche Aufgaben, aber sie sind Hilfsmittel und Instrumente. Sie schärfen die Sinne. Gezielt und ganz beiläufig ermöglichen sie, sich Schritt für Schritt von der Aufgabe zum Konzept zu bewegen.

1 Vgl. | Cf. Joachim Müller-Jung, Wie entsteht Originalität im Gehirn? Kreativität ist die neue Intelligenz, in: Frankfurter Allgemeine Zeitung 28.1.2013, 14 **2** Yvonne Farrell/Laura Weissmüller/Shelley McNamara, Wir sind ewige Optimistinnen (Interview), in: Süddeutsche Zeitung, 2.4. 2018, 10 **3** Vgl. | Cf. Lemma Prozeß, in: Jürgen Mittelstraß (ed.): Enzyklopädie Philosophie und Wissenschaftstheorie, Stuttgart: J.B. Metzler 1995 **4** Ibid. **5** Vgl. | Cf. Matthias Sauerbruch, Fünf Thesen zur Entwurfslehre, in: hoch 1. Jahrbuch des Fachbereichs Architektur der Universität Hannover, Hannover: Internationalismus 2001, 25-27, 26 **6** Vgl. | Cf. Stephan Huber. 7,5 Zi.-Whg f. Künstler, 49 J., Ausstellung im Kunstverein Hannover 2001 **7** Stephan Berg, Shit Happens, in: Kunstverein Hannover (ed.), Stephan Huber. 7,5 Zi.-Whg f. Künstler, 49 J., Hannover: Kunstverein Hannover 2001, Seite 7-9, 7 **8** Vgl. | Cf. Margitta Buchert, Preservation as an origin, in: Maurizio Carta/Sarah Hartmann/Jörg Schröder (eds.), Creative Heritage, Berlin: Jovis 2018, 34-35 **9** Brigitte Hausmann/Angelika Stepken (ed.), Qin Yufen, Leben, Ausstellung Schwartzsche Villa, Kultur Steglitz-Zehlendorf Berlin: Eigen 2018 **10** Vgl. hierzu | Cf. on this subject Umberto Eco, Das offene Kunstwerk, Frankfurt/Main: Suhrkamp 1977 **11** Vgl. | Cf. Heinrich von Kleist, Die allmähliche Verfertigung der Gedanken beim Reden, Erstdruck, in: Zeitschrift von Paul Lindau (ed.) Nord und Süd, 1878, Bd. 4, 3-7 **12** Gerda Steiner/ Jörg Lenzlinger, Giardino Calante. Falling Garden, Ausstellung San Staë, 50. Biennale Venedig 2003 **13** Zutaten: Plastikbeeren (Indien), Kuhfladen (Jura), Abfallpapier (Venedig), Baobabsamen (Australien), Birken-, Holunder- und Magnolienäste (Uster), Dornen (Almeria), Nylonblüten (Preisparadies), Schweinezähne (Indonesien), Algen (Seoul), Orangenschalen (Migros), Düngerkristallblumen (home grown), Taubenknochen (San Staë), Seidenknospen (Stockholm), Rohrkolben (Ettiswil), Katzenschwänze (China), Selleriewurzeln (Montreal), Potenzrinde (Karibik), Wildschweinborsten (Zoo), Bananenblätter (Murten), Gummischlangen (Cincinnati). | Ingredients: Plastic berries (India), cow dung (Jura), waste paper (Venice), baobab seeds (Australia), birch, elder and magnolia branches (Uster), thorns (Almeria), nylon flowers (Preisparadies), pig teeth (Indonesia), algae (Seoul), orange peels (Migros), Crystal fertiliser flowers (home grown), pigeon bones (San Staë), silk buds (Stockholm), reeds (Ettiswil), cattails (China), celery roots (Montreal), potency bark (Caribbean), wild boar bristles (zoo), banana leaves (Murten), rubber snakes (Cincinnati). In: www.steinerlenzlinger.ch/giradinocalante 31.7.2018 **14** Vgl. | Cf. Sean Scully, Gemälde Pastelle Aquarelle Fotografien 1990-2000, Düsseldorf: Richter 2001

HOW DOES ONE STOP?

About the relation between time and designing

Katja Benfer | Cyrus Zahiri

HOW DOES ONE STOP? Those who design are looking for a good solution. Their search is limited by the delivery deadline, the assignment[1] and the interpretation of the adjective 'good'[2]. Timeframes, constraints and quality expectations not only restrict us, they also control and influence the design process. Designing usually takes place within a fixed timeframe. The available time budget influences the leeway of the designer. As the deadline approaches, the 'room for movement' gets smaller, as specifications that determine the design must be decided before concluding the draft. However, time influences the design process not only as a resource. Some of the relations between time and design will be discussed in more detail in the following.[3]

IS IT GOOD ENOUGH? A: Pave this area. B: As cheaply as possible. C: Heavy vehicles in the morning. D: Where is the city center? E: Does the surface look like wood parquet? F: ... The requirements placed on a design solution not only result from the task, they also develop and change during the process. The designer roughly positions the design task between the two poles of 'simplification' and 'enrichment'. Those who simplify look for a solution that is as pragmatic as possible. Adjectives such as 'quick', 'proven', 'cost-effective', 'safe' determine the course of action. Those who enrich, on the other hand, seek to discover the opportunities that a task opens up. The renewal of a paved area also offers an opportunity to rediscover the city center, to think about 'homeliness' and 'wooden parquet' as metaphors guiding the design, or to examine the city structure and existing materials closer.

WIE AUFHÖREN?

Zur Beziehung von Zeit und Entwerfen

Katja Benfer | Cyrus Zahiri

W I E A U F H Ö R E N ? Wer entwirft, sucht nach einer guten Lösung. Eingeschränkt wird diese Suche durch das Abgabedatum, durch die Aufgabe[1] und durch die Auslegung des Adjektivs gut.[2] Zeitrahmen, Fragestellung und Gütevorstellung schränken aber nicht nur ein, sie steuern und beeinflussen auch das Entwerfen. Entworfen wird meist innerhalb einer festgelegten Zeitspanne. Dabei beeinflusst das zur Verfügung stehende Zeitbudget den Handlungsspielraum des Entwerfenden. Mit näher rückendem Abgabetermin verkleinert sich seine ‚Bewegungsfreiheit'. Schließlich müssen entwurfsbestimmende Festsetzungen vor der abschließenden Ausarbeitung entschieden werden. Zeit beeinflusst den Entwurfsprozess aber nicht nur als Ressource. Einige der Beziehungen zwischen Zeit und Entwerfen sollen im Folgenden näher betrachtet werden.[3]

G U T G E N U G ? A. Pflastern Sie doch diese Fläche. B. So günstig wie möglich. C. Schwere Fahrzeuge am Morgen. D. Wo ist das Stadtzentrum? E. Erinnert die Fläche an Holzparkett? F. ... Die Anforderungen an eine Entwurfslösung ergeben sich nicht nur aus der Aufgabenstellung, sie entwickeln und verändern sich auch beim Bearbeiten. Grob verortet der Entwerfende die Entwurfsaufgabe dabei zwischen den beiden Polen ‚Vereinfachen' und ‚Anreichern'. Wer vereinfacht, sucht nach einer möglichst pragmatischen Lösung. Handlungsbestimmend sind dabei Adjektive wie ‚rasch', ‚bewährt', ‚günstig', ‚sicher'. Dagegen zielt Anreichern darauf ab, Chancen zu entdecken, die sich mit einer Aufgabe eröffnen. Das Erneuern einer Pflasterfläche bietet dann gleichzeitig Anlass, das Stadtzentrum neu zu entdecken, über ‚gute Stube' und ‚Holzparkett' als entwurfsleitende Metaphern nachzudenken oder Stadtstruktur und Bestandsmaterialien näher zu untersuchen.

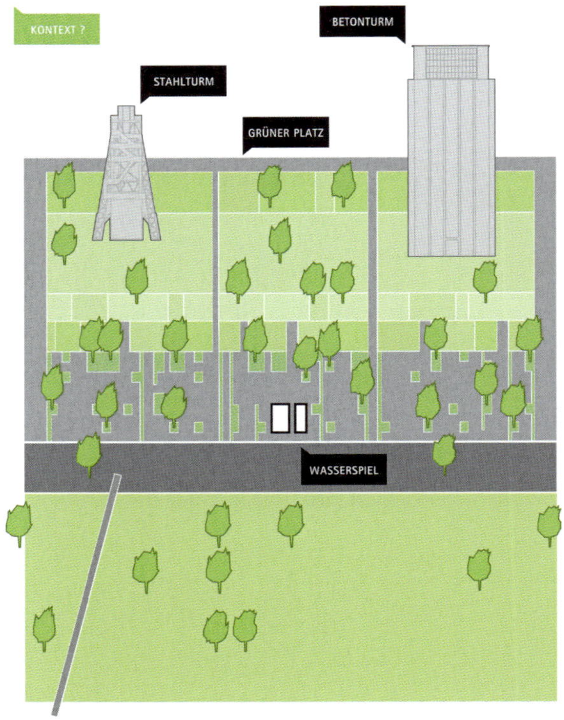

1 | Städtebaulicher Kontext, ehem. Zechengelände ‚Heinrich Kamp-Lintfort', Neubeplanung | Urban context, former mining site 'Zeche Heinrich Kamp-Lintfort', redesign

While exploring options for the task, specific quality criteria also always emerge. Is it enough to ensure the costs, load capacity class and completion date? Or should the design also contribute to the city's identity, to the development of a quarter, or to the contemporary interpretation of a city square? Narrow quality criteria are significantly easier to evaluate than a quality requirement resulting from the incorporation of additional reference systems. Budget certainty is easier to measure than urban development quality. Designing is bound up with an intense search process. The designer pursues a variety of 'routes', each with an uncertain outcome. The time budget is not only put under pressure by 'search expeditions' but also by the absence of reliably measurable quality features. In addition, it must be decided each time from case to case whether an ongoing option has good enough prospects to be pursued or whether it would be better to start over. In parallel, one must look around for promising alternatives.

REFERENCE SYSTEMS AND TIME Returning once again to the design objective of 'enrichment' ... According to Koestler, creative accomplishments are the result of the successful link between reference systems of essentially different natures.[4] The means for this are comparison, abstraction, analogy, or the use of metaphors. Layering that evokes 'bisociations' is what brings success.[5] For Koestler, associations always remain bound to their original reference system. 'Bisociations', on the other hand, refer to several reference systems and therefore point to new insights.[6] For urban design, Oswald Mathias Ungers illustrates this approach in 1982 in his book 'Morphology. City Metaphors'.[7] He combines on each double page a city layout, an image and a concept. With this juxta-

2-6 | Themen als Anknüpfungspunkte für den Entwurf ‚Wasserspiel' | Themes as starting points for the design 'Wasserspiel'

Beim Ausloten der Aufgabenstellung tauchen immer auch eigene Gütekriterien auf. Reicht es aus, Kosten, Belastungsklasse und Fertigstellungsdatum zu sichern? Oder soll der Entwurf auch beitragen zur Stadtidentität, zur Adressbildung oder zur zeitgenössischen Interpretation eines Stadtplatzes? Dabei lassen sich eng gefasste Gütekriterien deutlich einfacher bewerten, als der Güteanspruch, der sich durch das Hinzuziehen weiterer Bezugssysteme ergibt. Kostensicherheit ist einfacher zu messen als städtebauliche Qualität. Entwerfen ist verbunden mit einem intensiven Suchprozess. Dazu verfolgt der Entwerfende unterschiedliche ‚Routen' mit jeweils ungewissem Ausgang. Sein Zeitbudget wird dabei aber nicht nur belastet durch ‚Such-Expeditionen', sondern auch das Fehlen von verlässlich messbaren Gütemerkmalen. Zudem muss er fallbezogen immer wieder entscheiden, ob eine laufende Untersuchung verheißungsvoll genug erscheint, um weiterverfolgt zu werden oder doch besser abzubrechen ist. Parallel dazu ist Ausschau zu halten nach aussichtsreichen Alternativen.

BEZUGSSYSTEME UND ZEIT Noch einmal zurück zum Entwurfsziel ‚Anreichern' ... Koestler zufolge entstehen schöpferische Leistungen durch das erfolgreiche Verknüpfen von zunächst wesensverschiedenen Bezugssystemen.[4] Mittel hierzu sind Vergleich, Abstraktion, Analogie oder der Einsatz von Metaphern. Erfolgreich sind Überlagerungen, die ‚Bisoziationen' wecken.[5] Für Koestler bleiben Assoziationen stets eingebunden in ihr ursprüngliches Bezugssystem. Dagegen beziehen sich ‚Bisoziationen' auf mehrere Bezugssysteme und verweisen damit auf neue Einsichten.[6] Für den Städtebau-Entwurf illustriert Oswald Mathias Ungers diesen Ansatz 1982 in seinem Buch ‚Morphologie. City Metaphors'.[7] Auf Doppelseiten kombiniert er dazu jeweils einen Stadtgrundriss, eine Abbildung und einen Begriff. Mit dieser Gegenüberstellung überlässt er es dem Betrachter, Wechselbeziehungen zwischen den unterschiedlichen Ausdrucksformen zu (er)finden. Augenfällig dabei ist, dass sich Ungers bei seinen Gegenüberstellungen die Freiheit nimmt, die Artefakte jeweils aus ihrem historischen Kontext loszulösen und frei

position, he leaves it up to the viewer to find or invent connections between the different forms of expression. It is noticeable that Ungers takes the liberty in his proposition to release the artifacts from their historical context and combine them freely. Interpreted in this manner, design is a search for exciting ordering systems rich in connections. This search can lead in two directions: firstly, as an attempt to enrich the design with additional layers of meaning, secondly as an attempt to build up additional relationships between the design and the substance. Designing aims towards a desirable future[8]. At the same time, the choice of reference systems also always bears historical connotations. The designer is therefore moving within a very wide timeframe.

ADVANTAGES AND DISADVANTAGES OF ROUTINES During the design process, objects, spaces and situations are simulated. The aim is to anticipate certain aspects of form, space and quality, to test and specify them. Promising design approaches are translated into sketches and models. Depending on the respective focal aspect, one selects suitable media, methods of presentation and translation tools accordingly.[9] The choice of tool provides different presentation, abstraction and manipulation techniques.[10] This regularly also comprises the appropriated use of tools that belong to other areas.[11]

As an intermediate result, a series of different artifacts show up. As 'epistemic objects', they offer a prospect of potentially interesting solutions.[12] They can be modified experimentally and enable the exploration and extension of the potential of an assignment.[13] Additionally unexpected results in the form of deviations and errors offer the opportunity to extend the scope of solutions.[14] Stable processes establish themselves with the use of apparently proven tools. There are various reasons for the emergence of these routines. Over time, designers develop a particular proclivity for certain techniques and materials. These 'favorite tools' include preferred types of pen, chalk and paper, modelling materials, or certain digital applications.

Routines also emerge through pursuing learnt ways of working or imitating examples. In addition, they are also regulated by time constraints. Sketching paper, an everyday item of work equipment today, was vehemently rejected by Semper around 1834.[15] On the other hand, in the 1980s the last 'urban development design kits' with prefabricated slab and tower buildings were set aside. In the 1990s there was a trend to copy collages of the landscape architect Yves Brunier and the design diagrams of Dutch architects. In view of a tight time budget and collaborative work processes, routines play a crucial role in the design process. When exploring a solution, they promise 'shortcuts' and therefore time saving. Within work groups, they also offer an orientation framework, as all those involved can refer to established procedures. Partial results can be exchanged between group members and worked out by different participants. Furthermore, the artefacts emerging over the course of the design remain comparable.

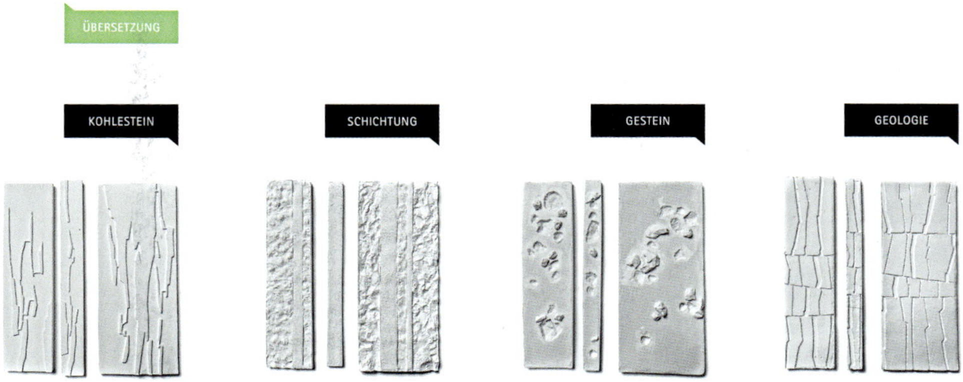

7-10 | Übersetzung der Themen in Reliefs, Gipsmodelle | Translation of the themes into reliefs, plaster models

zu kombinieren. In dieser Leseweise ist Entwerfen ein Suchen nach spannungsvollen und beziehungsreichen Ordnungssystemen. Dabei kann sich diese Suche in zwei Richtungen bewegen: einerseits als Versuch, den Entwurf um zusätzliche Bedeutungsebenen anzureichern und andererseits als Ansatz, um zusätzliche Beziehungen zwischen Entwurf und Bestand aufzubauen. Entwerfen zielt auf eine wünschenswerte Zukunft ab.[8] Gleichzeitig sind mit der Wahl von Bezugssystemen immer auch historische Konnotationen verknüpft. Damit bewegt sich der Entwerfende in einem sehr breit gespannten Zeitrahmen.

WOHL UND WEHE DER ROUTINEN Während des Entwurfsprozesses werden Objekte, Räume und Situationen simuliert. Ziel ist es, bestimmte Aspekte zu Form, Raum und Beschaffenheit vorwegzunehmen, um sie zu überprüfen und zu präzisieren. Dazu werden aussichtsreiche Entwurfsansätze in Abbildungen und Modelle übersetzt. Je nach der gerade im Fokus stehenden Fragestellung sind dazu jeweils geeignete Medien, Darstellungsweisen und Übersetzungswerkzeuge auszuwählen.[9] Mit der Werkzeugwahl werden jeweils unterschiedliche Darstellungs-, Abstraktions- und Manipulationstechniken verfügbar.[10] Das schließt regelmäßig auch das Zweckentfremden von Werkzeugen ein, die eigentlich in anderen Bereichen eingesetzt werden.[11]

Als Zwischenergebnis entstehen Reihen aus unterschiedlich ausgearbeiteten Artefakten. Als ‚epistemische Objekte' bieten sie einen Ausblick auf potentiell interessante Lösungen.[12] Sie lassen sich probeweise verändern und ermöglichen es damit, das Potential einer Aufgabe zu erkunden und auszuweiten.[13] Unerwartete Ergebnisse in Form von Abweichungen und Fehlern bieten zudem die Chance den Lösungsraum zusätzlich zu erweitern.[14] Mit dem Einsatz scheinbar bewährter Werkzeuge etablieren sich gleichbleibende Abläufe. Für das Entstehen dieser Routinen gibt es unterschiedliche Gründe. Im Laufe der Zeit entwickeln Entwerfende eine besondere Zuneigung zu bestimmten Techniken und Materialien. Zu diesen Lieblingswerkzeugen gehören bevorzugte Stift-, Kreide- und Papiersorten, Modellbaumaterialien oder auch bestimmte digitale Anwendungen.

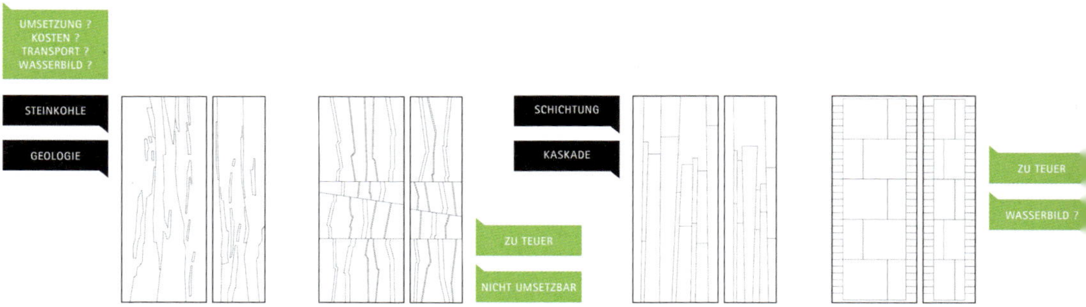

11-14 | Umsetzung der Reliefs, CAD Zeichnung | Realisation of the reliefs, CAD drawing

A given set of tools and routines are associated with the hope that the earlier proven success of an approach can also be applied to the assignment at hand. Familiar routines, such as the creation of analysis sketches and work models, are often used as an introductory approach to a new task. In later design phases, digital or analog detailed models enable the examination of spatial disposition, material use and connections. When applying routines, however, it is also possible to overlook problems and opportunities. Abraham Maslow provides a reminder that proven tools are also often used when other work methods would be more suitable.[16]

OPTIONS AND REPERTOIRE Over the course of the design process, the designer can make use of the aforementioned methods. Depending on experience, repertoire and budget, they can be combined or used sequentially. At the beginning of the examination, various approaches are developed and pursued in parallel. Horst Rittel suggests the creation and variation of options.[17] For Rheinberger, the repetition and modification of routines is an important method of gaining knowledge.[18] According to Ahrens, the experimenter must attempt to "maintain a 'sphere of vagueness' [...] that on the one hand prevents pure frenzy and on the other hand does not drift into being machine-like."[19] For certain periods of time it remains unclear "which signals should be strengthened and which should be weakened."[20]

The working method described here is understood by Rheinberger as 'researching design'. It does not distinguish between scientific and artistic practices. "The thoughts of inventors and scientists are directed, like artists, not towards the knowledge of the existing, instead their notions concentrate on future possibilities."[21] In the experiment, it is possible that "commonly used tools [...] take on new functions" and that "unanticipated events" occur.[22] Experimental setups therefore allow the creation of knowledge. Depending on the means used, involving teams enables an additional probing of options or more in-depth approaches to solutions. However, if these co-designers are not attuned to each other or are on different wavelengths, this process can also be very unproductive and fruitless.

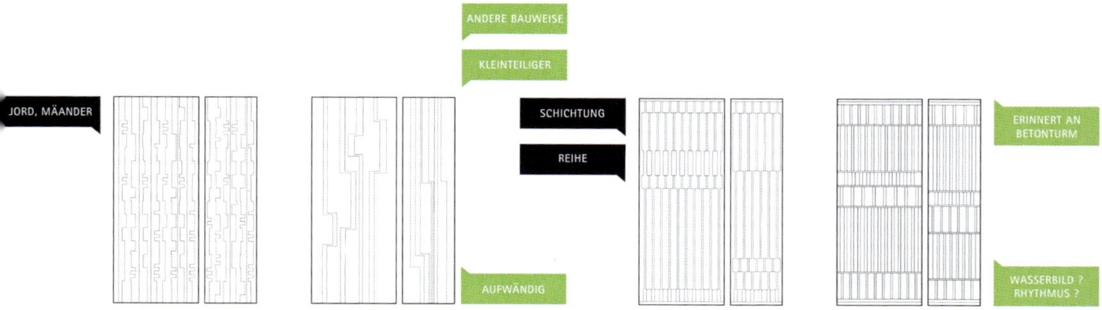

15-18 | Umsetzung der Reliefs, CAD Zeichnung | Realisation of the reliefs, CAD drawing

Routinen entstehen auch durch das Aufgreifen erlernter Arbeitsweisen oder das Nachahmen von Vorbildern. Zudem sind sie auch abhängig von zeitbedingten Sichtweisen. Skizzenpapier, ein heute alltägliches Arbeitsmittel, wurde von Semper um 1834 vehement abgelehnt.[15] Dagegen wurden in den 1980er Jahren die letzten ‚Städtebau-Entwurfskoffer' mit vorgefertigten Zeilen- und Punktbauten weggelegt. Wer auf sich hielt, kopierte in den 1990er Jahren Collagen des Landschaftsarchitekten Yves Brunier und die Entwurfs-Diagramme niederländischer Architekten. Angesichts eines knappen Zeitbudgets und arbeitsteiliger Arbeitsprozesse spielen Routinen eine wichtige Rolle im Entwurfsprozess. Beim Erkunden eines Lösungsraum versprechen sie ‚Abkürzungen' und damit Zeitersparnis. Innerhalb von Arbeitsgruppen bieten sie zudem einen Orientierungsrahmen, da alle Beteiligten auf festgelegte Abläufe zurückgreifen können. Zwischen den Gruppenmitgliedern können Teil-Ergebnisse ausgetauscht und von anderen weiterentwickelt werden. Wichtig ist auch, dass die im Entwurfsverlauf entstehenden Artefakte untereinander vergleichbar bleiben.

Mit einem festgelegten Werkzeuggebrauch und den dazugehörigen Routinen ist die Hoffnung verbunden, dass sich ein früher erfolgreiches Vorgehen auch auf die anstehende Aufgabe übertragen lässt. Vertraute Routinen, wie das Herstellen von Analysezeichnungen und Arbeitsmodellen werden oft einleitend zur Annäherung an eine neue Aufgabe genutzt. In späteren Entwurfsphasen ermöglichen digitale oder analoge Detailmodelle das Prüfen von Raumdisposition, Materialeinsatz und Anschlüssen. Beim Einsetzen von Routinen können aber auch Probleme und Chancen übersehen werden. Abraham Maslow erinnert daran, dass vertraute Werkzeuge oft auch dann eingesetzt werden, wenn andere Arbeitsmittel besser geeignet wären.[16]

VARIANTEN UND REPERTOIRE Im Laufe des Entwurfsprozesses kann der Entwerfende dazu auf die oben beschriebenen Methoden zurückgreifen. Je nach Erfahrung, Repertoire und den Budget lassen sie sich kombinieren oder nacheinander einsetzen. Zu Beginn der Untersuchung werden unterschiedliche Ansätze parallel entwickelt und verfolgt. Horst Rittel schlägt dazu das Erzeugen und Evaluieren von Varianten vor.[17] Für

Those who have gathered experience in design have a repertoire at their disposal allowing a greater degree of freedom. It includes solutions that have already been applied successfully, solution fragments from former examinations, as well as an overview of series of solutions surrounding one's own field of work.[23] In addition, there is a more or less well-trained ability for the 'hostile takeover' of reference systems from extraneous fields. A wider design repertoire enables shortcuts. Potential solution routes can be gauged better in advance. In some cases, occurring problems can be overcome quicker. At the same time, this form of predisposition is also restrictive, because preferred and proven solutions are repeated more readily.

TURNING POINTS The emerging solution appears non-descriptive and weak. The intermediate result does not meet expectations. Suddenly additional requirements must be taken into consideration. Over the course of the design process, critical turning points often turn up unexpectedly. The situation is complicated by having to take into consideration that investments have already been made, the time contingent is dwindling and already set out plans must be redone and adapted in case of changes. In light of this, it is crucial to develop alternatives quickly. A more intense consideration becomes necessary, both conceptually, while searching for suitable reference systems, as well as for the purposeful use of tools.

In relation to the concept, already discarded approaches are studied again ad hoc – perhaps solutions were overlooked. In addition, new design attempts must be launched. On the one hand, there is a resorting to the individual repertoire of familiar solutions. At the same time, however, one must also look for new routes. Koestler and Ungers do not explain, however, how to find a suitable reference system. Koestler distinguishes between an incubation phase and an inspiration phase. The first phase is characterized by a concentrated examination of the assignment. The second phase, on the other hand, evades control. Koestler situates it more at the transition to the subconscious.[24] What makes matters worse is that ideas that seem suitable at first may later turn out to be misdirected.[25]

IMPROVISING As the time budget steadily dwindles, it must be checked at intervals whether the tools and routines used are supporting the search process effectively. Design monitoring is usually carried out manually.[26] Accordingly, results can only be assessed after a certain period of time. At the same time, unproductive and prolonged ways of working must be broken off as quickly as possible and replaced by more suitable methods. Over the course of the design process, there is a constant search for effective representation methods. Sometimes characteristics and properties emerge that cannot be depicted by conventional means. These include, in particular, the effect of light and shade, water, or the interplay of plants.[27] In some cases, new translation and representation forms must be 'invented'.[28] A method is suitable if the associated tools are available quickly and without induction and the intermediate results they produce are reversible and remain easy to adapt.[29]

BEZIEHUNG WASSER / STEIN ?

PARAMETER ?

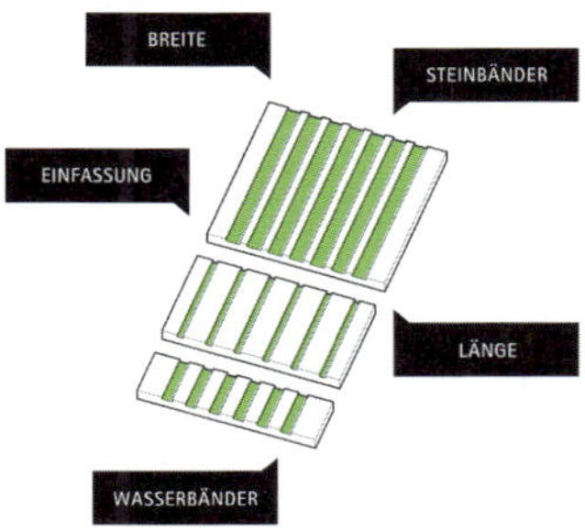

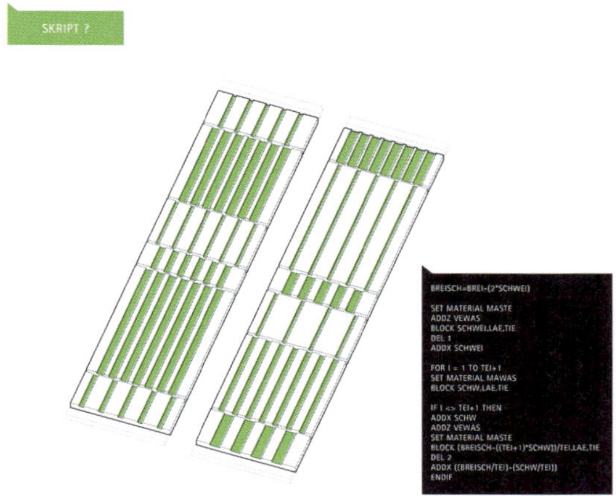

19-20 | Präzisierung Rhythmus Stein- & Wasserstreifen, 3D-CAD-Skript | Specification rhythm stone & water strips, 3D CAD script

Rheinberger ist das Wiederholen und Abwandeln von Routinen eine wichtige Methode der Wissensgewinnung.[18] Ahrens zufolge muss der Experimentator dazu versuchen „einen ‚Raum des Vagen' aufrechtzuerhalten [...], der einerseits das reine Rauschen verhindert und andererseits nicht ins Maschinenhafte abdriftet."[19] Dabei bleibt über bestimmte Zeitstrecken hinweg unklar, „welche Signale verstärkt und welche abgeschwächt werden sollten".[20]

Die hier beschriebene Arbeitsweise wird mit Rheinberger als ‚forschendes Entwerfen' verstanden. Er unterscheidet dabei nicht zwischen wissenschaftlichen und künstlerischen Praktiken. „Die Gedanken von Erfindern und Wissenschaftlern richten sich ganz ähnlich wie die von Künstlern nicht auf die Erkenntnis des Bestehenden, ihre Vorstellungen konzentrieren sich auf zukünftige Möglichkeiten."[21] Im Experiment können „gängig verwendete Werkzeuge [...] neue Funktionen annehmen" und „unvorwegnehmbare Ereignisse" auftreten.[22] Experimentalanordnungen ermöglichen damit die Herstellung von Wissen. Je nach Mitteleinsatz ermöglicht der Einsatz von Teams ein zusätzliches Erarbeiten von Varianten oder vertiefenden Lösungsansätzen. Sind diese Co-Entwerfenden nicht aufeinander eingespielt oder auf unterschiedliche ‚Wellenlängen' eingestellt, kann dieses Verfahren allerdings auch sehr unproduktiv und unergiebig sein.

Wer im Entwerfen Erfahrung gesammelt hat, verfügt über ein Repertoire und damit einen höheren Freiheitsgrad. Zu diesem Fundus gehören bereits erfolgreich eingesetzte Lösungen, Lösungsfragmente aus früheren Auseinandersetzungen sowie ein Überblick über Lösungsreihen rund um das eigene Arbeitsfeld.[23] Hinzu kommt noch eine mehr oder weniger gut antrainierte Fähigkeit zur ‚feindlichen Übernahme' von Bezugssystemen aus fachfremden Bereichen. Ein größeres Entwurfsrepertoire erlaubt Abkürzungen. Potentielle Lösungswege lassen sich vorab besser abschätzen. Fallweise lassen sich auftretende Probleme rascher bewältigen. Gleichzeitig schränkt diese Form der Vorprägung aber auch ein, denn bevorzugte und bewährte Lösungen werden häufiger wiederholt.

WASSERBILD ?

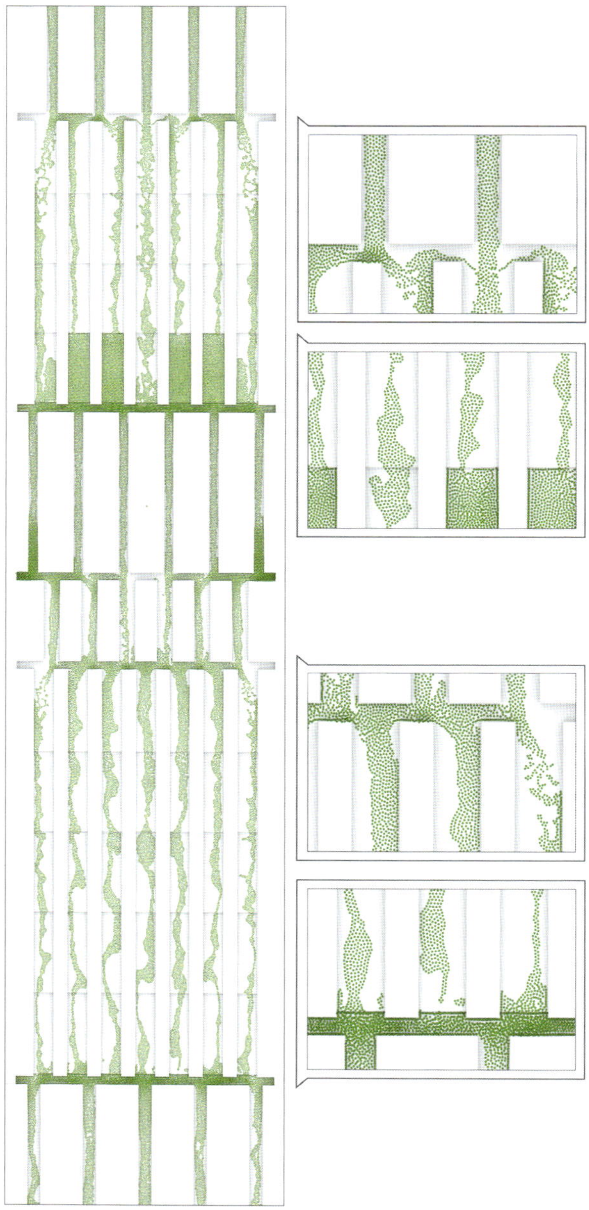

WASSER-SIMULATION

- EMITTERS
  - EMITTER QUELLE 1
  - EMITTER QUELLE 2
  - EMITTER QUELLE 3
  - EMITTER QUELLE 4
  - EMITTER QUELLE 5
  - EMITTER QUELLE 6
  - EMITTER QUELLE 7
- FLUIDS
  - FLUID SPRITZ
  - FLUIDS QUELLE
  - FLUIDS NEBEL
- DAEMONS
  - GRAVITY
  - SPEED
  - WIND

21 | Simulation Wasserbild, Animation & Rendering C4D | Simulation of water appearance, animation & rendering C4D

W E N D E P U N K T E Die erarbeitete Lösung wirkt kraftlos und nichtssagend. Das Zwischenergebnis fällt anders aus als gedacht. Und plötzlich müssen zusätzliche Anforderungen berücksichtigt werden. Im Laufe des Entwurfsprozesses tauchen oft unerwartet kritische Wendepunkte auf. Erschwerend ist dabei zu berücksichtigen, dass bereits Mittel investiert wurden, das Zeitkontingent schwindet und bei Änderungen bereits erarbeitete Planungen zu wiederholen und anzupassen sind. In dieser Stimmung sind rasch Alternativen zu entwickeln. Notwendig wird eine intensivere Auseinandersetzung, sowohl konzeptionell, bei der Suche nach geeigneten Bezugssystemen, wie auch beim zweckmäßigen Einsatz von Werkzeugen.

Konzeptbezogen werden dazu ad hoc bereits verworfene Ansätze erneut geprüft – vielleicht wurden Lösungen übersehen. Ergänzend müssen neue Entwurfsversuche gestartet werden. Einerseits wird dabei zurückgegriffen auf das individuelle Repertoire an bekannten Lösungsansätzen. Gleichzeitig muss aber auch nach neuen Wegen gesucht werden. Koestler und Ungers erläutern allerdings nicht, auf welche Weise ein geeignetes Bezugssystem zu finden ist. Immerhin unterscheidet Koestler zwischen einer Inkubations-Phase und einer Phase der Inspiration. Die erste Phase ist gekennzeichnet durch eine konzentrierte Auseinandersetzung mit der Fragestellung. Dagegen entzieht sich die zweite Phase einer Steuerung. Koestler verortet sie eher am Übergang zum Unbewussten.[24] Erschwerend ist, dass zunächst als passend erscheinende Ideen sich zu einem späteren Zeitpunkt als Irrläufer erweisen können.[25]

I M P R O V I S I E R E N Bei stetig schrumpfendem Zeitbudget ist in Abständen immer wieder zu prüfen, ob die eingesetzten Werkzeuge und Routinen den Suchprozess sinnvoll unterstützen. Entwurfsuntersuchungen werden überwiegend händisch unternommen.[26] Entsprechend sind die Ergebnisse erst nach einiger Zeit auszuwerten. Gleichzeitig müssen unproduktive und langwierige Arbeitsweisen möglichst rasch abgebrochen und durch besser geeignete Methoden ersetzt werden. Im Laufe des Entwurfsprozesses wird immer wieder nach geeigneten Darstellungsmitteln gesucht, um offene Fragen rasch und wirksam prüfen zu können. Stellenweise tauchen dabei auch Merkmale und Eigenschaften auf, die sich durch herkömmliche Mittel nicht darstellen lassen. Dazu gehören insbesondere die Wirkung von Licht und Schatten, Wasser sowie das Zusammenspiel von Pflanzen.[27] Fallweise sind dazu neue Übersetzungs- und Darstellungsformen zu ‚erfinden'.[28] Eine Methode ist gut geeignet, wenn die dazugehörigen Werkzeuge rasch und ohne Einarbeitung verfügbar sind und die damit erzeugten Zwischenergebnisse reversibel und leicht bearbeitbar bleiben.[29]

FESTHALTEN, AUSSCHAU HALTEN ODER ANHALTEN? In der Zusammenschau zeigt sich, dass sich Entwerfende zwischen unterschiedlichen Zeithorizonten bewegen und dabei unterschiedliche Haltungen im Umgang mit Zeit miteinander verknüpfen müssen. Dabei ist der Entwurfsprozess durch widersprüchliche Bewegungsrichtungen

HOLD ON, LOOK AROUND OR CALL A HALT? Viewed as a whole, it is evident that designers are moving between different time horizons and must therefore combine different ways of handling time. The design process is determined by conflicting directions. Should one continue to hold on to the work result? Is there hope for alternatives? Or is it better to call it a day? The situation is reminiscent of the halting problem described by Alan Turing.[30] How can one tell if a process is running successfully or whether one should break it off? Rittel expresses himself rather succinctly on the subject. No conclusive solutions can be found for nasty problems.[31] Accordingly, they do not have any stoppage rules. Instead the designer reacts to external framework conditions: "He runs out of time, money, or patience."[32]

In view of the constantly shrinking time budget, the designer finds himself in a particular situation. On the one hand, perseverance is necessary to continue to pursue already worked out design approaches through barren spells. At the same time, however, openness is important to be able to discover deviations as potential alternatives. There must also be the willingness to leave what has already been worked on behind and to start again. This leads to conflicting feelings such as tension, trust, hope, fear, helplessness, rage and emptiness.[33] However, this emotional situation can also contribute to shifting one's perspective. Indicators of this are a great concentration and special attention to the everyday. Objects, phenomena and processes are considered with more attention than usual in terms of their suitability for the design process.

This exceptional situation resounds in Petra Blaisse's description of Yves Brunier's way of working: "[...] Infuriatingly bad color schemes, brutal forms covered with tin foil, bright paint: technical props and crude materials like foam rubber, plastic, Q-tips, wire, textiles, screws etcetera symbolizing building and landscape: all thrown together in what seemed great anguish and haste!"[34] Koolhaas adds elsewhere: "He took everything that was on the table, and incorporated it in the maquette, as if this very determination to put things together itself generated the logic of the decision"[35] One must also consider that designing is not a zero-sum game. (Almost) every design assignment offers the opportunity for an intense examination of self-chosen topics. The corresponding experiences extend the individual repertoire and can be reused elsewhere. And perhaps one can then also save a little time.

PROSPECTS It is worth undertaking a closer examination of the interplay between time and design process – especially as design processes and scientific working resort to similar approaches and methods in part. Reference points on this are offered by Koestler's theory of the layering of reference systems (bisociation and blending), the use of tools and routines to generate 'epistemic objects' described by Rheinberger, or the handling of historical series presented by Kubler.

bestimmt. Soll am Arbeitsergebnis weiter festgehalten werden? Lässt sich auf Alternativen hoffen? Oder ist es doch besser, alles hinzuschmeißen? Die Situation erinnert an das von Alan Turing beschriebene Halteproblem.[30] Woran ist zu erkennen, ob ein Prozess erfolgreich verläuft oder abgebrochen werden soll? Rittel äußert sich dazu recht lapidar. Für bösartige Probleme lassen sich nun mal keine abschließenden Lösungen finden.[31] Entsprechend besitzen sie auch keine Stopp-Regel. Ersatzweise reagiert der Entwerfende auf externe Randbedingungen: „Ihm fehlt Zeit, Geld oder Geduld."[32]

Angesichts des stetig geringer werdenden Zeitbudgets gerät der Entwerfende in eine besondere Lage. Einerseits ist Durchhaltevermögen nötig, um bislang erarbeitete Entwurfsansätze über Durststrecken weiter zu verfolgen. Gleichzeitig wichtig ist aber auch Offenheit, um Abweichendes und Weitab-Liegendes als potentielle Alternativen entdecken zu können. Dazu muss auch die Bereitschaft vorhanden sein, das bislang Erarbeitete hinter sich zu lassen und neu anzufangen. Dabei überlagern sich widersprüchliche Gefühle wie Anspannung, Vertrauen, Hoffnung, Angst, Hilflosigkeit, Wut und Leere.[33] Allerdings kann diese Empfindungslage auch dazu beitragen, die Wahrnehmung zu verschieben. Kennzeichen hierfür sind eine größere Konzentration und eine besondere Zuwendung für Alltägliches. Mit mehr Aufmerksamkeit als üblich werden dabei Gegenstände, Phänomene und Abläufe auf ihre Eignung für den Entwurfsprozess hin überprüft.

Dieser Ausnahmezustand klingt an in Petra Blaisse' Beschreibung von Yves Bruniers Arbeitsweise: „[...] scheußliche Farbgruppen, rabiate Formen eingefasst in Alufolie, grelle Farben: technisches Halbzeug und Rohmaterialien wie Moosgummi, Plastik, Wattestäbchen, Draht, Textilien, Schrauben usw., die Gebäude und Landschaft darstellen sollten: alles zusammengeworfen unter scheinbar großer Angst und Eile!".[34] An anderer Stelle ergänzt Koolhaas: „Er nahm alles, was auf dem Tisch lag und fügte es in das Modell ein, als ob diese Entschlossenheit Dinge zusammenzustellen, die Entscheidung begründete."[35] Zu berücksichtigen ist auch, das Entwerfen kein Null-Summen-Spiel ist. (Fast) jede Entwurfsaufgabe bietet die Chance sich intensiv mit selbst-gewählten Themenfeldern auseinanderzusetzen. Die entsprechenden Erfahrungen erweitern das individuelle Repertoire und können an anderer Stelle wiederverwendet werden. Und vielleicht lässt sich dann auch etwas Zeit einsparen.

A U S B L I C K Es lohnt sich, die Wechselbeziehungen zwischen Zeit und Entwurfsprozess näher zu untersuchen – insbesondere, da Entwurfsprozesse und wissenschaftliches Arbeiten über Strecken auf ähnliche Ansätze und Methoden zurückgreifen. Anknüpfungspunkte dazu bieten Koestlers These zur Überlagerung von Bezugssystemen (Bisoziation und Blending), der von Rheinberger beschriebene Einsatz von Werkzeugen und Routinen zur Erzeugung von ‚epistemischen Objekten' oder der von Kubler vorgestellte Umgang mit historischen Reihen.

1 Horst W. Rittel/Wolf D. Reuter, Planen, Entwerfen, Design - Ausgewählte Schriften zur Theorie und Methodik, Stuttgart Berlin Köln: Kohlhammer 1992, 20 ff. | et seqq. **2** ibid. 113 ff. | et seqq. **3** Es gibt unterschiedliche Versuche den Entwurfsprozess in Abschnitte aufzuteilen. Allerdings herrscht hierzu Uneinigkeit - nicht nur hinsichtlich der Anzahl der Entwurfsphasen und ihrer Benennung, sondern auch zur Abfolge und Verknüpfung der Phasen. Vgl. dazu | There are varying attempts to divide the design process into stages. However, there is disagreement – not only regarding the number of design phases and how they are termed, but also regarding the sequence and linking of phases. Cf. on this subject Bryan Lawson, How Designers Think, London: Routledge 1980, 24ff., | et. seqq., 110 **4** Arthur Koestler, The Act of Creation, London: Hutchinson & Co. 1964, 190 **5** ibid. 376 **6** Koestlers Ansatz wird von Fauconnier und Turner weiter ausgearbeitet. Für die Überlagerung von unterschiedlichen Bezugssystemen schlagen sie den Begriff ‚Conceptual Blending' vor. Vgl. | Koestler's approach is elaborated by Fauconnier and Turner. For the layering of different reference systems they suggest Begriet seqq. 'Conceptual Blending'. Cf. Gilles Fauconnier, Mark Turner, The Way We Think - Conceptual Blending And The Mind's Hidden Complexities, New York: Basic Books 2003 **7** Oswald Mathias Ungers, Morphologie - City Metaphors, Cologne: Verlag der Buchhandlung König 1982. Koestlers Buch erscheint bereits 1962. | Koestler's book was already published in 1962. **8** Katja Benfer, Cyrus Zahiri, Entwurf und Krise in: Margitta Buchert (ed.), Praktiken reflexiven Entwerfens, Berlin: Jovis 2016, 165-176 **9** Vgl. | Cf. Ulrike Böhm, Cyrus Zahiri, Katja Benfer, Tools & Translation. Relations between Design and Digital Techniques, in: Buhmann, Pietsch, Heins (ed.), Digital Design in Landscape Architecture, Heidelberg u.a.: Wichmann 2008, 141-149 **10** Vgl. | Cf. Christian Gänshirt, Werkzeuge für Ideen - Einführung in das architektonische Entwerfen, Basel, Boston, Berlin: Birkhäuser 2007 **11** Vgl. | Cf. Ulrike Böhm, Cyrus Zahiri, Katja Benfer, The Design Process. Between Imagination, Implementation and Evaluation, in: Amsterdam European League of Institutes of the Arts: Designing Design Education. Proceedings part 1, Designtrain congress, Amsterdam: 2008, 42-56 **12** Das gilt auch für pragmatische Lösungen, denn Zwischenlösungen dienen dazu Kosten zu sichern, Mengen zu berechnen oder Plandarstellungen für die Baustelle zu erarbeiten etc. Zu epistemischen Dingen vgl. | This also applies to pragmatic solutions, because intermediate solutions serve the purpose of securing costs, calculating quantities or working out plans for the building site etc. On epistemic matters cf. Hans-Jörg Rheinberger, Experimentalsysteme und epistemische Dinge: Eine Geschichte der Proteinsynthese im Reagenzglas, Frankfurt/Main: Suhrkamp Verlag 2006 **13** Vgl. | Cf. Ulrike Böhm, Cyrus Zahiri, Katja Benfer, op. cit. (Anm. 9 | note 9) **14** Vgl. | Cf. ibid. **15** Gottfried Semper, Vorläufige Bemerkungen über bemalte Architektur und Plastik bei den Alten,

Altona: Hammerich 1834, 7 **16** 'Law of the instrument', Abraham Maslow, Psychology of science - A reconnaissance, Madison: Harper & Row 1966, 15 **17** Vgl. | Cf. Horst W. Rittel/Wolf D. Reuter, op. cit. (Anm. 1 | note 1) **18** Vgl. | Cf. Hans-Jörg Rheinberger, op. cit. (Anm. 12 | note 12) **19** Vgl. | Cf. Sönke Ahrens, Experiment und Exploration: Bildung als experimentelle Form der Welterschließung, Bielefeld: Transcript 2010 **20** ibid., 134 **21** Hans-Jörg Rheinberger, op. cit. (Anm. 12 | note 12), 97 **22** ibid., 16, 34 **23** George Kubler, Die Form der Zeit. Anmerkungen zur Geschichte der Dinge, Berlin: Suhrkamp, 1982, 70 **24** Arthur Koestler, The Act of Creation, London: Hutchinson & Co. 1964, 119 **25** Rittel illustriert diesen Schock mithilfe eines Diagramms | Rittel illustrates this shock with the help of a diagram. Vgl. | Cf. ibid. op. cit. (Anm. 1 | note 1), 78 ff. | et seqq. **26** Das gilt insbesondere auch für die Eingabe in digitale Anwendungen. | This applies in particular to the input of digital applications. **27** Fallweise kann Modelling- und Rendering-Software unterstützen. Voraussetzung ist aber auch hier ein geschickter Umgang mit Zeit, denn die Simulation ist überwiegend sehr rechen- und damit zeitintensiv. | In some cases, modelling and rendering software can provide support. However, the condition here also is an accomplished handling of time, as the simulation is mostly very calculation-intensive and therefore time-intensive. **28** Christian Gänshirt zitiert dazu den Architekten Siza: „Man darf sich nicht zum Sklaven eines einzigen Arbeitsmittels machen." | Christian Gänshirt cites the architect Siza on this subject: "One must not make oneself a slave to a single working method". Christian Gänshirt, op. cit. (Anm. 10 | note 10), 21 **29** Vgl. | Cf. Ulrike Böhm/ Cyrus Zahiri/Katja Benfer, op. cit. (Anm. 10 | note 9); Lernkurven, digitale Aufbereitung, Workflow, Verfügbarkeit und Fertigungszeiten müssen insbesondere bei digitalen Anwendungen wie 3D-Drucker und CNC-Fräsen berücksichtigt werden. Aufgrund dieser Randbedingungen bleiben ad hoc bearbeitbare Materialien wie Karton, Styrodur und Balsa-Holz weiterhin wichtige Arbeitsmaterialien innerhalb des Entwurfsprozess. | Learning curves, digital processing, workflow, availability and production times must be taken into consideration especially for digital applications such as 3D printers and CNC mills. Owing to these framework conditions, materials that can be used ad hoc such as cardboard, polystyrene and balsa wood remain important working materials within the design process. **30** Jack Cohen/Ian Stewart, Chaos und Anti-Chaos, Munich: Deutscher Taschenbuch Verlag 1994, 279 ff. | et seqq. **31** Horst W. Rittel/Wolf D. Reuter, op. cit. (Anm. 1 | note 1), 28 **32** ibid. 24 **33** Vgl. | Cf. Katja Benfer/Cyrus Zahiri, op. cit. (Anm. 1 | note 8) **34** Petra Blaisse, Une impression personelle, in: Jacques, M. (ed.), Yves Brunier, Basel/Boston/Berlin: Birkhäuser 1996, 19 ff. | et seqq. **35** Odile Fillion, Entretien avec Rem Koolhaas, in: Jacques, M. (ed.), Yves Brunier, Basel/Boston/Berlin: Birkhäuser 1996, 90 ff. | et seqq.

FUEL FOR A NOVEL DESIGN STRATEGY

On spatial patterns and structural knots

Caroline Voet

The making of architecture has an ambivalent relationship with the processes that trigger and feed it. It deals with concrete reality, but in itself architectural design is an abstract medium of representation, formed by tools and methodologies. The 1990s forms a period of transition between digital design and architecture through tectonics, tactility and craftsmanship. Both approaches induced their own architectural language, backed up by their proper architectural theories. In my own research by design, which started at the Architectural Association in 1997, I have made use of tools from both worlds. This paper aims to trace these processes of transformation between theory and practice, between hybrid complexity and the need for order.

AA DESIGN RESEARCH LABORATORY FOR DIGITAL ARCHITECTURE In 1997, Robert E. Somol asked his students at the Architectural Association to inject ink into water, mapping its process of transformation into digital drawings and animations of

TREIBSTOFF FÜR EIN NEUES GESTALTEN
Über räumliche Muster und strukturelle Knoten

Caroline Voet

Das Entwerfen von Architektur beinhaltet ein ambivalentes Verhältnis zum Prozess, welcher es anstößt und nährt. Obgleich sie sich mit einer greifbaren Realität auseinandersetzt, stellt architektonische Gestaltung ein abstraktes Medium der Repräsentation dar, geprägt von Werkzeugen und Arbeitsweisen. Die 1990er Jahre formieren eine Periode des Übergangs zwischen digitalem Design und einer Architektur der Tektonik, Taktilität und Handwerkskunst. Beide Ansätze bringen eine eigene, von ihrem jeweiligen theoretischen Unterbau gestützte, architektonische Sprache ein. Für mein eigenes entwurfsbasiertes Forschen, das ich 1997 an der Architectural Association begann, griff ich auf Werkzeuge beider Welten zurück. Dieser Beitrag hat das Ziel, diese Prozesse der Transformation zwischen Theorie und Praxis, zwischen hybrider Komplexität und dem Bedarf nach Ordnung, nachzuzeichnen.

AA DESIGN RESEARCH LABORATORY FOR DIGITAL ARCHITECTURE 1997 forderte Robert E. Somol seine Studierenden der Architectural Association dazu auf, Tinte in Wasser zu lösen und den Prozess ihrer Transformation in digitale Zeichnungen sowie in Animationen von Raum zu übersetzen. Es war einer von mehreren Workshops, die wir am ‚Design Research Lab', einem Masterprogramm der Architectural Association in London durchführten. Das Programm war ein Jahr zuvor konzipiert worden von dem Amerikaner Brett Steele, später Dekan der AA, und dem Deutschen Patrick Schumacher, zu diesem Zeitpunkt bereits Partner bei Zaha Hadid Architects.[1] Wir wurden aufgefordert, uns auf

space. It was one of the workshops we conducted at the Design Research Lab, a professional Master at the Architectural Association in London, established one year earlier by the American Brett Steele, later AA director and the German Patrick Schumacher, already then main partner of Zaha Hadid Architects.[1] We were asked to focus on new and emergent spatial formations, new types of organizations and complex, large-scale urban site conditions.[2] We were introduced to drawing software such as Microstation, From.Z and 3D StudioMax, while receiving guest lectures on dataprocessing, programming, genetic algorithms, self-organizational modelling and animation. Intense workshops on for example Synthetic Engineering by Hanif Kara and Surface Urbanism by Raoul Bunschoten were alternated with theoretical courses from the course tutors themselves.

Put forward as an example was the work of Peter Eisenman, still seen as having a pioneering role in defining architectures through processes of deformation. Architectural form was seen as an initial neutral form on which forces, vectors, could be applied. The forces were translations of all kinds of urban movements, programmatic or environmental parameters. The new generation of digital architects was present, led by Gregg Lynn, who as guest editor had put together the special edition of 'Architectural Design', 'Folding in Architecture'. A former student and assistant of Eisenman, Lynn saw pliancy and smoothness in geometry as a means of involving architecture in complexity through flexibility.[3] Of these initial experiments it was the Deleuzian focus on spatial models, most of which were derived from Leibniz's monadology, that took hold in the field.[4]

Deleuze saw the baroque as an 'operative function' unconnected to any specific moment in history.[5] Nevertheless, Lynn remained an utopian architect, and the performance of "the series of vaguely biomorphic and inflected shapes rendered in a mysterious glowing and perpetual computer night time" as Harry Francis Mallgrave described them, accompanying the texts, remained even more vague.[6] On the one hand, we were seduced by the idea of complex architectural processes, the literal and physical folding. In its eagerness to entangle with the new zeitgeist, or the desire to create a new one, the urban critical mass was portrayed as some sort of software that generated an ever-growing number of complexities and contradictions, and architecture could reinvent itself by becoming an expression of these processes. On the other hand, we were also aware of the criticism expressed on this 'form-driven' American avant-garde.[7] We researched other developments taking place, not least the pragmatic strategy and programmatic concerns such as Rem Koolhaas' interior urbanism and bigness, or MVRDV's datascapes.

die neuen und im Entstehen befindlichen räumlichen Formationen, auf neue Arten der Organisation sowie komplexe, großmaßstäbliche urbane Kontexte zu fokussieren.[2] Uns wurde Zeichnungsoftware wie Microstation, Form.Z und 3D Studio Max vorgestellt. Daneben hörten wir Gastbeiträge zu Datenverarbeitung, genetischen Algorithmen, selbstorganisatorischer Modellierung und Animation. Intensive praktische Workshops zu ,Synthetic Engineering' von Hanif Kara, oder ,Surface Urbanism' von Raoul Bunschoten wechselten sich ab mit theoretischen Seminaren der Lehrenden selbst.

Als Beispiel wurde die Arbeit Peter Eisenmans vorgebracht, der noch immer als Vorreiter in der Deutung von Architekturen durch Prozesse der Deformation gesehen wurde. Architektonische Gestalt erwuchs hier aus einer zunächst neutralen Form, auf welche Kräfte, Vektoren, angewendet werden konnten. Diese Kräfte waren die Übersetzung vielzähliger urbaner Bewegungen sowie programmatischer oder umgebungsbedingter Parameter. Angeführt von Gregg Lynn, welcher als Gastherausgeber eine Spezialausgabe von ,Architecture Design' mit dem Titel ,Folding in Architecture' konzipiert hatte, waren auch die Vertreter einer neuen Generation digitaler Architekten anwesend. Als ehemaliger Student und wissenschaftlicher Mitarbeiter Eisenmans sah Lynn Biegsamkeit und Gleichförmigkeit als Möglichkeit, die Komplexität von Architektur durch flexible Veränderung zu verstärken.[3]

Innerhalb dieser ersten Experimente waren es die Deleuze'schen Betrachtungen räumlicher Modelle, von denen sich die meisten aus Leibniz' Monadentheorie ableiteten, die im Fachgebiet Fuß fassten.[4] Deleuze sah das Barocke als eine ,operative Funktion', welche keine Verbindung zu einem bestimmten Zeitpunkt in der Geschichte besaß.[5] Lynn jedoch blieb ein Architekt des Utopischen, und das Leistungsvermögen seiner „Serie mehr oder minder biomorphologischer und gebogener Formen, berechnet in einem mysteriösen Leuchten fortwährender nächtlicher Rechenzeit", wie Harry Francis Mallgrave es kommentierte, blieb schematisch.[6] Einerseits waren wir verführt von der Idee komplexer architektonischer Prozesse des wortwörtlichen und physischen Faltens. Im Bestreben, sich in diesem neuen Zeitgeist zu verstricken, oder in der Sehnsucht, einen neuen zu begründen, stellte die urbane kritische Masse eine Art Software zur Genese einer nicht-endenden Anzahl an Komplexitäten und Widersprüchen dar. Architektur konnte sich selbst neu erfinden, indem sie zum Ausdruck dieser Prozesse wurde. Andererseits waren wir uns der Kritik an dieser ,form-getriebenen' amerikanischen Avantgarde bewusst.[7] Wir recherchierten daher auch zu anderen zeitgenössischen Entwicklungen, nicht zuletzt zu den pragmatischen Strategien und programmatischen Betrachtungen in Rem Koolhaas' internen Urbanismus und dem Konzept der ,Bigness' wie auch in MVRDVs ,Datascapes'.

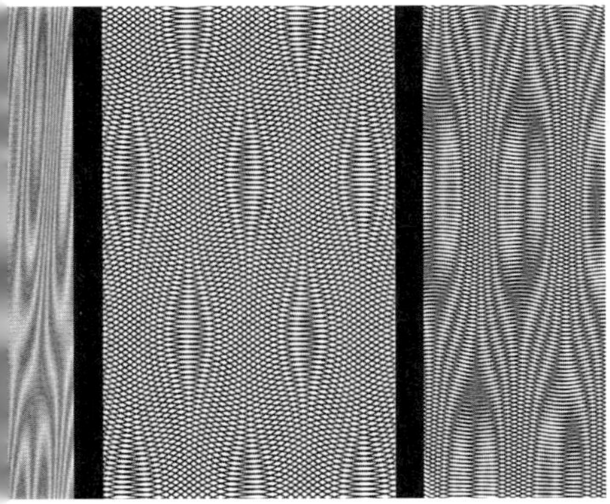

1 | Moirémuster | moiré patterns

2 | Fyber space

FYBER SPACE PROJECT Our project utilizes a generative pattern as spaceframe and field condition (fig. 1-3). Our project focused on Corporate Interior Urbanism. Addressing the demands of large business organizations undergoing constant reconfiguration, studio projects sought new models of continuous interiority, programmatic hybridity and structural connectivity. I found myself under the direct guidance of Patrick Schumacher, investigating the London planning-based firm DEGW. Two texts, both treated in his theoretical course 'Productive Territories', gave me some keys. These were no visionary manifestos, but texts that, through the lens of a new perspective, reread the history of building and art.

The first was published in the 'Architectural Design' no. 127 of 1997, 'Architecture after Geometry'. Like its famous predecessor 'Folding in Architecture' its content covered visionary and utopian topics, with work from for example Ocean UK, CHORA, Gregg Lynn, but also Daniel Libeskind. Amongst these biomorphic endeavors was the text of Stan Allen on Field Conditions, previously published in the 'Berlage Papers' of 1996.[8] He defined the Cordoba Mosque and Le Corbusier's Venice Hospital as a plan syntax of repeated parts. It existed without a unifying scheme; the overall form being an elaboration of conditions established locally. He compared it to the loss of the figurative in cubism and minimalism. The end result was an organism as a figure, an effect emerging from the field itself, as a moment of intensity. The detour towards Le Corbusier and the arts from cubism to minimalism, of course, had been done 40 years earlier. In order to define what could be called an emerging figure, Colin Rowe and Robert Slutsky described the effect of Phenomenal Transparency.[9] A series of paintings from Cézanne to Léger showed the disappearance of the figurative towards a figure-ground effect. The simulation of reality through shifting color planes and densities induced a layered effect of deep space. From the perspective of 1997, 40 years later, this quality of dynamic superposition could be seen as a diagram, a highly charged and productive field from which different figures could emerge.

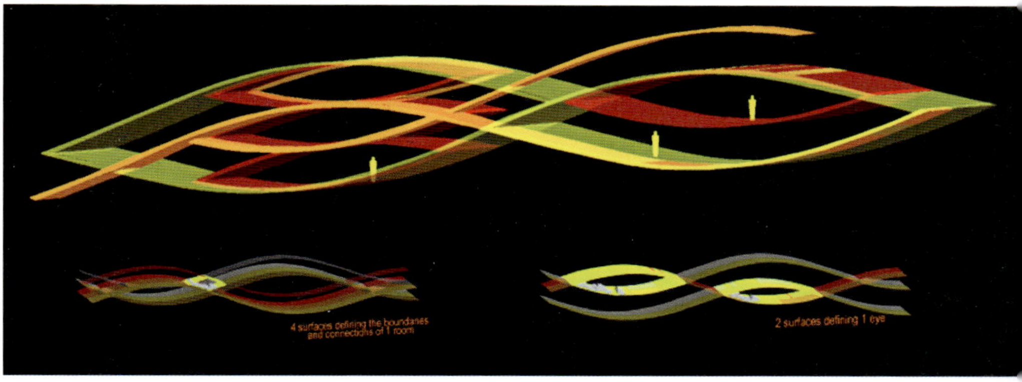

3 | Projektcluster und Auge | Project cluster and eye

FYBER SPACE PROJECT Unser Projekt führte ein generatives Muster als ‚Spaceframe' und ‚Field Condition' ein. Damit fokussierte es einen unternehmensbezogenen internen Urbanismus (Abb. 1-3). Die sich im ständigen Wandel befindlichen Bedürfnisse großer Unternehmen adressierend, suchte das Projekt nach Modellen kontinuierlicher Innenräume, programmatischer Vermischungen und struktureller Verbindungen. Ich befand mich unter direkter Anleitung von Patrick Schumacher und untersuchte die in London ansässige Planungsfirma DEGW. Zwei Aufsätze, die beide in Schumachers theoretischem Kurs ‚Productive Territories' behandelt worden waren, gaben mir Anhaltspunkte. Es waren keine visionären Manifeste, sondern Texte, welche die Geschichte des Bauens und der Kunst aus einer neuen Perspektive betrachteten.

Der erste war 1997 in der 127. Ausgabe von ‚Architectural Design' mit dem Titel ‚Architecture after Geometry' erschienen. Wie in der Vorgängerausgabe ‚Folding in Architecture' wurden in ihr visionäre und utopische Themen behandelt, u.a. innerhalb der Arbeiten von Ocean UK, CHORA, Gregg Lynn, aber auch Daniel Libeskind. Unter diesen biomorphologischen Bestrebungen befand sich auch der Text ‚Field Conditions' von Stan Allen, der bereits im Jahr 1996 in den ‚Berlage Papers' publiziert worden war.[8] Hierin beschrieb Allen die Moschee Cordobas und Le Corbusiers Krankenhaus in Venedig als eine Art Syntax sich wiederholender Einheiten. Sie bestanden ohne eine vereinheitlichende Systematik; ihre letztendliche Gestalt war eine Ausformulierung lokaler Abhängigkeiten. Stan Allen verglich dies mit dem Verlust des Bildhaften in Kubismus und Minimalismus. Das Ergebnis war die Abbildung eines Organismus, der als Moment der Intensität aus den Feldbedingungen selbst hervorgegangen war. Der Umweg über Le Corbusier und die Künste vom Kubismus bis zum Minimalismus hatte natürlich bereits vierzig Jahre früher begonnen. Um näher zu erläutern, was als eine neu auftretende Formensprache bezeichnet werden könnte, beschrieben Colin Rowe und Robert Slutzsky hier die Wirkung phänomenologischer Transparenz.[9] Mit einer Serie von Malereien von Cézanne bis Léger stellten sie dazu das Verschwinden des Bildhaften gegenüber eines Figur-Grund-Effektes dar. Die Abbildung

Being immersed within the digital design world and its theories, we embarked on a night and day journey to define a novel graduation project. The disappearance of structure and material left me on the fringes of the course. Refusing to inject ink into water, I wandered around London to find patterns with some material quality. This journey revealed the depth in the work of Rachel Whiteread, Gerhard Richter and Anish Kapoor, who were all presenting work in the smaller galleries around London. A way was also shown by 'Studies in the Search for Infinity' (1997) ceramics with woven patterns by Josiah McElheny, whom I met at the Saatchi Gallery. This type of patterns could form the foundation for a generative design process. For our end project I tested hundreds of patterns that could induce such a quality, not as virtual deformation, but as a pattern becoming hybrid through the superimposition of stable entities like grids. Reading the patterns through what Jessy Reiser defined as a space frame, a diagrammatic repetitive structure, made it possible to control it. The space frame was a system of rules that in each application enabled a different solution, which was the most productive one according to the change of occupation. The essence is the redundancy of connections and boundaries. This is where its potential dynamics lie: as with the Cordoba Mosq, nodes and connections could be eliminated or reinforced, without altering the whole or the generic underlying pattern.

Stan Allen's reference to moiré patterns, with their uncanny coexistence of a regular grid and an emergent figure, set me on course for defining this diagrammatic structure. It was the concept of the moiré effect that enabled to hybridise phenomenal transparency with the space frame, giving birth to the conception of the Fyber Space Project. The pattern was made by superimposing two grids of sinusoidal waves. By changing the equation on the computer, it was possible to control the pattern and the effects of the different figures that emerged. Together with fellow students Insoo Park and Andre Leirner, the organizational charts of the companies were translated into data diagrams of communication and network configurations.[10] From that, certain boundaries and connections were chosen, or the possibility was left open for them both to exist.

Two types of repetitive knots, representing intimate small-scale spaces, defined the core of the control. Eye-shaped nodes emerged, defining 'project clusters' for up to 25 workers, where honeycomb elements formed enclosed cells as hotel rooms. They defined the 'moments in space', connected by waves of connectivity, the 'movement in space'. The more we dissolved the waves, the bigger the eyes would get, ready to take over an auditorium or an urban plaza. The urban structure that emerged from this could house 36 working clusters, a hotel with 168 rooms and public facilities.

von Realität durch das Ineinanderschieben von Farbflächen und -dichten regte dabei ein vielschichtiges Empfinden von Raumtiefe an. 1997, vierzig Jahre später, konnte diese Qualität dynamischer Überlagerung als Ordnungsschema gelesen werden; als reichhaltiges und produktives Spielfeld, aus welchem unterschiedliche Bilder hervorgehen konnten.

Vertieft in die Welt des digitalen Entwerfens und dessen Theorien, begannen wir tagein tagaus ein neuartiges Abschlussprojekt zu konzipieren. Das Verschwinden von Struktur und Material ließ mich an den Randbereichen der Lehrveranstaltung zurück. Mich dem Einfüllen von Tinte in Wasser verweigernd, suchte ich in London nach Konzepten zu materiellen Qualitäten. Dieser Ausflug offenbarte die Tiefe in den Arbeiten Rachel Whitereads, Gerhard Richters und Anish Kapoors, welche alle Arbeiten in kleineren Galerien in London ausstellten. Eine Möglichkeit der Auseinandersetzung wurde außerdem aufgezeigt von den Keramiken mit gewebten Mustern der ‚Studies in the Search for Infinity' (1997) von Josiah McElheny, welchen ich in der Saatchi-Galerie traf. Diese Art der Muster schien eine geeignete Basis für einen generativen Gestaltungsprozess zu sein. Für unser Abschlussprojekt testete ich Hunderte solcher Muster, die eine generative Qualität nicht als virtuelle Verformung, sondern durch die Überlagerung von Mustern mit stabilen Elementen – wie Rastern – und die hierdurch entstehenden Vermischungen herbeiführen konnten. Eine Steuerung dieser Muster ermöglichte das Einbringen einer diagrammatischen repetitiven Struktur, die Jesse Reiser als ‚Spaceframe' bezeichnet hatte. Der Spaceframe war ein System von Regeln, das unterschiedliche, leistungsfähige Lösungen für Nutzungsänderungen hervorbringen konnte. Diese griffen letztlich auf eine Redundanz an Verbindungen und Grenzen zurück. Hierin lag ihre potentielle Dynamik: Wie im Fall der Moschee Cordobas, konnten Knoten und Verbindungen eliminiert oder verstärkt werden, ohne das Ganze oder das zugrundliegende Muster zu verändern.

Stan Allens Verweis auf Moiré-Muster und der hierin zu beobachtende Koexistenz regulärer Raster und neu entstehender Bilder ermöglichte es, diese diagrammatische Struktur genauer zu definieren. Es war also das Konzept des Moiré-Effektes, das eine Vermischung phänomenologischer Transparenz mit dem Spaceframe ermöglichte und schließlich die Idee des Fyber Space-Projects hervorbrachte. Das Muster entstand durch die Überlagerung zweier Raster aus sinusförmigen Wellen. Durch eine Veränderung der Gleichungen im Computer war es möglich, das Muster und die Wirkung der unterschiedlichen entstehenden Bilder zu steuern. Zusammen mit meinen Mitstudierenden Insoo Park und Andre Leirner übersetzten wir die Organisationstabellen der Firmen in Datendiagramme der Kommunikation und Netzkonfigurationen.[10] Davon ausgehend wurden bestimmte Grenzen und Verbindungen ausgewählt, oder die Existenz von diesen wurde offen gelassen.

THE KNOT. REFLECTIONS BETWEEN SUSPICION AND INTRIGUE

How to integrate scripting and the setting of parameters within a structural materiality? This procedure of losing and regaining control was intriguing. I felt that computer drawing and scripting could enhance this balanced process, because the factor of unpredictability could be incorporated. That we learned from Eisenman. Drawing gives you what you know, whereas the computer offers the option to open up other possibilities you did not know. You set up a series of variables, linked in certain relationships, and the computer offers different possible conclusions. Beyond our own knowledge of mathematics and geometry, the computer is able to make synthetic movements.[11] So my research focussed on specifically this: What could be specific tools to regain control? Could control be part of the initial parameters? This was all about surfaces being manipulated by forces; weightless in itself, endlessly foldable. I noticed that at some point, in order to make it a building, to define its materiality, classical tools of control were brought in: matrixes through patterns and grids. But even then, the intersection between two lines was only virtual. Knots were virtual points that could be manipulated through vortexes. If materiality and structure were to be manipulative and unpredictable, could it be possible to bring back the knot, not only in its representational manner, but also through its ontological meaning?

I was highly disappointed by Stan Allen's conclusion that Renzo Piano's high-tech detailing would be the answer of this line of thought, as he worked from the individual joint outwards: "For Piano, the joint is not an occasion to articulate the intersection of two materials (as is the case with for example Carlo Scarpa), but is instead a locus of an intensive design energy that proceeds outwards to condition the form of the whole."[12] I felt the need to articulate, and to somehow link the detail with the whole as could be felt in the work of Scarpa. Architecture detached from representation or an ontological meaning only resides in formalism. I wanted to see these patterns through the lenses that were set by Kenneth Frampton and his Studies in Tectonic Culture (1995).[13] Frampton's belief in the primacy of architecture as a language through form and tectonics, architectural phenomenology, led him to retrace a historical line through Karl Bötticher and Gottfried Semper. Semper's theory on 'dressing' opened up the connection between architecture and space, away from Bötticher's supremacy of architecture as structure. Although not part of the 'digital design agenda', these wanderings to the 'other side' were encouraged.

Loos' definitions of space through their material surfaces was a key element in this. Where H&dM read Semper through Loos in defining their projects through materiality and spatial qualities, we read Semper, also through Loos, but in order to give a grounding to our experiments in surface architecture. The DRL encouraged us to look at the dynamics of surfaces not through their effect, but through literal topographic defor-

Zwei Arten sich wiederholender Verknüpfungen, welche kleinteilige private Räume darstellten, bildeten das zentrale Moment kontrollierender Eingriffe. Augenförmige Knotenpunkte entstanden, welche ‚Projektcluster' für bis zu 25 Mitarbeitende dort abgrenzten, wo Bienenwabenelemente umschlossene Zellen als Hotelzimmer darstellten. Sie definierten die ‚Momente im Raum' und waren verbunden durch Wellen von Konnektivität, den ‚Bewegungen im Raum'. Je stärker wir die Wellen auflösten, desto größer wurden diese augenförmigen Bereiche, sodass sie schließlich Auditorien oder urbane Plätze beherbergen konnten. Die urbane Struktur, die daraus entstand, fasste bis zu 36 Arbeitscluster, ein Hotel mit 168 Zimmern sowie öffentliche Einrichtungen.

KNOTENPUNKTE. REFLEXIONEN ZWISCHEN MISSTRAUEN UND FASZINATION

Wie können Scripting und das Bestimmen von Parametern in eine bauliche Materialität einbegriffen werden? Das Vorgehen des Verlusts und Wiedererlangens von Kontrolle war faszinierend. Ich hatte das Gefühl, computerbasiertes Zeichnen und Scripting könne diesen austarierten Prozess erweitern, weil hiermit der Faktor des Unvorhersehbaren inbegriffen werden konnte. Das hatten wir von Eisenman gelernt. Zeichnen gibt einem, was man weiß, während der Computer Möglichkeiten bereithält, weitere, einem bislang unbekannte Varianten zu eröffnen. Man setzt eine Reihe von Variablen, verbunden durch bestimmte Bedingungen, und der Computer offeriert verschiedene mögliche Lösungen. Außerhalb unseres eigenen Wissens über Mathematik und Geometrie ist der Computer in der Lage andersartige, virtuelle Abläufe zu vollführen.[11] Meine Forschung fokussierte sich also auf eben jenes: Was konnten spezifische Werkzeuge sein, um die Kontrolle in diesem Zusammenhang wiederzuerlangen? Konnte die Kontrollmöglichkeit Teil der Ausgangsparameter sein? Letztlich ging es hierbei um die Manipulation von Oberflächen durch Kräfte, die als solche schwerelos, unendlich faltbar waren. Ich bemerkte an einem bestimmten Punkt, dass, um aus diesen Überlegungen ein tatsächliches Gebäude zu machen und seine Materialität zu bestimmen, klassische Werkzeuge der Kontrolle notwendig wurden: Matrixen von Mustern und Rastern. Doch selbst dann war die Überschneidung zwischen zwei Linien noch rein virtuell. Die Knotenpunkte waren virtuelle Punkte, welche mittels Vektoren beeinflusst werden konnten. Wenn also Material und Struktur unvorhersehbar sein sollten, wie war es dann möglich, den Knotenpunkt nicht in bloßer gegenständlicher Art, sondern ebenso in seiner ontologischen Bedeutung zu besetzen?

Von Stan Allens Schlussfolgerung, dass Renzo Pianos High-Tech-Ornamentik die Antwort zu diesem Gedanken sein könnte, da er von der einzelnen Verbindung nach außen arbeitete, war ich enttäuscht. „Für Piano ist das Gelenk nicht der Anlass, eine Verschneidung zweier Materialien zu artikulieren, wie es zum Beispiel bei Carlo Scarpa der Fall ist, sondern stattdessen ein Ort intensiver gestalterischer Kraft, welche nach Außen drängt, um die Form als Ganzes zu beeinflussen."[12] Ich spürte den Drang, dieses Detail selbst zu artikulieren

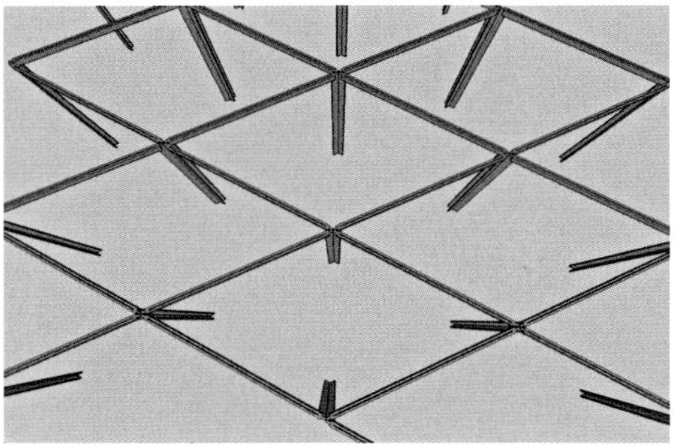

4 | Muster | Pattern

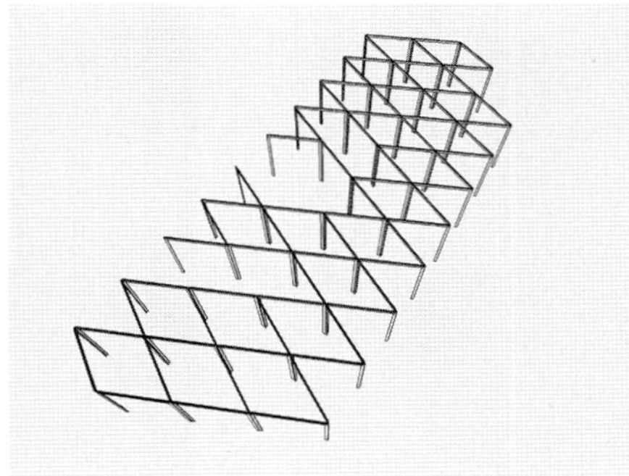

5 | Space frame

mations. The Fyber Space Project wanted to create a tension between the two different realms, looking for cross-fertilisation. Was it not the novel lens of the diagram, that enabled Colin Rowe to compare Palladio and Le Corbusier, putting both of them in an entire new and clarifying light?[14] Encouraged by Kipnis' text 'The Cunning of Cosmetics', a reading of the work of H&dM which receives its sharpness through the questions he raises as an apostle of 'the digital side', I tried to elope from the digital camp to the tectonic.[15] Working for Zaha Hadid in London and later Christian Kieckens in Brussels informed and fed my research.

But it was not until my own practice 'Voet en De Brabandere' was founded in 2012 that I felt free to fully explore these two worlds in a productive dialog, taking on board elements that reinforced one hybrid design process. As such, the scenography for the exhibition of the Henry Van de Velde Label (2014) grew from a spaceframe and a knot (fig. 4-9). The overall pattern was an offset of the Lokettenzaal of the Flemish Parliament, a structure designed by the modernist architect Victor Bourgeois. We deformed it into a smaller maze, bringing in the human scale and frames for objects. The central point of control was utterly structural and repetitive: the inverted column, as an homage to Mies van der Rohe, and its connection to the beam structure. Depending on the size of the objects and the exhibition scenario, structural elements were eliminated, resulting in an environment that intensified the relation between the viewer and the object.

THE OTHER LENS TOWARDS HABITABILITY Within the work of Voet en De Brabandere, the ontological was equally the means to infuse the human aspect within the generic approach of pattern structures. Beyond the literary and formal approach of digital or parametric design, the complexity of field conditions induced a layered architectural discourse as language and as technique that did not aim for a total rupture with history and the reinvention of the new. It sought fundaments and ontologies, not as dogmas, but as engaging with an ongoing process where discontinuities,

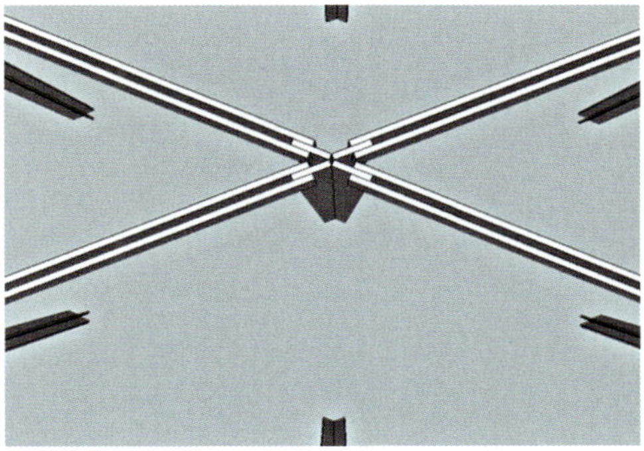

6 | Knoten | Knot

7 | Knoten-Prototyp | Knot prototype

und irgendwie mit dem Ganzen zu verbinden, wie es in der Arbeit Scarpas zu spüren war. Architektur, welche sich von Repräsentation oder ontologischer Bedeutung lossagt, bleibt im Formalismus. Ich wollte die Muster daher auch durch die Perspektive Kenneth Framptons und seiner Studien in ‚Tectonic Culture' (1995) betrachten.[13] Framptons Glaube an das Primat der Architektur als Sprache der Formen und der Tektonik, an die architektonische Phänomenologie, zeichnete eine historische Verbindung zwischen Karl Bötticher und Gottfried Semper. Sempers Prinzip der Verkleidung eröffnete eine Verbindung zwischen Architektur und Raum jenseits von Böttichers Bevorzugung der Architektur als Struktur. Obwohl kein Teil der ‚Agenda' des Digital Designs, wurden diese Exkursionen zur ‚anderen Seiten' ermutigt.

Loos' Betrachtung von Raum in dessen Oberflächenmaterialien stellte hierbei ein Schlüsselelement dar. Während Herzog & de Meuron Semper mithilfe von Loos interpretierten und ihre Projekte in Materialität und räumlicher Qualität entsprechend ausformulierten, lasen wir Semper, ebenfalls durch Loos, um eine Basis für unsere Experimente einer form- und materialbestimmten Architektur zu schaffen. Das DRL ermutigte uns, die Dynamik von Oberflächen nicht in ihrem Effekt, sondern in ihren tatsächlichen topografischen Verformungen zu betrachten. Das Fyber-Space-Project wollte eine Spannung zwischen diesen beiden Bereichen schaffen und nach gegenseitiger Befruchtung suchen. War es nicht die alternative Perspektive des Diagramms gewesen, welche es Colin Rowe ermöglicht hatte, Palladio und Le Corbusier zu vergleichen und beide in ein neues, erhellendes Licht zu rücken?[14] Ermutigt von Kipnis' Text ‚The Cunning of Cosmetics', einer Interpretation der Arbeit Herzog & de Meurons, die ihre Schärfe durch die Fragen erhielt, welche er als ‚Apostel des Digitalen' aufwarf, versuchte ich, aus dem Digitalen in das Tektonische zu fliehen.[15] Das Arbeiten bei Zaha Hadid in London und später bei Christina Kieckens in Brüssel beeinflusste und nährte hierbei meine weitere Forschung.

Doch erst als ich 2012 mein eigenes Büro ‚Voet en De Brabandere' gegründet hatte, fühlte ich mich frei, diese beiden Welt gänzlich als produktiven Dialog zu ergründen und Elemente aus diesem zu nutzen, um einen hybriden Gestaltungsprozess zu stärken.

8-9 | Ausstellung Henry-Van-de-Velde-Label | Exhibition Henry Van de Velde label, 2014

superposition could frame complex spatial thinking through a more inclusive design method. It was not the complex world in itself as the object of interest, but the way in which humans live (habiter) in this world, focussing on maintaining its habitability. Thus, when embarking on a new project, we focussed on activities and perception, not on functions and m^2. For the new scenography for Museum Plantin-Moretus (2016), we wanted to integrate an atmospheric pattern, not by literally constructing it, but by infusing a network of nodes that communicate through light and rituals (fig. 10-12). The house of Plantin-Moretus consists of a series of rooms arranged around a courtyard garden. The atmosphere, as well as the activities within the house, depends on the infiltration of daylight. This important layer disappeared for conservatory reasons when the house became a museum, as most of the exhibited books and paintings need to be protected from the light. We defined the ritual of reading itself, in relation to light, as the new ontological node of the network. Throughout the museum, we proposed a series of lecterns, some with a book, some empty, each with their own reading light. The shape of the lectern is an invitation for reading, quietness, and contemplation. It is folded by the gesture of opening a book. Thus, upon entering the museum, one sees people reading. The soft light that falls from the reading lamps onto the lecterns is a tangible element in itself: it captures a gesture, illuminating not only the book, but also the face and hands reading it. The lecterns are shaped by going back to the origins of reading a book. In the same manner, we went back to defining a double writing desk for children to draw. The top folds upward, adding a counter movement to the topography of the lecterns.

Als solcher erwuchs die Szenografie für die Ausstellung des Henry-Van-de-Velde-Labels (2014) aus dem Spaceframe und dem Knoten (Abb. 4-9). Das übergreifende Prinzip war dabei ein Versatz des Lokettenzaals des flämischen Parlaments, einer Struktur, die vom modernen Architekten Victor Bourgeois entworfen worden war. Der zentrale Punkt der Kontrolle war völlig strukturell und repetitiv: die umgekehrte Stütze als eine Hommage an Mies van der Rohe und ihre Verbindungen zur Balkenstruktur. Abhängig von der Größe des Objektes und dem Ausstellungszenario konnten strukturelle Elemente eliminiert werden, um eine Umgebung zu schaffen, welche die Relation zwischen dem Betrachter und dem Objekt verstärken konnte.

DER ANDERE BLICK AUF BEWOHNBARKEIT Innerhalb der Arbeit von ‚Voet en De Brabandere' war das Ontologische ebenso das Mittel dazu, einen menschlichen Aspekt in den generischen Ansatz von strukturellen Mustern einzubringen. Abseits eines wortwörtlichen und formalen Ansatzes digitalen oder parametrischen Designs brachte die Komplexität der Bedingungen einen geschichteten Architekturdiskurs als Sprache und als Technik mit sich, der nicht auf einen totalen Bruch mit der Geschichte und der Erfindung des Neuen abzielte. Er suchte Fundamente und Ontologien nicht als Dogmen, sondern als Auseinandersetzungen mit dem andauernden Prozess, in welchem Diskontinuitäten und Überlagerungen komplexes räumliches Denken rahmen und in den man inklusivere Entwurfsmethoden einbringen konnte. Nicht die komplexe Welt selbst war das Objekt der Betrachtung, sondern die Art, in welcher der Mensch diese Welt bewohnt und hierin zudem ein Fokus auf der Erhaltung eben dieser Bewohnbarkeit. Als wir also ein weiteres Projekt begannen, konzentrierten wir uns auf Aktivitäten und Wahrnehmungen, nicht auf Funktionen und m^2. Für die neue Szenografie des Museums Plantin-Moretus (2016) versuchten wir ein atmosphärisches Muster einzubringen. Nicht als tatsächliche Konstruktion, sondern durch die Installation eines Netzwerkes von Knotenpunkten, welche mittels Licht und Ritualen verbunden waren (Abb. 10-12). Das Haus Planin-Moretus besteht aus einer Reihe von Räumen, welche um einen Hofgarten angeordnet sind. Die Atmosphäre, wie auch die Aktivitäten innerhalb des Hauses, sind dabei abhängig vom Einfall des Tageslichts. Diese wichtige Ebene verschwand jedoch aus konservatorischen Gründen als das Haus zum Museum wurde, da die meisten ausgestellten Bücher und Bilder vor dem Licht geschützt werden mussten. Wir definierten das Ritual des Lesens selbst, in Relation zum Licht, als neuen ontologischen Knotenpunkt des Netzwerks. Im ganzen Museum schlugen wir eine Reihe von Pulten vor, manche mit einem Buch, manche leer, jedes davon mit seiner eigenen Leselampe. Die Form der Pulte stellt eine Einladung zum Lesen dar, zur Stille und zur Kontemplation. Ihre Faltung entspricht einer Geste des Aufschlagens eines Buches. Beim Betreten des Museums sieht man lesende Menschen. Das weiche Licht, welches von den Leselampen auf die Pulte fällt, ist selbst ein sinnliches Element: Es fängt eine Geste ein, beleuchtet nicht nur das Buch, sondern auch das Gesicht und Hände der Lesenden. Die Pulte sind von der Rückbesinnung auf den Ursprung des Lesens geformt. Auf gleiche Art und Weise gestalteten wir einen doppelten Schreibtisch, auf dem Kinder zeichnen sollten. Die Oberseite faltet sich nach oben und fügt der Topografie der Pulte eine Gegenbewegung hinzu.

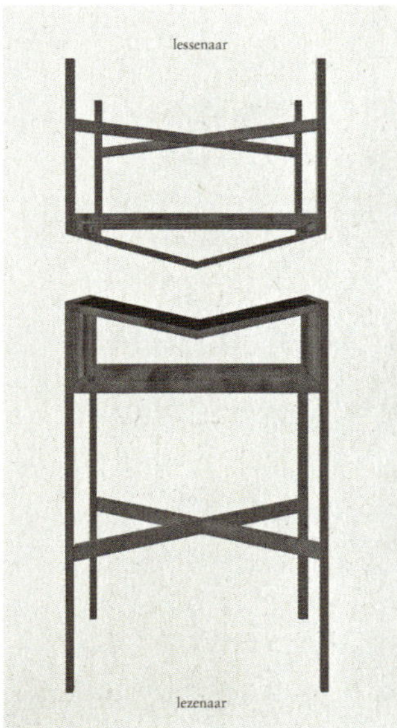

10-11 | Museum Plantin-Moretus, Knotenpunkte, Schreibtisch | nodes, writing desk

What emerged here is a possible strategy that connects complex or large structures with the human scale, with tactility and sensory experience. At the DRL, the formative role of research-based design strategies focused on processes of transformation: architecture as an autonomous virtual form deformed by forces. This methodology freed from preconceptions and constraints, enabling unimagined and unpredictable forms. Nevertheless, the act of designing threatened to be arbitrarily cut off from the act of will: no control and no materiality. Through a position of resistance to the virtual, a cross-fertilization was proposed between the complex DRL design tools and theories of tectonic culture. The strategy of losing and regaining control was introduced not through the virtual, but through the generic and the ontological. The processes of deformation envisaged hybrid patterns of superimposed stable grids. As a central tool, the knot as the classical module and its relation to the whole enabled the quest for an ontological grounding, both structural and spatial. Taking the formal gestures of pattern and knot as a starting point and redirecting them by experience and use, aimed at introducing a fundamental habitability.

12 | Museum Plantin-Moretus, Lesepult | lectern

Was hier entstand, ist eine mögliche Strategie, komplexe Großstrukturen mit dem menschlichen Maßstab zu verbinden, mit taktiler und sensorischer Erfahrung. Im DRL fokussierte das forschungsbasierte Design Prozesse der Transformation, eine Architektur als autonome virtuelle Skulptur, die von Kräften geformt ist. Diese Methode, frei von Vorannahmen und Beschränkungen, ermöglichte unvorstellbare und unvorhersehbare Formen. Nichtsdestotrotz war die Handlung des Entwerfens in Gefahr, vom freien Willen abgeschnitten zu werden, ohne Kontrolle und ohne Materialität. Aus einer Position des Widerstandes gegen das Virtuelle wurde eine gegenseitige Befruchtung zwischen den komplexen Gestaltungsmethoden des DRL und den Theorien der Tektonik entwickelt. Die Strategie des Verlierens und Wiedererlangens von Kontrolle wurde uns so nicht durch das Virtuelle, sondern durch das Generische und Ontologische ermöglicht. Der Prozess der Verformung fokussierte dabei hybride Muster sich überlagernder, stabiler Raster. Als ein zentrales Werkzeug ermöglichte der Knoten als klassisches Modul und dessen Relation zum Ganzen die Suche nach einer ontologischen Basis, sowohl strukturell als auch räumlich. Der Nutzen formaler Gesten von Mustern und Verknüpfungen als Ausgangspunkt, und die Veränderung dieser durch Erfahrung und Nutzung, hatten hierbei das Schaffen einer grundlegenden Bewohnbarkeit des Habitats zum Ziel.

1 Der amerikanische Architekturkritiker und Entwerfer Jeffrey Kipnis legte 1992 mit der Gründung des AA Graduate Design Program den Grundstein für dieses Seminar | The American Architectural Critic and designer Jeffrey Kipnis planted the seeds for this course in 1992, founding the AA Graduate Design Program. **2** Vgl. | Cf. Graduate Design Research Lab, in: AA projects review 1997-1998, London: Architectural Association, 152-16 **3** Vgl. | Cf. Gregg Lynn, Architectural Curvilinearity. The folded, the pliant and the supple, in: Architectural Design nr. 102, special issue: Folding in architecture (1993) 20 **4** Vgl. | Cf. Gregg Lynn, Introduction, in: Architectural Design nr. 102, special issue: Folding in architecture (1993) 9 **5** Vgl. | Cf. Gilles Deleuze, The Fold. Leibniz and the Baroque, the pleats of matter, in: Architectural Design nr. 102, special issue: Folding in architecture (1993) 33-37 **6** Vgl. | Cf. Harry Francis Mallgrave/David Goodman, Introduction to architectural theory. 1968 to the present, Hoboken New Yersey: Wiley-Blackwell 2011, 163 **7** Vgl. | Cf. Michael Speaks, It's out there ... the formal limits of the American Avant-Garde, in: Architectural Design nr. 68, special issue: Hypersurface architecture (1998) 30 **8** Vgl. | Cf. Stan Allen, From object to field, in: Architectural Design nr. 127, special issue: Architecture after geometry (1997) 24-31 **9** Vgl. | Cf. Colin Rowe/Robert Slutsky, Transparency. Literal and phenomenal, in: Perspecta vol. 8 (1963) 45-54 **10** DEGW stellte uns mehrere Analysen zu den Themen der Zeiterfassung und der Entwicklung von Arbeitsstilen zur Verfügung | DEGW provided us with several analyses such as a time Utilisation survey and a workstyle development. **11** Vgl. | Cf. Yu Tung Liu, Conversations with Peter Eisenman, Greg Lynn, in: Yu-Tung Liu (ed.), Defining Digital Architecture. FEIDAD Award, Basel: Birkhäuser 2001, 19 **12** Stan Allen, From object to field, in: Architectural Design nr. 127, special issue: Architecture after geometry (1997) 27 **13** Vgl. | Cf. Kenneth Frampton, Studies in tectonic culture, Cambridge: MIT Press 1995 **14** Vgl. | Cf. Colin Rowe, The mathematics of the Ideal Villa, in: Architectural Review (1947) 101-104 **15** Vgl. | Cf. Jeffrey Kipnis, The cunnings of cosmetics, in: El Croquis 84, Herzog & de Meuron (1998) 22-29

„Paul Klee sagte einmal, dass uns mehr an den ‚formenden Kräften' als an den formalen Resultaten gelegen sein sollte. Das heißt, dass wir (...) mehr Wert auf den Vorgang der Gestaltung als auf die fertigen Resultate legen müssen." | 'Paul Klee once said that we should be more interested in the "shaping forces" than in the formal results. That means that we (...) must place more value on the design process than on the finished results.'

Aldo Rossi

VERSCHRÄNKUNGEN
ENTANGLEMENTS

When areas of application and finding processes are more closely linked in design and research, one can speak of entanglements. In physics and other natural sciences, the concept of entanglement refers to a quantum physics phenomenon. It characterizes the nature of a system in which a couple or several constituting parts cannot be described as a combination of one condition and another, but rather just as a shared condition, as if they were permanently connected and could only reach their objective together.[1] If designers in architecture, landscape architecture and urban design interact exploratively with central design media, it opens up the possibility of a differentiated understanding of comparatively dense relationships between design and research.

In this respect, one can refer in particular to visual media and models as a central working method, design and research tool.[2] They represent tools, contribute to determining ways of working and generate images, image sequences and visualizations. Their professional function lies primarily in the representative display of specifications for further design concretization and for realization as structural-spatial artifacts. In addition, they can visualize speculative and visionary content, generate new worlds of imagination creatively and experimentally.[3] Finally, they can also act as entanglements, if there is a translation of research-developed and discursive content into visually recognizable thought and representation orders. In any case, they are sediments of a preceding process.[4]

Dort, wo Anwendungsbereiche und Entdeckungsprozesse im Entwerfen und Forschen ausgeprägter ineinandergreifen, kann von Verschränkungen gesprochen werden. In der Physik und anderen Naturwissenschaften bezieht sich das Konzept der Verschränkung auf ein quantenphysikalisches Phänomen. Charakterisiert wird damit die Beschaffenheit eines Systems, bei dem ein Paar oder mehrere konstituierende Teile sich nicht als Kombination aus dem einen und dem anderen Zustand beschreiben lassen, vielmehr nur als ein gemeinsamer Zustand, so als stünden sie permanent in Verbindung und würden nur gemeinsam ihr Ziel erreichen.[1] Dort, wo Entwerfende in Architektur, Landschaftsarchitektur und Städtebau mit zentralen Medien der Entwurfstätigkeit forschend interagieren, öffnet sich ein Feld zum differenzierteren Verständnis vergleichbar dichter Relationen von Entwerfen und Forschen.

Insbesondere können hierbei bildliche Medien und Modelle als signifikante Arbeitsmittel, Entwurfs- und auch Forschungsinstrumente benannt werden.[2] Sie bilden Werkzeuge, bestimmen Arbeitsweisen mit und bringen Bilder, Bildfolgen und Imaginationen hervor. Ihre professionelle Funktion liegt vorrangig in der repräsentierenden Darstellung von Vorgaben für weitere entwurfliche Konkretisierungen und für die Umsetzung in baulich-räumliche Artefakte. Darüber hinaus können sie spekulative und visionäre Inhalte veranschaulichen, kreativ und experimentell neue Vorstellungswelten schaffen.[3] Schließlich können sie auch als Verschränkungen wirken, wenn eine Übersetzung forschend entwickelter und diskursiver Inhalte in visuell erkennbare Denk- und Darstellungsordnungen erfolgt. In jedem Fall sind sie Sedimente eines Prozesses, in denen zu ihnen gefunden wurde.[4]

Processes of model graphic exploration are discussed by Ole W. Fischer, based on the example of analog and digital sketching work by Peter Eisenman and Scott Cohen from the 1970s to the 1990s. Through the medium of drawing processes, dynamic modifications and layering, it presents varying critical considerations of production and reproduction, of rules and coincidence, as well as an implicitly cultivated criticism of valuations and values of the architectural discipline in times in which the economic instrumentalization of architecture dominated and digital algorithmic design was emerging and developing. With an analytical approach and by means of geometric and formal operations, it was attempted to probe the autonomous and independent character of architecture in this historical situation and to examine conditions that support and reinforce it. Through the sequence of these directed examinations and their contextualization in relation to the given circumstances, the studies can be understood as design-based research processes and their limits can be discussed.

If one initially maintains a focus on digital design processes, one could also consider the search for a grammar in the sense of an examination of structural-spatial basic codes or for a set of rules against this background. Based on the example of the project 'A Grammar for the city' by the architecture firms Dogma and Office KGDVS, which is researched by Sarah Wehmeyer, it remains open, however, to what extent this intention played a guiding role for the architects or an approach to a theoretical model ensued, or whether one should rather speak of an epistemic imagination that also includes sensory capabilities.[5] It shows work with collages, which can be understood as tools of design presentation and at the same time as compartments of a research process, in a both artistically abstract and everyday-related articulation. It allows the tentative recognition of different forms of perception and knowledge production.

Prozesse modellhafter zeichnerischer Erkundung diskutiert Ole W. Fischer am Beispiel analoger und digitaler zeichnerischer Arbeiten von Peter Eisenman und Scott Cohen aus den 1970er bis 1990er Jahren. Mittels des Mediums von Zeichnungsprozessen, von dynamischen Modifikationen und Schichtungen erfolgten hierbei in unterschiedlicher Weise kritische Auseinandersetzungen mit Produktion und Reproduktion, mit Regel und Zufall sowie eine implizit kultivierte Kritik an Wertsetzungen und Wertigkeiten der Architekturdisziplin in Zeiten, in denen die ökonomische Instrumentalisierung der Architektur dominierte und das digital algorithmische Entwerfen sich ankündigte bzw. entwickelte. Mit analytischem Vorgehen und mittels geometrischer und formaler Operationen wurde versucht, dem autonomen und eigenständigen Charakter der Architektur in dieser historischen Situation auf den Grund zu gehen und Bedingungen zu untersuchen, die sie unterstützen und stärken. In der Reihung dieser gesteuerten Untersuchungen und zudem ihrer Kontextualisierungen zu vorhandenem Bestand werden die Studien als entwurfsbasierte forschende Prozesse lesbar, und ihre Grenzen können diskutiert werden.

Wird der Fokus auf digitale Entwurfsprozesse zunächst beibehalten, dann könnte auch das Suchen nach einer Grammatik im Sinne einer Untersuchung baulich-räumlicher Grundcodes oder eines Regelwerks vor diesem Hintergrund betrachtet werden. Am Beispiel des Projekts ‚A Grammar for the city' der Architekturbüros Dogma und Office KGDVS, das von Sarah Wehmeyer erforscht wird, bleibt jedoch offen, inwieweit bei den Architekten diese Intention leitend wirkte oder aber eine Annäherung an ein theoretisches Modell erfolgte oder vielmehr von einer epistemischen Imagination gesprochen werden sollte, die auch sinnliche Vermögen einschließt.[5] Aufgezeigt wird das Arbeiten mit Collagen, die in einer zugleich künstlerisch abstrakten wie alltagsnahen Artikulation als Instrumente der Entwurfspräsentation und gleichzeitig als Kompartimente eines Forschungsprozesses verstanden werden können. Dies ermöglicht, unterschiedliche Formen von Wahrnehmung und Wissensproduktion näherungsweise zu erkennen.

In a form of research report, Andreas Nütten presents how polycentric structural-spatial urban regions can be researched and illuminated by means of an abstract-analytical and at the same time descriptive imagery. The chosen approaches allow the reset and the invention of means of representation and at the same time channel knowledge about visual forms and about the studied spaces. By comparing various options regarding systemized and inventive, as well as epistemic knowledge practices, it also raises the question as to what is taken into consideration. Qualitative phenomenal experience aspects with a subjective nuancing are included, controlled and recalled in the interconnected phases. In firmly reflexive process phases, they are imaginatively envisioned and condensed into thinking, content and representation orders. These can serve as a basis for concrete projects and are also articulated and discussed comparatively. In this way they become manageable qualified knowledge for spatial design and beyond.

In einer Art Forschungsbericht stellt Andreas Nütten vor, wie sich polyzentrische baulich-räumliche Stadtregionen mittels einer abstrakt-analytischen und zugleich anschaulichen Bildlichkeit erforschen und veranschaulichen lassen. Die gewählten Vorgehensweisen ermöglichen das Reset und die Erfindung von Darstellungsweisen und kanalisieren gleichzeitig Erkenntnisse zu Bildformen und zu den untersuchten Räumen. Über den Vergleich verschiedener Optionen von systematisierter und erfinderischer sowie zugleich auch epistemischer Wissenspraktiken wird auch befragt, was zur Anschauung kommt. Qualitative phänomenale Erfahrungsaspekte mit subjektiver Nuancierung werden in die ineinander verschränkten Phasen aufgenommen, kontrolliert und erinnert. In dezidiert reflexiven Prozessabschnitten werden sie imaginativ vergegenwärtigt und zu Denk-, Inhalts- und Darstellungsordnungen kondensiert. Diese können als Basis für konkrete Projekte dienen und werden vergleichend auch sprachbasiert artikuliert und diskutiert. In dieser Weise werden sie zu handhabbarem qualifizierten Wissen für die Raumgestaltung und darüber hinaus. MB

1 Vgl. | Cf. Helmut Fink: Interpretation verschränkter Zustände: Die Quantenwelt – unbestimmt und nichtlokal? In: Physik in unserer Zeit 35(2004)/4, 168–173 **2** Vgl. | Cf. Stan Allen, Practice versus project, in: id. (ed.), Practice. Architecture, technique and representation, Abingdon: Routledge 2000, XII-XXV, XXII-XXIII; Michael Brawne, Architectural thought. The design process and the expanded eye, Burlington, Mass.: Architectural Press 2003, 83-96; Inge Hinterwaldner, Prolog. Modellhaftigkeit und Bildlichkeit in Entwurfsartefakten, in: Sabine Ammon/id. (eds.), Bildlichkeit im Zeitalter der Modellierung. Operative Artefakte in Entwurfsprozessen der Architektur und des Ingenieurwesens, Paderborn: Wilhelm Fink 2017, 13-31 **3** Vgl. | Cf. Karen Barad, Verschränkungen, Berlin: Merve 2015, passim und | and 200-201 **4** Vgl. dazu auch | Cf. on this subject also Olaf Breidbach/Federico Vercellone, Anschauung denken, München: Wilhelm Fink 2011, 27- 55 **5** Zu Imagination vgl. | On imagination cf. Martin Seel, Ethisch-ästhetische Studien, Frankfurt/Main: Suhrkamp 1996, 132-136; Gerald Wildgruber, Zur Logik des Imaginären, in: Emmanuel Alloa/Gottfried Böhm/Orlando Budelacci/id.(eds.), Imagination. Suchen und Finden, Paderborn: Wilhelm Fink 2914, 47-89

DRAWING ON CONTINGENCY
Peter Eisenman, Preston Scott Cohen and the analog-digital moment

Ole W. Fischer

DESIGN PROCESS RESEARCH? Architectural design is not science, but a cultural practice. Yet there are scientific approaches towards the tools and processes employed in architectural design, once they transcend the merely representational (of structures to be build) and become investigations into the representational apparatus itself. Retrospectively, this seems especially relevant in a time of media change, such as the analog-digital moment, where figures like Peter Eisenman (*1932) and Preston Scott Cohen (*1961) tested processual drawing as means of artistic exploration.

DIGITAL ARCHITECTURE? Contemporary discourse in architecture identifies a paradigm shift from 'analog' to 'digital media' over the last two to three decades. As the story goes, the availability of powerful desktop computers and CAD software in the late 1980s and early 1990s both in offices and education fostered a break with the classical architectural representation of orthogonal projection, perspectival drawing and physical model as codified by Leon Battista Alberti in 'De re aedificatoria' (1443–1452). Especially the spread of scripting, parametric design optimization, and digital fabrication would have fundamentally changed the design process and questioned the notion of architectural authorship. The author's agency would have moved from manually manipulating form directly and intentionally towards setting rules: form results contingently from processes initiated and framed by the designer, often in a way beyond her original imagination. Or, to employ a popular evolutionary metaphor, the designer breeds a specific code or DNA, cultivates a family tree of projects through simulated genetic adaption that populate diverse ecological niches, as found in arguments of Alejandro Zaera-Polo, Patrik Schumacher or ArandaLasch.[1] Not accidentally, terms, themes, and theories of Artificial Life, genetic biology, IT and systems theory converge when architects discuss parametric form finding.

KONTINGENZ DARSTELLEN

Peter Eisenman, Preston Scott Cohen und der analog-digitale Moment

Ole W. Fischer

ENTWURF PROZESS FORSCHUNG? Architekturentwurf selbst ist keine Wissenschaft, sondern eine kulturelle Praxis. Jedoch gibt es wissenschaftliche Annäherungen an die im Architekturentwurf verwendeten Werkzeuge und Prozesse, sobald diese das rein Darstellende (von zu errichtenden Gebäuden) überwinden und zu Forschungen in den repräsentativen Apparatus selbst fortschreiten. Rückblickend scheint das besonders relevant für eine Zeit des Medienwechsels, wie beispielsweise jenes analog-digitalen Momentes, in dem Protagonisten wie Peter Eisenman (*1932) und Preston Scott Cohen (*1961) prozessuale Darstellungsformen als Mittel künstlerischer Forschung getestet haben.

DIGITALE ARCHITEKTUR? Der zeitgenössische Architekturdiskurs beschreibt einen Paradigmenwechsel von ‚analogen' zu ‚digitalen Medien' über die letzten zwei bis drei Jahrzehnte. Wenn man dieser Argumentation folgt, dann hat die Verfügbarkeit von leistungsstarken Computern und CAD Software in den späten 1980er und frühen 1990er Jahren sowohl in den Büros als auch in den Hochschulen einen Bruch mit den klassisch architektonischen Repräsentationsformen der orthogonalen Projektionen, der Perspektive und des physischen Modells herbeigeführt, wie sie bereits von Leon Battista Alberti in ‚De re aedificatoria' (1443-1452) festgelegt wurden. Besonders die Verbreitung von Scripting, parametrischer Entwurfsoptimierung und digitaler Fabrikation habe den Entwurfsprozess fundamental verändert und die architektonische Autorenschaft hinterfragt. Die Handlungsfähigkeit der Entwurfsverfasserin habe sich von einer unmittelbaren und intentionalen handwerklichen Manipulation der Form zur Setzung von Regeln verschoben: Die Form resultiert kontingent aus den von der Entwerferin angestoßenen und festgelegten Prozessen, oftmals in einer Art und Weise jenseits ihrer ursprünglichen Vorstellungskraft. Oder, um es mit einer gebräuchlichen evolutionären Metapher zu beschreiben: Die Entwerferin züchtet einen spezifischen Code oder DNA, sie

1 | Peter Eisenman: Romeo and Juliet, Collage, Biennale di Venezia 1985

A N A L O G   B L O B ?   A U T O N O M Y   A N D   N O T A T I O N   This narration about the birth of digital form finding out of the spirit of IT, software (and genetics) sounds convincing and enjoys the support of many well-known architects and theorists. Yet on closer inspection it might turn out to be too technologically deterministic. In the 1970s and 80s there were thought experiments in architecture that foreshadowed current developments in parametric-digital design processes.

Significantly, Greg Lynn, one of the pioneers of digital architecture and curator of the 2013 exhibition 'Archaeology of the Digital' at the CCA in Montreal, selected the 1987 project 'Bio Center Frankfurt University' by Peter Eisenman Architects for display.[2] Yet these experiments with scripting, with the combinatory logic of DNA "letters" of GACT, and with a rudimentary three-dimensional computer software that would eventually lead to 'FormZ' in the New York office of Eisenman would not have been possible without the formalist inquiry of the previous decades. Eisenman embarked on a trajectory of an analog virtualization of architecture with his design series of the 'Houses' since the mid-1960s, followed by urban design projects of the late 1970s and 80s. On this journey he introduced processual methods, such as 'scaling' in the project 'Romeo and Juliet' (aka: 'Moving Arrows, Eros, and Other Errors') displayed at the Venice Biennale 1985, which undermine the humanist notion of architectural authorship through autonomization – or rather automatization – of the design process by rendering it independent of the human observer (including the author himself) and which, according to the hypothesis of this essay, anticipate thereby some of the intellectual challenges of digital parametric design (fig. 1).[3] Instead of the classical reference to the human body, either directly via representation and proportion (Humanism) or indirectly via functionality and ergonomics (Modernism), Eisenman explores an inner-architectural operation, which refers only to

kultiviert einen Stammbaum von Projekten durch die Simulation genetischer Anpassung an verschiedene ökologische Nischen, wie es sich in den Beschreibungen von Alejandro Zaera-Polo, Patrik Schumacher oder ArandaLasch findet.[1] Nicht zufällig konvergieren die Begriffe, Themen und Theorien des künstlichen Lebens, Gentechnik, IT und Systemtheorie, wenn sich Architektinnen über parametrische Formfindung austauschen.

ANALOGER BLOB? AUTONOMIE UND NOTATION Diese Erzählung von der Geburt der digitalen Formfindung aus dem Geiste der IT, Software (und der Genetik) klingt überzeugend und hat auch viele Fürsprecher unter bekannten Architektinnen und Theoretikerinnen für sich. Jedoch bei genauerer Betrachtung könnte sie sich als zu technologiedeterministisch herausstellen. In den 1970er und 1980er Jahren gibt es eine Reihe von Gedankenexperimenten in der Architektur, welche die gegenwärtigen Entwicklungen in den parametrisch-digitalen Entwurfsprozessen vorausahnen lassen.

Bezeichnenderweise wählte Greg Lynn, selbst einer der Pioniere der digitalen Architektur und Kurator der Ausstellung ‚Archaeology of the Digital' am CCA in Montreal 2013, das Projekt ‚Biocenter Frankfurt University' von Peter Eisenman Architects aus dem Jahre 1987 für seine Ausstellung aus.[2] Aber diese Experimente mit Scripting, mit der kombinatorischen Logik der DNA-‚Buchstaben' des ACGT und mit einer rudimentären dreidimensionalen Computersoftware, aus der sich später FormZ im New Yorker Büro Eisenmans entwickeln sollte, wären nicht möglich gewesen ohne die formalistische Recherche der vorangegangenen Jahrzehnte. Eisenman bewegte sich auf einer Flugbahn hin zur analogen Virtualisierung der Architektur bereits mit seiner Entwurfsserie der ‚Houses' seit den Mit-Sechzigerjahren, fortgesetzt von seinen städtebaulichen Studien der späten 1970er und 1980er Jahre. Auf dieser Reise führte er prozessuale Methoden ein, wie beispielsweise das ‚Scaling' für das an der Biennale di Venezia 1985 ausgestellte Projekt ‚Romeo and Juliet' (auch bekannt als: ‚Moving Arrows, Eros, and Other Errors'), welche die humanistische Tradition architektonischer Autorenschaft durch eine Autonomisierung – oder vielmehr Automatisierung – des Entwurfsprozesses untergraben, indem sie diesen unabhängig vom menschlichen Beobachter (inklusive dem Autor selbst) zu machen trachten, und dadurch, wenn man der Argumentation dieses Essays folgt, einige der intellektuellen Herausforderungen des digital-parametrischen Entwerfens vorwegnehmen (Abb. 1).[3] An Stelle der klassischen Referenzen zum menschlichen Körper, entweder direkt über Repräsentation und Proportion (Humanismus) oder indirekt über Funktionalität und Ergonomie (Moderne), untersucht Eisenman eine inner-architektonische Operation, welche nur auf den Entwurfsprozess selbst referenziert – das heißt: auf das Zeichnen selbst. Dafür überlagert er verschiedene architektonische Maßstäbe innerhalb einer gerasterten Zeichnung, mischt existierende stadträumliche Elemente (Situation) mit verlorenen

the design process itself – that is: to drawing. For this, he superimposes different architectural scales in one gridded drawing, mixes existing urban elements (situation) with lost historic artifacts and layers (historic map of Verona, the cemetery of Verona, the tomb of Julia, the church of 'Montecchio Maggiore', plans of the 'castelli' of Romeo's and Julia's families, etc.) and adds non-architectural narrative elements (William Shakespeare's drama 'Romeo and Juliet', 1597 which he 'translates' into an architectural notation). By these processes, Eisenman tries to escape the classical representational function of architecture – as representation of something extrinsic to its own disciplinary processes and rules – by introducing accidental elements, ambiguous juxtapositions, and incongruent superimpositions, which lead traditional readings of the drawings 'ad absurdum'. Eisenman claims to question the metaphysics of architecture (anthropocentrism, origin, presence) as well as the ones of the artwork (closure, unity, authorship) and those of language (meaning, identity, representation) with the means of seriality, discontinuity, and complexity, in order to open architecture for alternative readings. However, if these playful-explorative encounters with process, chance, and contingency liberate architecture from the servile functions induced by author, program and site (not to speak of clients, budget, construction, materials and other forms of contingencies), or if the author enters through the backdoor as a 'demiurge' who determines not only the design, but commands also over its interpretation, remains open for debate.[4]

The drawings of Preston Scott Cohen in the 1990s demonstrate a similarly highly complex process of form finding, where the architect meticulously follows the protocols of transformational geometry set prior to the design. Here the architect performs a series of continuous projective transformations of an object in space by means of two-dimensional analog drawings, each step using the resulting figure of the previous as a starting point of the new construction, an intentionally laborious process of redrawing that disables any sense of final outcome, in order to undermine the classical notion of authority over form making. Cohen engages in his early work with architectural notations, or rather a process of continuously looped drawing and its laws of geometric transformations, in direct reaction to the theory of formal autonomy. By this he refers to the work of Peter Eisenman of the 1970s, who claimed an autonomous architecture as a form of conceptual art, which would have been liberated from the representation of something other than itself through the process of self-referentiality.[5] Eisenman proposes thinking of architecture in terms of medium specificity, with reference to Clement Greenberg's definition of modern art, who argued that the modernity of painting shows in its abstract color application on a two-dimensional canvas, instead of the representation of a subject, motive or genre. With Greenberg in mind, Eisenman tries to identify the specific 'architectonic' of modern architecture in the use of its elements as self-referential signs – in the selection, size,

historischen Artefakten und Schichten (die historische Karte von Verona, den Friedhof von Verona, das Grabmal von Julia, die Kirche ‚Montecchio Maggiore', Pläne der ‚Castelli' der Familien Romeos und Julias, etc.) und fügt außer-architektonische narrative Elemente hinzu (aus William Shakespeares Drama ‚Romeo and Juliet' von 1597, das er in eine architektonische Notation ‚übersetzt'). Durch diese Prozesse versucht Eisenman einer klassischen repräsentativen Funktion der Architektur – als Repräsentation von etwas außer ihren eigenen disziplinären Prozessen und Regeln – zu entfliehen, indem er akzidentielle Elemente, mehrdeutige Gegensätze und inkongruente Überlagerungen einführt, welche eine traditionelle Lektüre der Zeichnungen ‚ad absurdum' führen. Eisenman behauptet so die Metaphysik der Architektur (Anthropozentrismus, Ursprung, Präsenz) zu hinterfragen, ebenso wie die des Kunstwerkes (Abgeschlossenheit, Einheit, Autorenschaft), als auch die der Sprache (Bedeutung, Identität, Repräsentation) durch die Mittel der Serialität, der Diskontinuität und der Komplexität, um die Architektur für alternative Lektüren zu öffnen. Ob jedoch diese spielerisch-forschende Auseinandersetzung mit Prozess, Zufall und Kontingenz die Architektur von ihrer durch Autor, Programm und Ort bestimmten dienenden Funktion befreit (um gar nicht erst von Bauherrinnen, Kosten, Konstruktion, Materialien und anderen Formen der Kontingenz zu sprechen) oder ob der Autor nicht wieder durch die Hintertür als Demiurg eintritt, der nicht nur den Entwurf bestimmt, sondern auch dessen Interpretation beherrscht, bleibt zu diskutieren.[4]

Die Zeichnungen aus den 1990er Jahren von Preston Scott Cohen zeigen einen ähnlich hochkomplexen Prozess der Formfindung, in denen der Architekt akribisch den im Vorfeld des Entwurfes festgelegten Protokollen der transformativen Geometrie folgt. Der Architekt stellt eine Serie von kontinuierlichen projektiven Transformationen eines Objektes im Raum mittels zweidimensionaler analoger Zeichnungen dar, bei der jeder Schritt die Abbildung des Vorausgegangenen wieder zum Ausgangspunkt der neuen Konstruktion macht, ein bewusst mühsamer Prozess des Neuzeichnens, der jede Vorstellung von einem Endergebnis bereits im Ansatz verunmöglicht, um die klassische Auffassung von Autorenschaft über den Formgebungsprozess zu unterlaufen. In seinen frühen Arbeiten beschäftigt sich Cohen mit architektonischen Notationen, oder vielmehr mit einem potentiell endlosen Zeichnungsprozess und mit den Gesetzen geometrischer Transformationen, in direkter Auseinandersetzung mit der Theorie der formalen Autonomie. Damit spielt er auf das Werk Peter Eisenmans aus den 1970er Jahren an, der die autonome Architektur als eine Spielart der konzeptuellen Kunst vorstellte, welche sich durch den Prozess der Selbst-Referentialität von der Darstellung von etwas anderem als sie selbst befreit habe.[5] Eisenman schlägt vor, die Architektur unter der Bedingung der Medienspezifizität zu denken, mit Verweis auf Clement Greenbergs Definition der modernen Kunst, der behauptet hatte, dass sich die Modernität eines Gemäldes an Hand seines abstrakten Farbauftrages auf eine zwei-

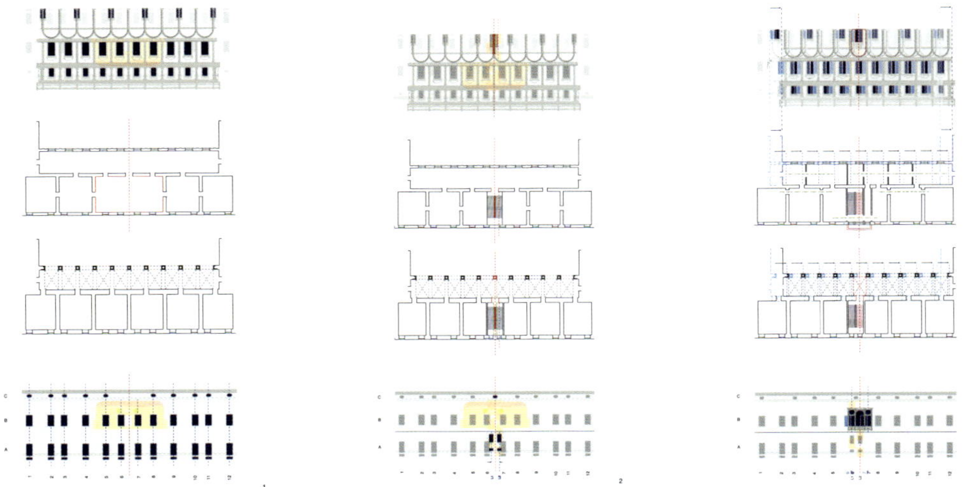

2-7 | Cohen: Palazzo Gambara, Brescia, Analysezeichnungen spüren die Störung des architektonischen Systems durch die Addition einer zentralen Treppe und den (fiktiven) Anpassungsprozess in Fassade und Plan Schritt für Schritt auf

number and positioning of pillar/beam, of wall/ceiling, and of volume/void and opening and their intentional marking, repetition, and differentiation.[6] For Eisenman the autonomy of architecture remains hidden in these 'intrinsic' formal operations independent of 'extrinsic' conditions like function, geometry, construction or materiality (or their overcoming and disappearing in the art work).

DRAWING TRACES Yet while Eisenman emphasizes architecture's abstraction, and sets its formal autonomy as absolute against context, building process as well as against functional demands, Cohen takes a differentiated stand where architectural form is both autonomous as well as "assimilated and situated".[7] From this dialectical figure, Cohen hopes to unfold the paradigmatic forms of architecture, their axioms and rules, in order to bring forward their hidden paradoxical formal genetic processes. Cohen dives into the history of architecture, like Eisenman before, who referred to Alberti, Palladio, Scamozzi or Venetian Palazzi to outline an unbroken line of tradition of Humanist architecture from Renaissance to Modernism – a continuity which would have been finally overcome with Le Corbusier's 'Maison Dom-ino' and Giuseppe Terragni's 'Casa del Fascio', which Eisenman reads as premieres of a self-referential, autonomous architecture, a historic project that he claims to continue with his series of 'Houses' in the 1960s and 70s (or is it rather that he invents this project?).[8]

Yet Cohen takes a different stance with regard to history: rather than searching for big treatises or for (postmodern) typologies, he directs his attention towards loopholes, mistakes, and discontinuities in geometric systems, such as his reconstruction of the design stages of the 'Palazzo Gambara' in Brescia: Cohen retraces retrospectively its

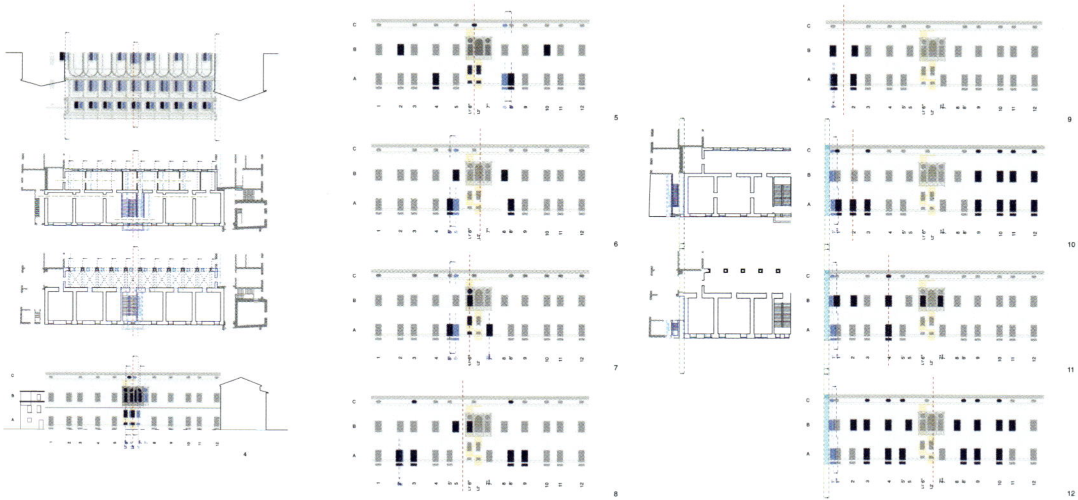

2-7 | Cohen: Palazzo Gambara, Brescia, analytic drawings which trace the disturbance of the architectonic system through the addition of a central stair case and the (fictional) process of adaptation in facade and plan step by step

dimensionale Fläche zeige, anstatt der Repräsentation eines Gegenstandes, Motivs oder Genres. Eisenman versucht nun, mit Greenberg im Geiste, das spezifisch ‚Architektonische' der modernen Architektur im Gebrauch ihrer Elemente als selbstreferentielle Zeichen zu identifizieren – in der Auswahl, Größe, Anzahl und Positionierung von Stütze/Balken, von Wand/Decke und von Masse/Leere bzw. Öffnung und deren intentionaler Markierung, Wiederholung und Differenzierung.[6] Für Eisenman liegt die Autonomie der Architektur in diesen ‚intrinsischen' formalen Operationen verborgen, unabhängig von den ‚extrinsischen' Bedingungen wie beispielsweise Funktion, Geometrie, Konstruktion oder Materialität (oder deren Überwindung und Verschwinden im Kunstwerk).

SPUREN ZEICHNEN Doch während Eisenman die Abstraktion der Architektur hervorhebt und ihre formale Autonomie als absolut gegenüber Kontext, Bauprozess und gegenüber funktionellen Anforderungen setzt, nimmt Cohen eine differenziertere Haltung ein, bei der die Architektur sowohl autonom als auch „assimiliert und situiert" wäre.[7] Aus dieser dialektischen Figur hofft Cohen, die paradigmatischen Formen der Architektur zu entfalten, ihre Axiome und Regeln, um ihren verborgenen paradoxalen Formwerdungsprozess ans Licht zu bringen. Dafür taucht Cohen in die Architekturgeschichte ein, wie schon Eisenman vor ihm, der sich auf Alberti, Palladio, Scamozzi oder die Venezianischen Palazzi berief, um eine ungebrochene Traditionslinie der humanistischen Architektur von der Renaissance bis zur Moderne zu zeichnen – eine Kontinuität, die erst mit Le Corbusiers ‚Maison Dom-ino' und Giuseppe Terragnis ‚Casa del Facsio' gebrochen worden wäre, welche Eisenman als Erstlingswerke einer selbstreferentiellen, autonomen Architektur versteht, einem historischen Projekt, von dem er behauptet, es mit seiner Serie der ‚Houses' in den 1960er und 70er Jahren fortzusetzen (oder ist es vielmehr so, dass er dieses Projekt damit erst erfindet?).[8]

transformations over time with a series of analytical drawings step by step. The original closed composition in a Palladian fashion gets disturbed by the slightly off-center addition of a staircase, which causes a series of further adaptations in the geometric-symmetrical sequences of facades (both courtyard and garden), in the layout of the main spaces, and even in the structure of the edifice. As a result, these adaptations caused by the added stairway would leave a trace of geometric deviations, incoherencies, and asymmetries within the architectural system, which fails to accomplish classical ideals of balance, harmony and representation (fig. 2-7).

But for Cohen this is not a defect, instead he welcomes it as an additional layer of architectural information. As an ordering system, architecture would need inherent conflicts and the struggle for order. The identity and specificity of edifices is rooted, according to Cohen, not in the authority of the architect, nor in the originality of the local and historic context, but it derives from the negotiation of the irreconcilable contradictions between the abstract (or ideal) architectonic system and the local conditions. For Cohen buildings are immanent entities, that is to say, they constitute closed systems of their own order, which wait for the informed observer to be uncovered and read, rather than just concentrating on the higher-level ideal schemata, as they populate the studies on the Italian villae and palazzi by Rudolf Wittkower, Colin Rowe, or Peter Eisenman. Hence Cohen does not select his examples from the oeuvre of canonic masters such as Alberti, Michelangelo, Palladio, etc. but rather from anonymous background, as in the case of the 'Palazzo Gambara', several unknown local master masons of the 16th to 19th century. With examples like this, Cohen puts forward a discussion about the dialectic between norm (type, style, homogeneity) and deviance (singularity, identity, specificity) in form of a geometric trace of differentiation (individuality) and contingency (by the rules of 'decorum' or through functional conditions). In this way, the analysis of the 'Palazzo Gambara' turns into historically informed reproduction, the process of drawing itself becomes a (fictional) appropriation, or rather: Cohen's very own design project.

PERFORMING PROCESSUALITY Beyond these historic exercises, Scott Cohen's early design work – such as 'Stereometric Permutations' (1993) – speak of a continuous inquiry into the medium of drawing, especially into the potential of projective geometry as primary driver and content of architecture (fig. 8). With these, Cohen joins a long tradition of geometric treatises since the Renaissance written by architects as proof of humanist science and in delineation from 'mere' building practice. Yet in difference to Greg Lynn, who stems from the same background of the New York office of

Doch Cohen verfolgt einen anderen Ansatz in Bezug auf die Geschichte. Anstatt nach den großen Traktaten oder den (postmodernen) Typologien zu suchen, lenkt er sein Interesse auf die Auslassungen, Fehlstellen und Diskontinuitäten in geometrischen Systemen, wie beispielsweise seine Rekonstruktion der Entwurfsstadien des ‚Palazzo Gambara' in Brescia: Cohen verfolgt aus der Retrospektive dessen Transformationen über die Zeit mittels analytischer Zeichnungen Schritt für Schritt zurück. Die ursprünglich geschlossene Komposition in palladianischer Manier wird von einer leicht außerzentrischen Hinzufügung eines Treppenlaufes gestört, die wiederum eine Serie anderer Anpassungen in der geometrisch-symmetrischen Sequenz beider Fassaden (Hof und Garten), in der Anordnung der Haupträume und sogar in der Struktur des Gebäudes nach sich zieht. Schlussendlich würden diese von der hinzugefügten Treppe veranlassten Adaptionen eine Spur geometrischer Abweichungen, Inkohärenzen und Asymmetrien innerhalb des architektonischen Systems hinterlassen, das nun nicht mehr die klassischen Ideale der Balance, Harmonie und Repräsentation erfülle (Abb. 2-7).

Jedoch ist das für Cohen kein Defekt, sondern im Gegenteil, er heißt dies als zusätzliche Schicht architektonischer Information willkommen. Als ein Ordnungssystem bedürfe die Architektur inhärenter Konflikte und das Ringen um Ordnung. Die Identität und Spezifizität der Gebäude gründe, so Cohen, weder in der Autorität des Architekten noch in der Originalität des lokalen und historischen Kontextes, sondern nähre sich aus der Verhandlung von unvereinbaren Widersprüchen zwischen dem abstrakten (oder idealen) Architektursystem und den lokalen Bedingungen. Für Cohen sind Gebäude immanente Entitäten, das heißt, sie konstituieren geschlossene Systeme eigener Art, die darauf warten, vom eingeweihten Betrachter entdeckt und gelesen zu werden, anstatt sich nur auf die übergeordneten idealen Schemata zu konzentrieren, wie sie die Studien italienischer Villae und Palazzi von Rudolf Wittkower, Colin Rowe oder Peter Eisenman bevölkern. Deshalb wählt Cohen seine Beispiele nicht aus dem Œuvre der kanonischen Meister wie Alberti, Michelangelo, Palladio etc. aus, sondern eher aus dem anonymen Hintergrund, wie im Fall des ‚Palazzo Gambara', mehrere unbekannte Baumeister zwischen dem 16. und 19. Jahrhundert. Mit Beispielen wie diesen stößt Cohen eine Diskussion über die Dialektik zwischen Norm (Typus, Stil, Homogenität) und Abweichung (Einzigartigkeit, Identität, Spezifizität) in Form einer geometrischen Spur der Differenzierung (Individualität) und Kontingenz (nach den Regeln des ‚Decorum' oder nach funktionalen Kriterien) an. Auf diese Art und Weise gerät die Analyse des ‚Palazzo Gambara' zu einer historisch informierten Wiederaufführung, der Prozess des Zeichnens selbst wird zu einer (fiktiven) Aneignung, oder vielmehr: wird zu Cohens ganz eigenem Entwurfsprojekt.

8 | Preston Scott Cohen, Stereometric Permutations, Zeichnung | Drawing, 1993
9 | Preston Scott Cohen, Rectilinear Spiriculate, Zeichnung | Drawing, 1998

PERFORMANZ DER PROZESSUALITÄT Außer diesen historischen Fingerübungen spricht Scott Cohens frühe Entwurfsarbeit – wie beispielsweise ‚Stereometric Permutations' (1993) – von einer kontinuierlichen Auseinandersetzung mit dem Medium der Zeichnung, speziell der projektiven Geometrie als primärer Antrieb und Inhalt der Architektur (Abb. 8). Damit reiht sich Cohen in eine lange Tradition seit der Renaissance der von Architekten geschriebenen geometrischen Traktate ein, die als Beweis ihrer humanistischen Wissenschaftlichkeit dienen und sie von der ‚bloßen' Baupraxis abgrenzen sollten. Doch im Gegensatz zu Greg Lynn, der aus demselben Umfeld des New Yorker Büros von Peter Eisenman stammt, stützt sich Cohen für die Konstruktion seiner Argumentation zur produktiven Rolle der Geometrie nicht auf Alberti.[9] Ebenso wie bei seiner Auswahl historischer Studienbeispiele bevorzugt Cohen etwas verborgenere Quellen, wie beispielsweise den britischen Mathematiker Brook Taylor, der wegen seines obskuren Schreibstiles wenig rezipiert wurde, obwohl es ihm gelang, bereits 1715 eine vollständige Beschreibung der Dreipunktperspektive zu liefern inklusive der präzisen mathematischen Bestimmung der Fluchtpunkte für die Darstellung von Objekten im Raum, die sich nicht parallel zur Bildebene befinden.[10] Zudem gelang es Taylor, das umgekehrte Problem zu lösen, den Betrachterstandpunkt beziehungsweise den Augpunkt eines gegebenen Bildes zu rekonstruieren, das heißt, er beschrieb eine Methode zur Berechnung dreidimensionaler Objekte und ihrer relationalen Positionierung im Raum, was eine der Grundlagen der projektiven Geometrie in der heutigen Mathematik darstellt. Cohen verweist auf Taylor andererseits, um seine Experimente mit prozessgesteuerten analogen Zeichnungen mit Darstellungsprotokollen der Linearperspektive anzureichern.

Eine künstlerische Aneignung dieser Darstellungsprinzipien zeigt sich in Cohens analoger Zeichnung ‚Rectilinear Spiriculate' (1998), eine Serie aneinandergereihter projektiver Transformationen eines einfachen Objektes, welche mit ihrer kreisförmigen Anordnung sowohl das Vorbild, das Abbild und die Konstruktionslinien dieser komplexen Transformationen ohne einen Anfang oder ein Endergebnis darstellt (Abb. 9). Vielmehr muss die gesamte Zeichnung selbst als Spur eines offenen Prozesses gelesen werden. Die von Cohen angewandten projektiven Protokolle basieren auf der Dreipunktperspektivkonstruktion wie sie Taylor entwickelt hat, und auf die Stereometrie und Stereotomie, wie sie während des französischen Manierismus von Philibert De L'Orme und Girard Desargues für den Steinschnitt beschrieben wurden.[11] In Cohens Zeichnung wird jedes zweidimensionale Bild als dreidimensionales Objekt interpretiert und Ausgangspunkt der nächsten Stufe der im Vorfeld festgelegten Abbildungsprotokolle, wie bereits der Titel ‚Rectilinear Spiriculate' andeutet – eine geradlinige spiralförmige Kalkulation. Damit unterstreicht Cohen den generativen

Eisenman, Cohen does not rely on Alberti to build his argument about the productive role of geometry.[9] Similarly to his choice of historic studies, Cohen prefers more under-researched sources, such as the British mathematician Brook Taylor who was not well received because of his obscure writing style, despite the fact that he developed a complete description of three-point-perspective as early as 1715, including a precise mathematical formulation of the vanishing points for the representation of objects in space which are not positioned parallel to the picture plane.[10] In addition, Taylor solved the inverse problem of reconstructing the observer standpoint respectively the eye point from a given image, that is, he described a method to calculate three-dimensional objects and their relational position in space, which is one of the fundamentals of projective geometry in today's mathematics. Cohen on the other end refers to Taylor to inform his experiments in processual analog drawing with representational protocols from linear perspective.

A creative appropriation of these representational principles manifests in Cohen's analog drawings 'Rectilinear Spiriculate' (1998) – a series of continuous projective transformations of a simple geometric object, which shows with its circular organization both the original, image and construction lines of the complex transformations, without establishing a beginning nor an end result (fig. 9). Rather, the entire drawing itself has to be read as a trace of an open process. The projective protocols employed by Cohen are based on the three-point perspective construction as developed by Taylor, and on stereometry and stereotomy as described during French Mannerism by Philibert De L'Orme and Girard Desargues for stone masonry.[11] In Cohen's drawing each two-dimensional image is interpreted as a three-dimensional object and becomes the starting point for the next iteration of the projective protocol set in advance, as the title 'Rectilinear Spiriculate' alludes to – that is a straight-lined spiral calculation. With this, Cohen underlines the generative process of geometry, as a project that is not limited to the servant representational functionality of architectural drawing (as description of a future building to be erected), but acts as operative reality. Cohen assigns to himself the laborious task of constructing with the analog tools of compasses, ruler, set square and pencil the previously set protocols (or projective scripts), where each step builds on the previous one. With this process he aims for contingent problem areas, not to 'solve' or 'optimize' them, but rather to test their openness and instability for architectural design beyond traditional notions of form, intentionality, and authorship.

In the case of 'Rectilinear Spiriculate', geometry is not an applied science of architecture any longer, a side-kick for structural calculations, for construction and for the transfer of plans from scaled drawing towards the site, but geometric drawing processes themselves

Prozess der Geometrie als Projekt, die nicht auf die dienende repräsentativ-funktionale Rolle der Architekturzeichnung (als Darstellung eines zukünftig zu errichtenden Gebäudes) beschränkt ist, sondern als operative Realität fungiert. Cohen beauftragt sich selbst mit der mühevollen Arbeit, mit den analogen Instrumenten von Zirkel, Lineal, Dreieck und Bleistift die im Vorhinein festgelegte Abfolge an Protokollen (oder projektiven Scripts) zu konstruieren, bei der jeder Schritt auf den vorhergehenden aufbaut. Mit diesem Prozess strebt er nach kontingenten Problemlagen, nicht etwa, um diese zu ‚lösen' oder zu ‚optimieren', sondern vielmehr um ihre Offenheit und Instabilität für den Architekturentwurf zu testen, jenseits von traditionellen Vorstellungen von Form, Intention und Autorenschaft.

Im Falle von ‚Rectilinear Spiriculate' erscheint die Geometrie nicht mehr als eine angewandte Wissenschaft im Dienste der Architektur, als eine Handlangerin für statische Berechnungen, für Konstruktion und für die Übertragung des Plans von der maßstäblichen Zeichnung auf die Baustelle, sondern die geometrischen Zeichenprozesse selbst erzeugen komplexe Formen. Cohen betont die Komplexität als einen Wert an sich, mit Verweis auf die unauflöslichen Konflikte auf einer Ebene, die auf einer höheren Ordnung ausbalanciert werden, in Analogie zur Anamorphose in der Malerei oder zur Ontogenese der Flunder in der Evolutionsbiologie. Beeinflusst von post-strukturalistischer Theorie kritisiert Cohen die angeblich fordistische Logik der Einfachheit, Rationalität und Serialität der modernen Architektur zugunsten von Abweichung, Komplexität und Mannigfaltigkeit, auf dem Weg zu einer Architektur des Außergewöhnlichen und Einzigartigen, die sowohl hochdeterminiert als auch überraschend und einmalig sei (eine Nicht-Standard Architektur).[12] Gleichzeitig lehnt Cohen eine „post-problematische" Architektur ab,[13] die sich in oberflächlich materielle Schönheit und formale Einfachheit flüchte, wie er sie beispielsweise in den neo-modernen und minimalistischen Tendenzen erblickt. Deshalb verweist Cohen auch wiederholt auf die mathematische Morphologie von D'Arcy Thompson.[14] Er zeigt sich weniger interessiert an harmonischen Idealtypen, sondern vielmehr an regelbasierten Übergängen, nicht an der Perfektion von formalen Lösungen, sondern eher an genealogischen Spuren vorangegangener Entwicklungsstadien und an den Prozessen der Anpassung und Transformierung. ‚Form' ist für Cohen weder ein platonisches Ideal, noch sieht er Komplexität als eine geometrische Kombination und Überlagerung von einfachen Elementen an (wie in den ‚Houses' von Eisenman), sondern vielmehr als eine Reaktion auf externe Kräfte, als eine Wechselwirkung zwischen Objekt und Kontext.

Der grundlegende Wechsel von analogen zu digitalen Zeichentechniken in den 1990er Jahren hat nicht nur die geometrische Formfindung an die Spitze der allgemeinen Architekturpraxis katapultiert, sondern auch das Werk Cohens verändert. Mit der Hilfe von

generate complex forms. Cohen emphasizes complexity as a value per se, referring to unresolved conflicts on one level, which find balance on a higher order, in analogy to anamorphosis in painting, or to the ontogenesis of the flounder (flatfish) in evolutionary biology. Informed by post-structuralist theories, Cohen criticizes the supposedly Fordist logic of simplicity, rationality, and seriality of modern architecture, in favor of deviance, complexity, and multiplicity, towards an architecture of the extraordinary and singular, which would be both highly determined as well as surprising and unique (an 'architecture non-standard').[12] At the same time, Cohen rejects a "post-problematic" architecture,[13] which would take refuge in superficial material beauty and formal simplicity, as for example he sees them in the neo-modernist and minimalist tendencies. This is also why Cohen refers frequently to the mathematical morphology of D'Arcy Thompson:[14] he is not interested in harmonious ideal types, but rather in rule-based transitions, not in the perfection of formal solutions, but rather in genealogic traces of previous evolutionary stages and in the processes of accommodation and transformation. 'Form' is to Cohen not a Platonic ideal, nor is complexity a geometric combination and superimposition of simple elements (as in the 'Houses' of Eisenman), but rather a reaction to external forces, a reciprocity between object and context.

The sea change from analog to digital drawing techniques in the 1990s did not only bring geometric form finding to the forefront of mainstream architectural practice, but also informed Cohen's work. With the help of vector-based computer software, he intensified his inquisition into geometric complexity beyond the representational potentials of analog drawing, as for example with his 'Torus House' (1999), a design based on a surface of revolution, hence on a topological two-dimensional manifold within three-dimensional space. The progress of vector-based CAD programs did not only allow for the precise construction of parametric curves ('splines'), but generated a new sensibility for geometric events, such as continuity, smooth seamless surfaces ('performance envelopes'), and morphologic transitions, instead of the discrete breaks, fractals, collages, montages, and disjunctions of neo-avantgarde architecture of the 1970s and 80s.

(INSTEAD OF A) CONCLUSION: ENDGAMES? Or: an essay on failure. The analog work of both Eisenman and Cohen sketches out some of the problems and questions of contemporary architecture: how do we engage discursively with objects that have not been conceived of by the designer as 'idea' or 'form', but rather stand

vektorbasierter Computersoftware hat er seine Recherche in die geometrische Komplexität jenseits der darstellerischen Potentiale der analogen Zeichnung intensiviert, wie beispielsweise mit seinem ‚Torus House' (1999), einem Entwurf basierend auf einem Revolutions-Flächenkörper, das heißt, auf einer topologischen zweidimensionalen Mannigfaltigkeit innerhalb des dreidimensionalen Raumes. Der Fortschritt der vektororientierten CAD Programme erlaubte nicht nur eine präzise Konstruktion der parametrischen Kurven (Polynomzüge), sondern schuf eine neue Empfindsamkeit für geometrische Qualitäten wie Kontinuität, glatte nahtlose Hüllflächen (‚Performance Envelopes') und morphologische Übergänge an Stelle von diskreten Brüchen, Fraktalen, Collage, Montage und Trennungen der Neo-Avantgarde der 1970er und 1980er.

(ANSTATT EINER) SCHLUSSFOLGERUNG: ENDSPIELE? Oder: ein Versuch über das Scheitern. Die analogen Arbeiten von sowohl Eisenman als auch Cohen skizzieren einige der Probleme und Fragen der zeitgenössischen Architektur: Wie nähert man sich diskursiv an Objekte an, die nicht von einer Entwerferin als ‚Idee' oder ‚Form' konzipiert wurden, sondern vielmehr unabhängig als Ergebnis eines Prozesses entstehen, der sich größtenteils menschlicher Beobachtung und ästhetischer Einflussnahme entzieht? Wie schreiben sich die digitalen Werkzeuge in die Disziplin der Architektur ein, und was bleibt vom ‚Architektonischen' jenseits der Künstlertradition des ‚disegno' der Renaissance, wenn die körperlichen, performativen Zusammenhänge von Vorstellung, Hand und Zeichnung von Interfaces, Medien und autonomer Software zerschnitten wurden? Was bleibt vom Kanon der Architektur, wenn Entwurf nichts anderes bedeutet als die bloße Auswahl an Quellen, Regeln und Protokollen? Wenn die Rolle der Architektin traditionell von architektonischen Ideen und Erfindungsgabe gekennzeichnet war, einem Motiv, das mittels des Zeichnungsprozesses herausgearbeitet werden musste, wer ist dann heute die Autorin eines Entwurfes – die Nutzerin der Software oder die Programmiererin des Algorithmus? Wie können Architektinnen in diesem unsicheren Raum der Kontingenz manövrieren? Einige der Antworten könnten aus den Arbeiten von Eisenman und Cohen gewonnen werden: Indem sie die scheinbar festgesetzten instrumentellen Verhältnisse der Disziplin hinterfragten, indem sie die architektonischen Darstellungsmittel erforschten, indem sie neue Protokolle jenseits reiner Anwendbarkeit und Optimierung entwickelten, und indem sie in arbeitsintensiven Selbstexperimenten diese testeten und systematisierten, kurz, indem sie den Entwurfsprozess selbst reflektierten, protokollierten und theoretisierten, anstatt sich nur auf das resultierende Objekt zu konzentrieren.

independently as results of processes largely hidden from human sight and aesthetic intervention? How do the new digital tools inform the discipline of architecture and what remains of the 'architectonic' beyond the Renaissance artist tradition of 'disegno', when the embodied, performative relation of mind, hand and drawing has been cut apart through interfaces, media and autonomous software? What remains of the canon of architecture when design becomes a mere selecting of sources, rules and protocols? If traditionally the role of the architect was defined by architectural ideas and invention, a motive that was worked out in the drawing process, who is the author of a design today – the user of the software or the programmer of the algorithm? How can architects maneuver this uncertain space of contingencies? Some answers may be drawn from the works of Eisenman and Cohen: by questioning instrumental relations of the discipline taken for granted, by exploring the architectural means of representation, by developing new protocols beyond pure applicability and optimization, and by testing and systematizing operations in laborious self-experiments, in short, by reflecting, protocoling, and theorizing the design processes itself, instead of focusing on solely the resulting object.

1 Foreign Office Architects (Alejandro Zaera-Polo, Farshid Moussavi), Phylogenesis FOA's Ark, Barcelona: Actar, 2003; Patrik Schumacher, The autopoiesis of architecture, 2 Bände | 2 volumes, Chichester: Wiley 2010-2012; ArandaLasch, Trace elements, New York City: Columbia Books 2017 **2** Canadian Center of Architecture, Montreal, 7.5.-27.10.2013. Die für die ‚Digitale Architektur' ausgewählten Projekte beinhalteten neben dem Biozentrum Frankfurt von Peter Eisenman (1987): Lewis Residence von Frank Gehry (1985-1995), Expanding Sphere von Chuck Hoberman (1992) und die Dachstruktur des Odawara Sportzentrums (1991) und Galaxy Toyama (1992) von Shoei Yoh. | Canadian Center of Architecture, Montreal, May 7 to October 27 2013. The selected projects of 'digital architecture' included next to the Biozentrum Frankfurt by Peter Eisenman (1987): Lewis Residence by Frank Gehry (1985-1995), Expanding Sphere by Chuck Hoberman (1992) and the roofing structure for Odawara sports complex (1991) and Galaxy Toyama (1992) by Shoei Yoh. **3** Peter Eisenman, Moving arrows, Eros and other errors. An architecture of absence, in: AA Files 12 (1986), 77-83 **4** Clive R. Knights, The fragility of structure, the weight of interpretation. Some anomalies in the life and opinions of Eisenman and Derrida, in: Ian Borden/ Jane Rendell (eds.): InterSections: Architectural histories and critical theories, London: Routledge 2000, 70-88, hier | here: 74-76 **5** Peter Eisenman, Aspects of Modernism: Maison Domino and the self-referential sign, in: Oppositions 15-16 (1979), 118-128 **6** ibid. 121-23 **7** Preston Scott Cohen, Stereometric permutations, in: Appendx: Culture/Theory/Praxis, No 3 (1997), http://www.appendx.org/appendx/issue3/cohen/stereo/index2.htm; s. auch | s. also: Preston Scott Cohen, Contested symmetries. The architecture of Preston Scott Cohen, New York: Princeton Architectural Press 2001, 16-29 **8** Bereits die Dissertationsschrift von Eisenman am Trinity College in Cambridge (UK) von 1963 spricht diese Beispiele und Themen an. Vgl. | Already the dissertation thesis of Eisenman at the Trinity College in Cambridge (UK) from 1963 addresses these examples and issues. Cf. Peter D. Eisenman, The formal basis of Modern architecture, Baden: Lars Müller 2006 **9** Vgl. | Cf. Greg Lynn, Animate form, New York: Princeton Architectural Press 1999 **10** Brook Taylor, Linear perspective: Or, a new method of representing justly all manner of objects as they appear to the eye in all situations, London: R. Knaplock 1715; Vgl. | Cf. Preston Scott Cohen, Contested Symmetries and other Predicaments in Architecture, New York: Princeton Architectural Press 2001, 54-69 **11** Robin Evans, The projective cast. Architecture and its three geometries, Cambridge (MA): MIT press 1995, hier Kapitel V | here Chapter V: Drawn stone, 179-239; Vgl. | Cf. Philibert de L'Orme, Nouvelles inventions pour bien bastir et a petits fraiz, trouvées n'agueres par Philibert de L'orme, Lyonnois, Architecte, Conseiller & Aulmonier ordinaire du feu Roy Henry, & Abbé de St Èloy les Noyon frais, Paris 1561; Vgl. | Cf. Girard Desargues, Exemple de l'une des manières universelles du S.G.D.L. touchant la practique de la perspective sans emploier aucun tiers point, de distance ny d'autre nature, qui soit hors du champ de l'ouvrage., Paris 1636 **12** Frédéric Migayrou/Zeynep Mennan (eds.), Architectures non standard, Paris: Centre Georges Pompidou 2003 (exhibition catalogue, Dec 10 2003-March 1 2004) **13** Preston Scott Cohen, Contested symmetries and other predicaments in architecture, New York: Princeton Architectural Press 2001, 12 **14** D'Arcy Wentworth Thompson, On growth and form, Cambridge: Cambridge University Press 1917 [1942]

COLLAGES . INTERACTIONS

A specific form of design and research processes

Sarah Wehmeyer

Due to an increasing interest in scientific considerations of the connections between research and design in design-based disciplines, the following contribution focuses on the digital collage, hitherto primarily a presentation medium, as a specific form of mutually influencing relationships between design and research processes in architecture. Based on the example of the project 'A grammar for the city' developed together by the architecture firms OFFICE and DOGMA based in Belgium, the potential the collage offers for conceptualizing and researching spatial qualities, as well as reflecting on individual ideals and values and develop them further, is examined. It is also questioned whether and how the collage as a reflexive approach to creative processes implicitly and/or explicitly supports the genesis of knowledge and especially design-specific knowledge.

The approach results from an architectural theory standpoint that perceives the process of design beyond its creative perspective, also in relation to its knowledge-generating capacities and its potential research possibilities. The research bases are, on the one hand, current discourses dedicated to the specific process of 'research-connected design', viewing its co-evolutionary qualities as a search for compositional order – the design – combined with the search for design-specific knowledge – the research.[1] What is equally significant for the following consideration of collages is the assumption that architecture-specific means of presentation and design-related practices, such as architectural sketching, photography or the model, provide accompanying support for and visually convey these various actions and the gained knowledge, as well as leave their own traces in what is being developed.[2]

COLLAGEN . INTERAKTIONEN

Eine spezifische Form entwerfender und forschender Prozesse

Sarah Wehmeyer

Ausgehend von einem zunehmenden Interesse für die wissenschaftliche Auseinandersetzung mit den Zusammenhängen von Forschen und Entwerfen in entwurfsbasierten Disziplinen, thematisiert der folgende Beitrag die bisher primär als Präsentationsmedium erfasste digitale Collage als eine spezifische Form der wechselwirksamen Relationen von entwerfenden und forschenden Prozessen in der Architektur. Am Beispiel des 2005 von den in Belgien ansässigen Architekturbüros OFFICE und DOGMA gemeinsam entwickelten Projektes ‚A grammar for the city' wird untersucht, welche Potentiale die Bild-Collage in ihrer Produktion sowie Rezeption offeriert, um sowohl räumliche Qualitäten zu konzipieren und zu erforschen als auch individuelle Ideale und Werte zu reflektieren und weiterzuentwickeln. Ebenso wird hinterfragt, ob und in welcher Weise die Collage als eine reflexive Annäherung an kreative Prozesse implizit und/oder explizit die Wissensgenese und in besonderer Weise die Genese entwurfsspezifischen Wissens unterstützt.

Die Annäherung erfolgt von einem architekturtheoretischen Standpunkt, welcher den Vorgang des Entwerfens über seine gestalterische Perspektive hinaus ebenso in Bezug auf seine wissensgenerierenden Kapazitäten sowie seine potentiellen forschenden Möglichkeiten wahrnimmt. Forschungsgrundlage sind zum einen gegenwärtige Diskurse, die sich dem spezifischen Prozess des ‚forschenden Entwerfens' widmen und diesen in seinen koevolutiven Qualitäten als eine Suche nach der kompositorischen Ordnung – dem Entwerfen – verknüpft mit der Suche nach entwurfsspezifischem Wissen – dem Forschen – erkennen.[1] Ebenso bedeutsam für die folgende Untersuchung der Collagen ist die Annahme, dass architekturspezifische Darstellungsmittel und entwurfsbezogene Praktiken wie die Architekturzeichnung, die Fotografie oder das Modell, diese unterschiedlichen Handlungen und die hierbei gewonnenen Erkenntnisse sowohl begleitend unterstützen und visuell vermitteln als auch selbst ihre Spuren im Entstehenden hinterlassen.[2]

COLLAGES The notion of collage goes back etymologically to the term 'papier collé' stemming from fine arts, which describes the method of esthetically layering flat everyday materials in art, such as newspaper extracts and wallpaper scraps, first used by Pablo Picasso and George Braque between 1911 and 1914.[3] Due to its specific dialectic – the coexistence of image fragments of widely varying origin, which evokes both the original meanings and a range of new associations through the composition – collage can be identified as a constantly recurring form of art from the beginnings of cubist 'adhered images' to surrealism and pop art.[4] In light of its multiple meanings and complexity, however, collage experienced an equally wide range of formal and ideal interpretations in the architecture of the 20th century.[5]

IN ARCHITECTURE RESEARCH In the recent past, architecture theory essays and publications have focused retrospectively on collages, including in the built and theoretical work of individual architects, in order to explore their graphic impulses regarding visual rhetoric and their influences on design conception, as well as the design stances of architects. Martino Stierli and Neil Levine show, for example, that Mies van der Rohe experiments with various techniques of photomontage and collage to develop typological and spatial-compositional principles in a project-specific context, as well as in the wider context of his personal architectural stance, and to communicate them visually.[6] Werner Blaser's documentation of Mies' theory at IIT in Chicago underlines further that Mies van der Rohe activates the process of collaging himself as a schooling of his perception and sensitization to proportions.[7]

The collage as a graphically conveying and at the same time critical-analytical medium is researched by Marie Theres Staffer based on the example of the creative actions of Superstudio. The Italian architecture group uses collage as an interplay between future visions and reality fragments to design anti-utopias such as the 'Continuous Monument' (1969) and thus to research current social, political and architectural topics.[8] Stauffer recognizes the potential of collage as the 'realized' end product, which makes the knowledge gathered by architects collectively accessible in combination with written manifestos and provokes public discourse.

The previous research shows exciting approaches to how collage was activated in the past in a targeted manner with different intentions as a specific medium of design, research and critical reflection on ideal and spatial forms of expression. For a more differentiated understanding of the potential of collage for various creative thought and design processes, collages are considered here in the work of the contemporary architecture firms OFFICE and DOGMA, referring to the competition design 'A grammar for the city'. The analysis of the competition design and the collages created in this context is within

C O L L A G E N Der Begriff der Collage ist etymologisch auf die der bildenden Künste entstammenden Bezeichnung des ‚papier collé' zurückzuführen, welche die von Pablo Picasso und George Braque zwischen 1911 und 1914 erstmals angewandte Methode der ästhetischen Schichtung flacher Alltagsmaterialien, wie Zeitungsausschnitte und Tapetenreste, in der Kunst beschreibt.[3] Aufgrund ihrer spezifischen Dialektik – die Koexistenz von Bildfragmenten unterschiedlichster Herkunft, welche sowohl die Erinnerung an ursprüngliche Bedeutungen wahrt als auch vielfache neue Bezüge durch das Zusammengesetzte hervorruft – ist die Collage von den Anfängen der kubistischen ‚Klebebilder' über den Surrealismus und die Pop-Art hinaus als eine stetig wiederkehrende Kunstform zu identifizieren.[4] In ihrer Mehrdeutigkeit und Komplexität erfuhr die Collage jedoch ebenso vielfältige formale und ideelle Interpretationen in der Architektur des 20. Jahrhunderts.[5]

I N D E R A R C H I T E K T U R F O R S C H U N G Um sowohl ihre grafischen Impulse auf die visuelle Rhetorik, als auch ihre Einflüsse auf die Entwurfskonzeption sowie die Entwurfshaltungen der Architekturschaffenden zu ergründen, fokussierten in jüngerer Vergangenheit architekturtheoretische Essays und Publikationen die Collage rückwirkend und individuell im gebauten und theoretischen Werk vereinzelter Architekten. Martino Stierli und Neil Levine etwa verdeutlichen, dass Mies van der Rohe mit unterschiedlichen Techniken der Fotomontage und Collage experimentiert, um typologische und räumlich-kompositorische Prinzipien im projektspezifischen Kontext sowie im übergeordneten Zusammenhang seiner persönlichen Architekturhaltung weiterzuentwickeln und visuell zu kommunizieren.[6] Werner Blasers Dokumentation der Mies'schen Lehre am IIT in Chicago unterstreicht weitergehend, dass Mies van der Rohe zudem den Prozess des Collagierens selbst als Schulung der Wahrnehmung und als Sensibilisierung für Proportionen aktiviert.[7]

Die Collage als grafisch vermittelndes und zugleich kritisch-analytisches Medium erforscht Marie Theres Stauffer am Beispiel der kreativen Handlungen von Superstudio. Die italienische Architekturgruppe nutzt die Collage als Wechselspiel zwischen Zukunftsvision und Realitätsfragment, um Anti-Utopien wie das ‚Continuous Monument' (1969) zu entwerfen und sich auf diese Weise forschend mit aktuellen gesellschaftlichen, politischen und architektonischen Themen auseinanderzusetzen.[8] Stauffer erkennt hierbei das Potential der Collage als das ‚realisierte' End-Produkt, welches im Zusammenspiel mit schriftlichen Manifesten den Erkenntnisgewinn der Architekten kollektiv zugänglich werden lässt und den öffentlichen Diskurs provoziert.

Die bisherigen Forschungen zeigen spannende Ansätze, wie die Collage in der Vergangenheit punktuell mit unterschiedlichen Intentionen als ein spezifisches Medium des Entwerfens, Forschens und kritischen Reflektierens von ideellen und räumlichen Ausdrucksformen aktiviert wurde. Um übergreifend die Potentiale der Collage für unter-

the project-specific framework itself, as well as with a focus on a superordinate project sequence, leading to a questioning on two scales of the special relationship between design and research processes and what role collage assumes in this.

ONE COMPETITION : 5 COLLAGES The project 'A grammar for the city' developed together by OFFICE and DOGMA is one of the winning designs of the competition held in 2005 by the South Korean government for a completely newly developed, representative administrative city. Its concept is based on a 'city of spaces' as a counter-model to the 'city of streets', consisting of uniform buildings at the crossing points, as well as public squares in the interspaces of a superordinate square grid, which lies radically across the design location defined by natural mountain and cultivated paddy field landscapes.[9]

Apart from reduced layout and profile sketches, special attention is drawn to five collages with which the work collective communicates its design in many magazines, publications and exhibitions. Two black and white collages (fig. 1-2) focus attention from a bird's-eye perspective on the planned city and its generic, cross-shaped building type. Three further multicolored collages show 'everyday' instantaneous shots within and beyond the already mature city (fig. 3-5). The architects construct (urban) spatial atmospheres through the digitally generated apparent layering of photographic image excerpts that visualize the public space and white areas that the architecture was reduced to. Through clear forms and edges, picture fragments and surfaces appear to be 'stuck on', generating an extreme two-dimensionality. But what does the specific pictorial language and esthetic of collages convey to us about the design, as well as the architectural thoughts and actions of the architects? Which qualities of the collages were appropriated and with what perspective were they used in creative design processes?

CITY WALLS, CITY SPACES The specific interplay of surface and image directly reflects the concept of the master plan: a clear division of the city into a system of walls [buildings] and spaces [squares].[10] The targeted composition and choice of perspective of the collages convey programmatic and design qualities of the building volumes and space volumes as individual and at the same time mutually communicating city building blocks. Different lines of vision in the monochrome collages stage the architecture as a modest gesture or dominant feature. While from overhead the white crosses appear in relation to their interspace as ordering 'city walls' (fig. 2), a panoramic view makes the actual clear building volume merge increasingly into a coherent surface that overlayers its surroundings (fig. 1). The monumental effect is enhanced through the surfaces that seemingly continue beyond the edge of the picture. Polychrome collages are similarly conceived. The symbolism of the white surface is chosen here to accentuate the role of architecture as a structure that acts in the background and the square interspaces as generous spaces open to appropriation and therefore forging identity.[11] Photographic

1 | OFFICE 19, Korea: Stadt von oben | city from above

2 | OFFICE 19, Korea: Vogelperspektive | bird's eye

schiedliche kreative Denk- und Schaffensprozesse differenzierter zu erfassen, werden hier Collagen im Werk der zeitgenössischen Architekturbüros OFFICE und DOGMA betrachtet. Untersucht wird der Wettbewerbsentwurf ‚A grammar for the city'. Die Analyse des Wettbewerbsentwurfes und der in diesem Kontext entstandenen Collagen erfolgt im projektspezifischen Rahmen selbst sowie mit dem Fokus auf eine übergeordnete Projektsequenz, sodass auf zwei Maßstabsebenen hinterfragt wird, in welcher besonderen Relation entwerfende und forschende Prozesse zueinander stehen und welche Rolle die Collage hierbei einnimmt.

EIN WETTBEWERB : 5 COLLAGEN Das von OFFICE und DOGMA gemeinsam entwickelte Projekt ‚A grammar for the city' ist einer der Siegerentwürfe des 2005 von der südkoreanischen Regierung ausgeschriebenen Wettbewerbes für eine gänzliche neu zu entwickelnde, repräsentative Verwaltungsstadt. Ihr Konzept beruht auf einer ‚Stadt der Räume' als Gegenmodell zur ‚Stadt der Straßen', bestehend aus uniformen Gebäuden auf den Kreuzungspunkten sowie öffentlichen Plätzen in den Zwischenfeldern einer übergeordneten quadratischen Rasterstruktur, welche sich radikal über den durch natürliche Berg- und kultivierte Reisfeldlandschaften definierten Entwurfsort legt.[9]

Neben reduzierten Grundriss- und Schnittzeichnungen stechen insbesondere fünf Collagen ins Auge, mit denen das Arbeitskollektiv seinen Entwurf in zahlreichen Zeitschriften, Publikationen und Ausstellungen kommuniziert. Zwei schwarz-weiß gehaltenen Collagen (Abb. 1-2) richten die Aufmerksamkeit aus der Vogelperspektive auf die Planstadt und ihren generischen, kreuzförmigen Gebäudetypus. Drei weitere mehrfarbige Collagen zeigen aus der Sicht eines Passanten ‚alltägliche' Momentaufnahmen innerhalb und außerhalb der bereits gewachsenen Stadt (Abb. 3-5). Die Architekten konstruieren (stadt-)räumliche Atmosphären über die digital erzeugte, scheinbare Schichtung aus fotografischen Bildausschnitten, welche den öffentlichen Raum visualisieren, und weißen

3-5 | OFFICE 19, Korea: Stadthalle, Außenansicht, Straße | city hall, outside, street

Flächen, auf welche die Architektur reduziert wurde. Durch klare Formen und Kanten wirken Bildfragmente und Flächen wie ‚aufgeklebt' und erzeugen eine extreme Zweidimensionalität. Doch was vermittelt uns die spezifische Bildsprache und Ästhetik der Collagen über den Entwurf sowie über das architektonische Denken und Handeln der Architekten? Welche Qualitäten der Collagen wurden sich zu eigen gemacht und mit welcher Perspektive wurden sie in kreativen Schaffensprozessen eingesetzt?

STADTWÄNDE . STADTRÄUME Die spezifische Wechselwirkung von Fläche und Bild spiegelt unmittelbar das Konzept des Masterplans wider: eine klare Aufteilung der Stadt in ein System aus Wänden [Gebäude] und Räumen [Plätze].[10] Die gezielte Komposition und Perspektivwahl der Collagen vermitteln hierbei programmatische sowie gestalterische Qualitäten der Baukörper und Raumkörper als individuelle und zugleich miteinander kommunizierende Stadtbausteine. So setzen unterschiedliche Blickrichtungen in den monochromen Collagen die Architektur als zurückhaltende Geste oder dominante Setzung in Szene. Während in der Aufsicht die weißen Kreuze im Verhältnis zu ihrem Zwischenraum als ordnende ‚Stadtwände' erscheinen (Abb. 2), verschmilzt mit dem Panoramablick der eigentlich klare Baukörper immer mehr zu einer zusammenhängenden und seine Umwelt überlagernden Fläche (Abb. 1). Die monumentale Wirkung wird durch die scheinbar über den Bildrand weitergeführten Flächen abermals überhöht. Ähnlich konzipiert sind die polychromen Collagen. Die Symbolik der weißen Fläche wird hier gewählt, um die Rolle der Architektur als eine im Hintergrund agierende Struktur und die quadratischen Zwischenräume als großzügige, aneignungsoffene und somit identitätsstiftende Orte zu akzentuieren.[11] Fotografische Fragmente, welche als symbolhafte und stereotypische Bildstaffage für zukünftige urbane Szenarien fungieren, bilden farblich sowie bildräumlich einen Ausgleich zur Härte der weißen Fläche, werden jedoch gleichermaßen wieder durch ihre Omnipräsenz durchbrochen.

FORSCHENDE ANTEILE Auffallend ist, dass die Collagen oftmals in Begleitung von Essays, wie dem von Pier Vittorio Aureli und Martino Tattara verfassten Text ‚Is this a city?', veröffentlicht werden.[12] In der Wechselwirkung aus Sprache und Collage wird deutlich, dass OFFICE und DOGMA den konzeptionellen und gestalterischen Prozess des Masterplanentwurfs nutzen, um ihr bürointernes Ideal der Stadt als ein stets unvollständig bleibendes ‚Artefakt' zu hinterfragen sowie mögliche Einflussgrößen von Architektur in Bezug auf die Gestaltung derartiger urbaner Texturen aufzuspüren. Angetrieben durch diese übergeordneten und auch projektbezogenen Fragestellungen, testen sie das gestalterische und programmatische Potential des Quadrates. Sie entwickeln ein reduziertes Architekturvokabular, bestehend aus dem kreuzförmigen Gebäude als struk-

fragments, as symbolic and stereotypical pictorial accessories that act as future urban scenarios, form an equalization spatially and in terms of color to the hardness of the white surface, but are equally striking due to their omnipresence.

RESEARCH COMPONENTS It is noticeable that these collages are often published accompanied by essays such as the text 'Is this a city?' compiled by Pier Vittorio Aureli and Martino Tattara.[12] In the interplay of language and collage it becomes clear that OFFICE and DOGMA use the conceptual and creative process of the master plan design to question their internal ideal of the city as a perpetually incomplete 'artefact', as well as to identify possible influences of architecture in relation to the design of such urban textures. Driven by these general and project-related questions, the design and programmatic potential of the square is tested. A reduced architectural vocabulary is developed, consisting of a cross-shaped building as a structuring wall and a square interspace as a space open to appropriation: building-as-wall and square-as-room. Through the repetitive positioning of these two design building blocks, the city is defined in its basic form but leaves an 'unfinished' structure open to future developments.[13]

In their search for design building blocks and strategies with which they can form and activate urban structures, as well as catalyze urban 'feelings', OFFICE and DOGMA identify both the potential and limits of their architectural positioning. They define, for example, the large scale and monumental, generated by the addition of 'generally valid' urban typologies such as the high-rise slab, as important properties of urban architecture. They also interpret the abstraction of the square on an intellectual level as a central architectural element to absorb the complexity of the city and to promote its range of uses. At the same time, when reflecting on their own work, there remain doubts as to whether such a reduced, formal set of rules does justice to the real urban diversity and takes other unpredictable factors of 'city production' into consideration.[14]

To convey the gained insights not only linguistically, but also graphically, OFFICE and DOGMA make use of collage as a visually striking 'image' that is also open to interpretation. In a targeted manner, they generate an abstract reality with 'white' gaps, instead of architectural objects with a detailed design.[15] Similar to the projects by Superstudio, 'A grammar for the city' is communicated in this manner as a conceptual-architectural design. This underlying design-related thinking of the architects is to be attributed just as much significance as the actual possible feasibility, so that the boundary between the implementation-related master plan and urban utopia blurs visually and in terms of content. The conscious further development of selected aspects of their design stance –

turierende Wand und dem quadratischen Zwischenraum als aneignungsoffenen Platz; Building-as-wall und Square-as-room. Mittels der repetitiven Setzung dieser zwei Entwurfsbausteine definieren sie die Stadt in ihrer Grundform, hinterlassen sie jedoch ebenso als eine ‚unfertige', für zukünftige Entwicklungen offene Struktur.[13]

In ihrem Suchen nach Entwurfsbausteinen und -strategien, mit denen sie städtische Strukturen formen und aktivieren sowie urbane ‚Gefühle' katalysieren können, erkennen OFFICE und DOGMA sowohl Potentiale als auch Grenzen ihrer architektonischen Setzungen. Großmaßstäblichkeit und Monumentalität, generiert durch Addition ‚allgemeingültiger' städtischer Typologien, wie der Hochhausscheibe, definieren sie beispielsweise als wichtige Eigenschaften von urbaner Architektur. Ebenso deuten sie die Abstraktion des Quadrates auf einer intellektuellen Ebene als zentrales architektonisches Element, um die Komplexität der Stadt absorbieren und ihre Nutzungsvielfalt fördern zu können. Gleichermaßen bleiben mit der eigenen Reflexion der Arbeit Zweifel, ob ein derart reduziertes, formales Regelwerk der realen urbanen Vielfalt gerecht wird und andere, nicht vorhersehbare Faktoren der ‚Stadtproduktion' berücksichtigt.[14]

Um die gewonnenen Erkenntnisse nicht nur sprachlich, sondern ebenso grafisch zu vermitteln, bedienen sich OFFICE und DOGMA der Collage als visuell prägnantes und gleichermaßen für Interpretationen offenes ‚Bild'. Gezielt spannen sie eine abstrakte Wirklichkeit mit ‚weißen' Lücken an Stelle gestalterisch detaillierter Architekturobjekte auf.[15] Ähnlich den Projekten von Superstudio wird ‚A grammar for the city' auf diese Weise als konzeptionell-architektonischer Entwurf kommuniziert. Den grundlegenden, entwurfsbezogenen Gedanken der Architekten ist dabei ebenso viel Bedeutung beizumessen wie der eigentlich möglichen Umsetzbarkeit, sodass die Grenze zwischen umsetzungsbezogenem Masterplan und urbaner Utopie inhaltlich und visuell verschwimmt. Das bewusste Weiterentwickeln ausgewählter Aspekte ihrer Entwurfshaltung – Stadt und Architektur als zusammenhängende jedoch ewig ‚unfertige' urbane Textur – das Testen sowie das fokussierte Suchen und Kommunizieren spezifischer entwurfsbezogener Wissensaspekte – Building-as-wall und Square-as-room als Entwurfsbausteine – können als forschende Anteile im Entwurfsprozess der Planstadt definiert werden.

P R O J E K T S E Q U E N Z   Interessanterweise kann ‚A grammar for the city' ebenso als Bestandteil eines größeren Zusammenhangs von Projekten und einer Sammlung von Collagen gesehen werden, die sich entwerfend und forschend mit urbanen Landschaften auseinandersetzen und hierbei wiederkehrend das Building-as-wall und den Square-as-room als Entwurfsvokabular der Stadt fokussieren. Mit dem 2004 initiierten Projekt

6 | DOGMA: Stop City

city and architecture as coherent but always 'unfinished' urban texture – as well as the testing and focused searching and communication of specific design-related knowledge aspects – building-as-wall and square-as-room as design building blocks – can be defined as research aspects in the design process of the planned city.

PROJECT SEQUENCE Interestingly, 'A grammar for the city' can be seen equally as a component of a wider context of projects and a collection of collages, which take a design and research approach to urban landscapes and focus repeatedly on building-as-wall and square-as-room as design vocabulary of the city. With the project 'Tower and Square' initiated in 2004, for example, OFFICE test initial conceptual and formal approaches to the dialog of wall and space in the form of pinpointed interventions in Rotterdam. On the occasion of an exhibition at the Witte de Witt Center, thematizing the increasing loss of public space in the Dutch metropolis, OFFICE together with the photographers Bas Princen and Milica Topalovic develop two modified tower types out of the city-specific typology of the high-rise – two possible variants of the building-as-wall. On the one hand, it is an ensemble of two cross-shaped towers that open up a public space between them. On the other hand, it is about the detached high-rise, the Towersquare, which frames an already existing public square within it. Their aim is to generate qualitative public spaces through variously designed relationships between architecture and the urban ground level.[16] Apart from large-format architecture models, a collage in a panorama format serves as an exhibition object. The added architecture is reduced to the white surface again and appears rather alien on the black and white city photography. The collage principle of coexistence, in this case the juxtaposition of

7 | DOGMA: Stop City

‚Tower and Square' beispielweise testen OFFICE erste konzeptionelle und formale Ansätze zum Dialog von Wand und Raum in Form von punktuellen Eingriffen in Rotterdam. Anlässlich einer Ausstellung im Witte de Witt Center, welche den zunehmenden Verlust des öffentlichen Raumes in der niederländischen Metropole thematisiert, entwickelt OFFICE mit den Fotografen Bas Princen und Milica Topalovic aus der stadtspezifischen Typologie des Hochhauses zwei abgewandelte Turm-Typen – zwei mögliche Varianten des Building-as-wall. Zum einen handelt es sich dabei um das Ensemble zweier kreuzförmiger Türme, die einen öffentlichen Raum zwischen sich aufspannen. Zum anderen geht es um das freistehende Hochhaus, den Towersquare, welcher im Inneren einen bereits bestehenden öffentlichen Platz umrahmt. Ihr Ziel ist es, durch unterschiedlich gestaltete Beziehungen von Architektur und städtischem Erdgeschoss qualitative öffentliche Räume zu generieren.[16] Als Ausstellungsobjekt dienen neben großformatigen Architekturmodellen ebenso eine Collage im Panoramaformat. Die hinzugefügte Architektur ist wieder auf die weiße Fläche reduziert und wirkt geradezu fremdartig auf der schwarz-weiß gehaltenen Stadtfotografie. Das Collagen-Prinzip der Koexistenz, in diesem Fall das Nebeneinander von vorhandenem Stadtbild und architektonischer Vision, wird inhaltlich und visuell genutzt, um eine mögliche Zukunftsvision zu kommunizieren, die Fragen offenlässt, jedoch ebenso zu diskutierende Lösungsansätze offeriert.

Formal ähnlich provokativ wirken die Collagen des 2008 entwickelten Gedankenmodells ‚Stop City' (Abb. 6-7). DOGMA überhöhen und radikalisieren das Building-as-wall und den Square-as-room, indem sie das gestalterische und programmatische Konzept eines Rasterfeldes im Masterplan auf die Dimensionen einer gesamten Stadt transferieren. Die

the existing city image and architectural vision, is used visually and in terms of content to communicate a possible future vision that leaves questions open, but also offers approaches to solutions open to discussion.

The collages of the thought model 'Stop City' developed in 2008 appear similarly provocative formally (fig. 6-7). DOGMA enhance and radicalize the building-as-wall and the square-as-room by transferring the design and programmatic concept of a grid in the master plan to the dimensions of a whole city. The high-rise slab is scaled to a large-scale wall that limits the horizontal extension of the city and organizes the urban living environment vertically. The public space, on the other hand, is transformed into a single forest-like intermediate space, so that the city appears as an oversized Central Park.[17] As was already the case with Superstudio in the 1960s, DOGMA also appears to be driven by a fundamental interest in addressing current topics regarding society, design, urban development and architecture reflexively, through the interplay of designing and researching processes. Stop City is therefore to be interpreted as a creative-critical anti-utopia in relation to the globally increasing shapeless urbanization, which is initially developed internally in the office in the form of manifestos and collages and is then published publicly as a discourse in images.

URBAN (SPACE) RESEARCHER Further projects could be shown at this point that have in common with the already mentioned designs that they are the reinterpretation or variation of the design idea and can generate public spaces through an extreme formal reduction and typological strictness, as well as enable a maximum urban unfolding. The architects develop various typologies – the block, the slab, the tower, the cross – as possible 'walls' of a city and with their designs they explore their physical qualities and intellectual intentions as an architectural element that both sets spatial boundaries and opens up new spaces. Competitions, exhibitions and collaborations with other firms act as ideal test fields in the process.

Even if most designs are not implemented practically, it is by no means paper architecture. This is because OFFICE and DOGMA activate these projects in order to reflect on and develop their way of thinking and designing architecturally.[18] They consciously refer to already available design-related knowledge – for example the rational positions and architecture concepts of the 1960s of Rossi and Grassi, as well as the visionary concepts of Superstudio – and apply it to specific projects with the prospect of sounding out new knowledge aspects.[19] These approaches and objectives characterize their way of designing as a process of research-connected design, in which building-as-wall and square-as-room have developed from a design research topic to one that is internal to their firm.

Hochhaus-Scheibe wird zur großmaßstäblichen Wand skaliert, welche die Stadt in ihrer horizontalen Ausdehnung begrenzt und die urbane Lebenswelt vertikal organisiert. Der öffentliche Raum hingegen wandelt sich zu einem einzigen waldähnlichen Zwischenraum, sodass die Stadt wie ein überdimensionierter Central-Park wirkt.[17] Wie bereits Superstudio in den 1960er Jahre scheint auch DOGMA hierbei durch ein grundlegendes Interesse angetrieben zu sein, sich in der Wechselwirkung aus entwerfenden und forschenden Prozessen mit aktuellen Themen von Gesellschaft, Gestaltung, Städtebau und Architektur reflexiv auseinanderzusetzen. So ist die Stop City als eine in Bezug auf die global zunehmende konturlose Verstädterung gestalterisch-kritische Antiutopie zu lesen, welche in Form von Manifesten und Collagen zunächst bürointern entwickelt und schließlich öffentlich als Diskurs in Bildern publiziert wird.

STADT (RAUM) FORSCHER Weitere Projekte könnten an dieser Stelle aufgezeigt werden, denen mit den bereits genannten Entwürfen gemeinsam ist, dass sie die Reinterpretation oder Variation der Entwurfsidee sind, über eine extreme formale Reduktion und typologischen Strenge qualitative öffentliche Räume zu generieren sowie eine maximale urbane Entfaltung zu ermöglichen. Die Architekten entwickeln verschiedene Typologien – den Block, die Scheibe, den Turm, das Kreuz – als mögliche ‚Wände' einer Stadt und erforschen mit den Entwürfen ihre physischen Qualitäten und intellektuellen Intentionen als architektonisches Element, welches sowohl räumliche Grenzen setzt, als auch neue Räume aufspannt. Wettbewerbe, Ausstellungen und Kollaboration mit anderen Büros fungieren hierbei als ideale Testfelder.

Auch wenn die meisten Entwürfe nicht praktisch umgesetzt werden, so handelt es sich hierbei keineswegs um Papierarchitektur. Denn OFFICE und DOGMA aktivieren diese Projekte, um ihre Art und Weise, architektonisch zu denken und zu entwerfen, reflektieren und weiterentwickeln zu können.[18] Sie greifen bewusst auf bereits vorhandenes, entwurfsbezogenes Wissen zurück – beispielsweise die rationalen Positionen und Architekturkonzeptionen der 1960er Jahre von Rossi und Grassi sowie die visionären Konzepte Superstudios – und wenden es mit der Perspektive, neue Wissensaspekte auszuspüren, projektspezifisch an.[19] Diese Handlungen und Ziele charakterisieren ihre Art und Weise des Entwerfens als einen Prozess forschenden Entwerfens, bei dem Building-as-wall und Square-as-room sich vom Entwurfs- zu einem bürointernen Forschungsthema entwickelt haben.

COLLAGE IM + ALS PROZESS Die Collage ist als visuelle und mediale Konstante in diesen unterschiedlichen, entwerfenden und zugleich forschenden Handlungen von OFFICE und DOGMA zu identifizieren. Wie bereits Mies van der Rohe mittels der Fotocollage und -montage seine Sensibilität für variierende Wirkungsweisen von

C O L L A G E   I N + A S A P R O C E S S   The collage can be identified as a visual and medial constant in these various designing and at the same time researching approaches by OFFICE and DOGMA. In the same way as Mies van der Rohe trains his perception of the varying effects of proportion, materials and constructive elements by means of photocollage and photomontage, OFFICE and DOGMA also appear to activate collage consciously as a practice for honing their own design-related competences. The interplay between two-dimensional surfaces and three-dimensional space in the process of creating a collage and in the reflection on one's own images acts in this context as training of their perception and their way of thinking about urban scenes as spaces and walls. It is equally evident that the architects appropriate collage with its characteristic 'floating state' between a concrete and abstract relationship to reality as a specific medium in order to dedicate themselves to researching superordinate questions regarding architecture and their design responsibility for our urban environment by means of an artistic-architectural approach.

The collages also serve OFFICE and DOGMA as a central visualization tool. They become depictions of a potential reality, as well as communication tools for specific insights generated during the design process. Through the constant creation of collages with recurring compositional means, they document and archive their designs, as well as their design-related knowledge aspects, by means of a superordinate formal systematization. The collages can therefore be read as a pictorial study of a permanent process of research accompanying the design, as the firm's internal visual knowledge archive that the architects can refer to for the purposes of critical reflection and further development. The many formally similar collages, through their publication, also act as an explicitly made, collectively accessible knowledge pool and therefore as an interesting research object for others.

8 | OFFICE 09, Rotterdam: Türme und Plätze | towers and squares

Proportionen, Materialien und konstruktiven Elementen schult, scheinen ebenso OFFICE und DOGMA die Collage bewusst als Praktik zu aktivieren, um ihre eigenen entwurfsbezogenen Kompetenzen zu schärfen. Das Wechselspiel zwischen zweidimensionalen Flächen und dreidimensionalem Raum im Prozess des Collagierens sowie in der Reflexion der eigenen Bilder wirkt in diesem Zusammenhang wie ein Training ihrer Wahrnehmung und ihres Denkens urbaner Szenen in Räumen und Wänden. Ebenso deutlich wird, dass sich die Architekten die Collage mit ihrem charakteristischen ‚Schwebezustand' zwischen konkretem Realitätsbezug und abstrakter Wirklichkeit als spezifisches Medium aneignen, um sich übergreifenden Fragen in Bezug auf die Architektur und ihre gestalterische Verantwortung für unsere urbane Umwelt über einen künstlerisch-architektonischen Zugang forschend zu widmen.

Die Collagen dienen OFFICE und DOGMA schließlich ebenso als zentrales Visualisierungsinstrument. Sie werden zu Abbildern einer möglichen Realität sowie zu Kommunikationsinstrumenten spezifischer im Entwurfsprozess generierter Erkenntnisse. Durch das konstante Collagieren mit wiederkehrenden kompositorischen Mitteln dokumentieren und archivieren sie auf diese Weise ihre Entwürfe wie auch ihre entwurfsbezogenen Wissensaspekte mit einer übergeordneten formalen Systematik. So können die Collagen weitergehend wie die Bildstudie einer permanenten, entwurfsbegleitenden Forschung gelesen werden; ein bürointernes, visuelles Wissensarchiv, auf welches die Architekturschaffenden selbst zurückgreifen können, um sich kritisch zu reflektieren und weiterzuentwickeln. Gleichermaßen fungiert die Vielzahl an formal ähnlichen Collagen durch ihre Veröffentlichung wie ein explizit gemachter, kollektiv zugänglicher Wissenspool und somit als spannendes Forschungsobjekt für Dritte.

1 Z.B. | E.g. Margitta Buchert, Formen der Relationen: Entwerfen und Forschen in der Architektur, in: Ute Frank et al. (eds.), EKLAT. Entwerfen und Konstruieren in Lehre, Anwendung und Theorie, Berlin: TU 2011, 77-78 **2** Vgl. beispielsweise zur Bedeutung von Entwurfsinstrumenten auf gestalterische Prozesse | Cf. for example on the significance of design instruments for design processes Christian Gänshirt, Werkzeuge für Ideen. Einführung ins architektonische Entwerfen, Basel/Boston/Berlin: Birkhäuser 2007; Lorenz Engell/Bernhard Siegert (eds.), Zeitschrift für Medien- und Kulturforschung 1: Entwerfen (2012), 6; zur Bedeutung der Architekturzeichnung vgl. z.B. | on the significance of architectural sketches cf. e.g. Robert Evans, The projective cast. Architecture and its tree geometrics, Cambridge/London: MIT Press 1995; zu fotografischen Dokumentationsreihen als Untersuchungsinstrument in der Architektur vgl. | on photographic documentation series as examination tools in architecture cf. Lara Schrijver, Architektonisches Wissen: Methode oder Mysterium?, in: Margitta Buchert (ed.), Reflexives Entwerfen. Reflexive Design, Berlin: Jovis 2014, 63-65 **3** Vgl. | Cf. Alfred Hentzen et al. (eds.), Picasso 1900-1955, München: Franzis-Druck 1956, 30-31 **4** Vgl. | Cf. Annegret Jürgens-Kirchhoff, Technik und Tendenz der Montage in der bildenden Kunst des 20. Jahrhunderts, Gießen: Anabas 1984, 42 **5** Vgl. | Cf. Jennifer A. E. Shields, Collage and Architecture, London: Routledge 2013; www.press.moma.org/2013/06/cut-n-paste-from-architectural-assemblage-to-collage-city, 23.06.2018 **6** Vgl. hierzu | Cf. on this subject Martino Stierli, Mies Montage: Mies van der Rohe, Dada, Film und die Kunstgeschichte, in: Zeitschrift für Kunstgeschichte 74/3 (2011); Neil Levine, The Significance of Facts: Mies's Collages Up Close and Personal, in: Assemblage: a critical journal of architecture and design culture, Nr. 37 (1998), 35-101; zur Bedeutung der Collage im Werk Mies van der Rohes vgl. ferner | on the meaning of collage in the work of Mies van der Rohe cf. Rolf Sasse, Mies montiert, in: ARCH+ 161 (2002), 58-61; Andreas Beitlin/Lena Büchel/Brigitte Franzen/Holger Otten (eds.), Mies van der Rohe. Montage. Collage, London: Koenig Books 2017 **7** Werner Blaser, Mies van der Rohe: Lehre und Schule, Basel/Stuttgart: Birkhäuser 1977, 11, 34 **8** Marie Theres Stauffer, Figurationen des Utopischen. Theoretische Projekte von Archizoom und Superstudio, Berlin/München: Deutscher Kunstverlag 2007, 10-19 **9** OFFICE/Sarah Lusic-Alavanja/Anh-Linh Ngo/Achim Reese, City Walls, in: ARCH+ 214 (2014), 100 **10** Vgl. | Cf. Pier Vittorio Aureli/Martino Tattara, Is this a city?, in: Kersten Geers/David van Severen et al. (eds.), OFFICE Kersten Geers David van Severen Volume 1, Köln: König 2017, 61 **11** ibid., 61 **12** Vgl. | Cf. ibid., 61; vgl. hierzu ebenso Dogma/OFFICE, Obstruction: A Grammar for the city, in: AA files 54, London 2012, 2-7 **13** Ibid. (Anm. 11 | Note 11), 61; Giovanna Borasi, Hunting for the present in the past, in: Kersten Geers/David van Severen et al. (eds.), OFFICE Kersten Geers David van Severen Volume 1, Köln: König 2107, 12 **14** Vgl. | Cf. ibid. (Anm. 11), 61 **15** ibid., 61 **16** Vgl. | Cf. Milica Topalović, Tower & Square, in: Kersten Geers/David van Severen et al. (eds.), OFFICE Kersten Geers David van Severen Volume 1, Köln: König 2017, 37; http://www.wdw.nl/en/our_program/exhibitions/untitled_tower_and_square, 10.07.18 **17** Dogma/Sarah Lusic-Alavanja/Anh-Linh Ngo/Achim Reese, Stop City, in: ARCH+ 214 (2014), 105-106 **18** Giovanna Borasi, Hunting for the Present in the Past, in: Kersten Geers/David van Severen et al. (eds.), OFFICE Kersten Geers David van Severen Volume 1, Köln: Walther König 2107, 11 **19** Vgl. | Cf. OFFICE Kersten Geers David Van Severen: Statement, in: ARCH+ 214 (2014), 76-77; Dogma: Statement, in ARCH+ 214 (2014), 98-99

SPATIAL SURVEY AND SPATIAL IMAGE

Andreas Nütten

The new spatial dimensions of the 'European metropolitan region' comprise wider polycentric areas that are neither clearly city nor clearly countryside. Commuter connections and various forms of interlinking define the expanse of these areas and everyday realities correspond to these dimensions. In many cases, however, these primarily functional spatial units are lacking an overarching new spatial understanding, an 'image' that generates a sense of belonging, identification and identity. However, this is important in order to grasp a wider cultural space with distinctive properties. It can stimulate involvement, initiative and empathetic bonds internally and make distinctive existing and new qualities visible outwardly. This requires new interpretations and new notions of the area. Image-based methods of surveying and presenting urban regions from the perspective of landscape are suggested in the following. With their systemizing aspects, the methods research and generate knowledge and furthermore, as phenomenological bases and starting points, can form significant creative platforms for more context-related spatial designing and planning.

LANDSCAPE PERSPECTIVE ON CITY The hypothesis here is: landscape is the future support structure of the urban region! In a task-dividing fusion of city and countryside, significant qualities and (new) tasks are to be expected in the countryside. A new dynamic will result from the interplay of global influences and local conditions, from

RAUMERKUNDUNG UND RAUMBILD

Andreas Nütten

Das neue Raumgefäß der ‚europäischen Metropolregion' fasst größere polyzentrische Räume, die weder eindeutig Stadt noch eindeutig Land sind, zusammen. Pendlerbeziehungen und vielfältige Formen der Verflechtung definieren die Ausdehnung dieser Räume, gelebte Alltagsrealitäten entsprechen diesen Dimensionen. Vielfach mangelt es diesen primär funktionalen Raumeinheiten jedoch an einem übergeordneten neuen Raumverständnis, an einem ‚Bild', das Zugehörigkeit, Identifizierung und Identität generiert. Dies ist aber wichtig, um einen größeren Kulturraum mit unverwechselbaren Eigenschaften zu begreifen. Nach innen können so Engagement, Initiative und empathische Bindung angeregt, nach außen unverwechselbare bestehende und neue Qualitäten sichtbar werden. Hierzu bedarf es neuer Lesarten und neuer Bilder des Raums. Für diese werden nachfolgend bildbasierte Methoden des Erkundens und Darstellens von Stadtregionen aus der Perspektive der Landschaft vorgeschlagen. Mit ihren systematisierenden Anteilen sind die Methoden forschend und wissensgenerierend und können darüber hinaus als phänomenologische Grundlagen und Ausgangspunkte wesentliche kreative Ebenen für ein verstärkt kontextbezogenes räumliches Entwerfen und Planen bilden.

LANDSCHAFTSPERSPEKTIVE AUF STADT Die Hypothese lautet hier: Landschaft ist die zukünftige Trägerstruktur der Stadtregion! In einer aufgabenteiligen Fusion von Stadt und Land sind wesentliche Qualitäten und (neue) Aufgaben in der Landschaft zu vermuten. Eine neue Dynamik wird sich aus dem Wechselspiel globaler

an urban way of life on the one hand, which has spread across the whole Central European territory, and at the same time the increasing significance of locational reference – meaningful local social ties –, as well as efficient and differentiated use of local resources.[1] The landscape will change due to new tasks. New possibilities can be created, provided that the structural local 'capabilities' and people are incorporated meaningfully.[2] Apart from the given local spatial structure conditions, new spatial-temporal location hierarchies will determine the spatial organization and define new tasks. To generate a new overall spatial identity, a new esthetic awareness is required. The increasing significance of local qualities and the landscape as a location factor must go hand in hand with an esthetic qualification if one wishes to generate a consciousness and new identity. To try out these hypotheses and to make it possible to take action along these lines of thinking and to generate spatial designs, a good understanding of the given spatial conditions is necessary. This was studied as the 'landscape metropolis' model, using the example of the metropolitan region Hanover – Braunschweig – Göttingen – Wolfsburg. Existing methods of survey and presentation were taken up and specific new ones were developed. Then they are presented and discussed, differentiated into the formats 'spatial survey and spatial notation', 'scenic spatial image' and 'structural spatial image'. This is associated with various interpretations and readings of the structural capabilities. Speculations about possible future programs, as well as atmospheric considerations and socio-cultural interpretation approaches, allow different narratives and designs to be incorporated on the way to the formation of an overall spatial identity.

STARTING SITUATION AND EXPERIMENTAL DESIGN An initial structural map shows the three overarching essential landscape types of the overall area (fig. 1). 'Naturally' given topographical and hydrological structures, as well as those of anthropogenic transformation (reclamation, drainage, access, topologically coherent settlement patterns, transport infrastructures), are apparent. Through highlighting and leaving out different structural elements per area, they are strongly contrasted, which is highlighted by a type of inversion graph: forests as spatial structuring elements are presented as black in the northern and southern areas, as gray in the central area in the interests of the openness and expanse of the space. The linked villages as a defining structure are highlighted in black here. In the central and southern area, the forest rims correspond largely with the topographical edges of the low mountain range.

This map is already an interpreting 'structural spatial image'. The aim of the map is to divide the space in terms of its overarching landscape structures and to decode it. The map provides bases for the spatial survey and for further maps of the structural 'capabilities'. The structural map is layered with an accessibility diagram (fig. 2). The graphically

Einflüsse und lokaler Standortbedingungen ergeben, aus urbaner Lebensweise einerseits, die sich über das gesamte mitteleuropäische Territorium ausgebreitet hat und gleichzeitig zunehmender Bedeutung des Ortsbezugs – sinnstiftender sozialer lokaler Bindung –, andererseits effizienter und differenzierter Nutzung der lokalen Ressourcen.[1] Mit neuen Aufgaben wird sich die Landschaft ändern. Es können neue Möglichkeitsräume geschaffen werden, sofern die strukturellen teilräumlichen ‚Begabungen', aber auch Akteure sinnvoll einbezogen werden.[2] Neben den gegebenen örtlichen raumstrukturellen Bedingungen werden neue raum-zeitlich bedingte Standorthierarchien die Organisation des Raums prägen und neue Aufgaben definieren. Um eine neue gesamträumliche Identität zu generieren, bedarf es eines neuen ästhetischen Bewusstseins. Die zunehmende Bedeutung lokaler Qualitäten und der Landschaft als Standortfaktor muss mit einer ästhetischen Qualifizierung einhergehen, will man ein Bewusstsein und neue Identität generieren.

Um diese Hypothesen zu überprüfen und um in diesen Denkrichtungen handlungsfähig zu werden und Raumentwürfe zu generieren, braucht es zunächst ein gutes Verständnis der gegebenen räumlichen Bedingungen. Dies wurde als Modell ‚Landschaftsmetropole' am Beispiel der Metropolregion Hannover – Braunschweig – Göttingen – Wolfsburg untersucht. Bestehende Methoden der Erkundung und Darstellung wurden aufgegriffen sowie eigene neu entwickelt. Nachfolgend werden sie – unterschieden in die Formate ‚Raumerkundung und Raumnotation', ‚szenisches Raumbild' und ‚strukturelles Raumbild' – aufgezeigt und diskutiert. Damit verbunden werden verschiedene Interpretationen und Lesarten der strukturellen Begabungen. Spekulationen über mögliche zukünftige Programme ebenso wie atmosphärische Betrachtungen und sozio-kulturelle Deutungsversuche, die unterschiedliche Erzählweisen (‚Narrative') und Entwürfe auf dem Weg zu einer gesamträumlichen Identitätsbildung zulassen, werden ebenfalls einbezogen.

AUSGANGSLAGE UND VERSUCHSANORDNUNG Eine erste Strukturkarte zeigt die drei übergeordneten wesentlichen Landschaftstypen des Gesamtraums (Abb. 1). ‚Natürlich' gegebene topografische und hydrologische Strukturen wie auch solche der anthropogenen Überformung (Urbarmachung, Entwässerung, Erschließung, topologisch kohärente Siedlungsmuster, verkehrliche Infrastrukturen) scheinen auf. Durch Hervorhebung und Weglassen ganz unterschiedlicher Strukturelemente pro Teilraum werden die Teilräume stark kontrastiert, was durch eine Art Inversgrafik bewusst überhöht dargestellt wird: Wälder als raumbildende Elemente sind im nördlichen und südlichen Teilraum schwarz, im zentralen Teilraum zugunsten der Offenheit und Weite des Raums grau dargestellt. Hier sind die vernetzten Dörfer als prägende Struktur schwarz hervorgehoben. Im mittleren und südlichen Teilraum stimmen die Waldränder weitgehend mit den topografischen Kanten der Mittelgebirge überein.

simplified figure shows three spatial zones of varying centrality defined spatially and temporally (30, 60 and 60+ minute spaces regarding the local public transport and starting from the Hanover, Hildesheim, Braunschweig and Wolfsburg train stations). Location conditions and hierarchies, the density of possibilities and interaction, intensity and speeds, as well as area 'capabilities' and tasks are indicated on the 'landscape metropolis' model, as well as through the basic physical structure, and determined by the spatial-temporal location in the overall system, states the hypothesis.

To be able to test this hypothesis and the given conditions initially, a spatial survey is required. The experimental design envisaged selecting the three surveys in such a way that beyond the city centers, all three landscape types are surveyed in parallel and all three spatial zones defined in terms of space and time are crossed transversely (fig. 3).

SPATIAL SURVEY AND SPATIAL NOTATION A significant aspect of the analysis of large areas is individual spatial surveying. As a walk or a cycle tour, it is a direct physical and mental encounter and involvement with the space, a spatial grasping with all the senses. It is important to encounter the space with as open a mind as possible and 'unaffected' with 'sweeping curiosity', as Lucius Burckhardt calls it, thereby allowing unintentional 'finding', meaning following the trail of unexpected phenomena, concealed qualities, as well as irritations.[3] In a process of seeing, identifying, understanding and presenting, structures that define the space and noticeable phenomena of large areas are presented in a variety of ways, in order to stimulate discussion about the spatial identity and possible futures for the areas. The 'perception cycle' according to Ulrich Neisser shows the cognitive process of these both deductive and inductive procedure of alternating searching and finding, speculating and assuming, the confirmation of certain conjectures, as well as the refuting and discovery of unsuspected 'new' phenomena during the spatial survey (fig. 4).[4]

To bring structural order to the range of survey impressions, an overarching and understandable survey grid is required initially. This is along directed routes that allow the identification of structural sequences, continuities and fractions. We experience the successive impressions during the walk like 'pearls lined up on a necklace'. The telling of experiences seeks a logical 'narrative thread'.[5] As this often does not follow by itself, we manipulate our narration. We are also caught up in our internal 'mental image in the head', which seeks permanent comparisons with the external spatial realities – a procedure that Burckhardt calls 'subsumption'.[6]

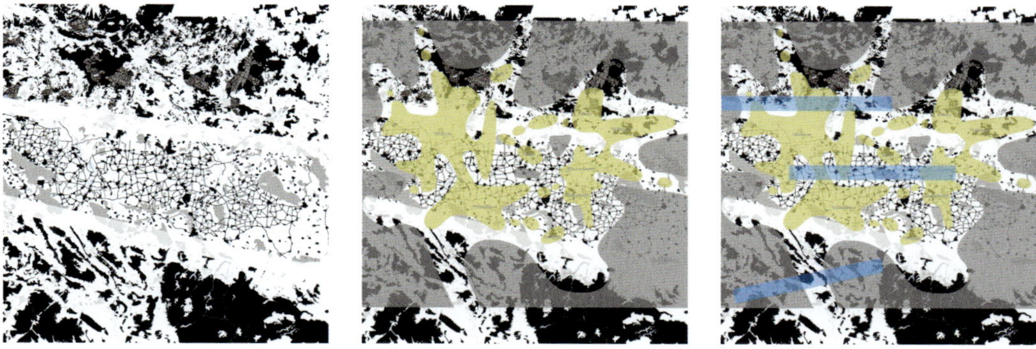

1-3 | Landschaftstypen, Erreichbarkeitsdiagramm, Erkundungsräume | Types of landscape, accessibility diagram, exploration spaces

Diese Karte ist bereits ein interpretierendes ‚strukturelles Raumbild'. Ziel der Karte ist es, den Raum auf der Ebene seiner übergeordneten Landschaftsstrukturen einzuteilen und zu dechiffrieren. Die Karte stellt Grundlagen bereit für die Raumerkundung und für weitere Karten der strukturellen Begabungen. Die Strukturkarte wird mit einem Erreichbarkeitsdiagramm überlagert (Abb. 2). Die grafisch vereinfachte Figur zeigt drei raum-zeitlich definierte Raumzonen unterschiedlicher Zentralität (30, 60 und 60+ Minuten-Räume bezogen auf den öffentlichen Personenverkehr und ausgehend von den Bahnhöfen Hannover, Hildesheim, Braunschweig und Wolfsburg). Standortbedingungen und Standorthierarchien, Angebotsdichte und Interaktionen, Intensitäten und Geschwindigkeiten, aber auch teilräumliche Begabungen und Aufgaben sind im Modell ‚Landschaftsmetropole' sowohl durch die physische Grundstruktur gegeben, wie auch durch die raum-zeitliche Lage im Gesamtsystem bestimmt, so die Hypothese.

Um diese Hypothese testen und zunächst die gegebenen Bedingungen überprüfen zu können, bedarf es der Raumerkundung. Die Versuchsanordnung sah vor, die drei Erkundungen so zu wählen, dass jenseits der Kernstädte alle drei Landschaftstypen parallel und alle drei raum-zeitlich definierten Raumzonen querend durchstreift werden (Abb. 3).

RAUMERKUNDUNG UND RAUMNOTATION Wesentlicher Teil der Analyse großer Räume ist die individuelle Raumerkundung. Als Spaziergang oder Fahrradtour ist sie eine unmittelbare physische und mentale Begegnung und Auseinandersetzung mit dem Raum, eine Raumerfassung mit allen Sinnen. Hierbei gilt es, dem Raum möglichst offen und ‚uninformiert' mit ‚umherschweifender Neugier' zu begegnen, wie Lucius Burckhardt es nennt, und so das absichtslose ‚Finden' zuzulassen, das heißt, den unerwarteten Phänomenen, verborgenen Qualitäten, aber auch Irritationen auf die Spur zu kommen.[3] In einem Prozess von Sehen, Erkennen, Begreifen und Darstellen werden raumprägende Strukturen und auffällige Phänomene großer Räume auf verschiedene Weise aufgezeigt, um die Diskussion über die räumliche Identität und mögliche Zukünfte der Räume anzuregen. Der ‚Wahrnehmungszyklus' nach Ulrich Neisser zeigt den kogni-

To orient ourselves or to create mental order, we try to establish a relationship between the spatial realities and prior knowledge, experience or memorable media images: 'it is like... here!'. We form analogies or associations: 'this reminds me of...!' A cognitive but also creative process of visualizing something, perceiving and editing the image sets in. What do I see, what do I want to see, what is disturbing the image? This has got to do with personal notions of value and world view. In part, these emerge from a more or less collective conscience of those groups we belong to, whether they are political, professional or generational notions. Alternatively, they can follow quite private association patterns. André Corboz describes these perception and interpretation processes between the landscape and the viewer as culturally determined and culturally determining interaction.[7]

Apart from the physical spatial encounter, the survey and its representation contain a distinctive spiritual-mental component that can be used productively for creative interpretations of the spaces found if there is a self-reflecting awareness of these cognitive processes, for example for collages. Getting involved with and exposing oneself in the space also comprises a situational component, which consciously includes the coincidence of encounters and events and requires situational decisions on the way: what route shall I follow? Which phenomena do I take in? How do I respond to them? How do I decide? How do I react to detours? Where do I get lost? Where is orientation lacking? What does that say about the space? What does it say about me? Through the personal encounter with the space, the conveying of spatial knowledge gained is endowed with a certain 'authenticity' and grounding.

The surveys were carried out by bike within a day and within an approximately 60-kilometre-long and three-kilometer-wide corridor from west to east. Per corridor, this resulted in around 600 photos and various forms of notes. Apart from surveying the spatial structure, indicators of an urban way of life in rural areas were gathered and attempts were made to show their 'mental state'. Insights and various representation formats are presented and discussed based on the example of a second spatial survey from Sarstedt to Braunschweig. After the survey, the question arose: according to which criteria and with what statement intention can 600 photographs be sorted and graphically processed?

The first illustration offers a pictorial overview of the spatial corridor in photo sequences (fig. 5). Fifty-one pictures, one per kilometer mostly looking forwards, create a 'distance-coherent' overall impression. Five further pictures, somewhat larger and some as panoramas, were selected so that they convey a typical spatial impression per ten kilometers. The aim initially was to grasp the area and to show gradual changes in the landscapes. The route is represented on a map with a kilometer scale, times and significant spatial structures.

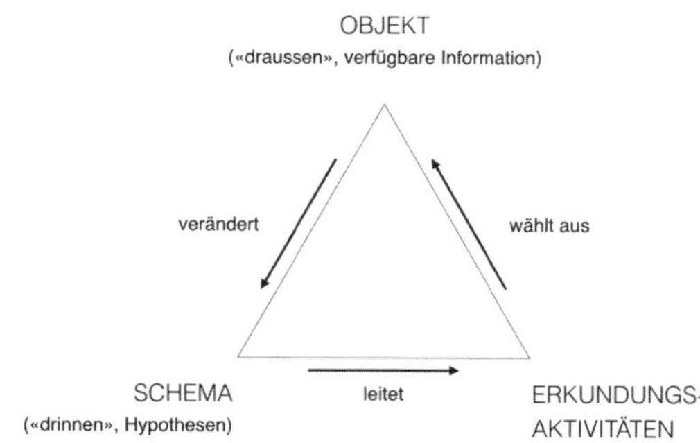

4 | Wahrnehmungszyklus nach Neisser | Perception cycle according to Neisser

tiven Prozess dieser gleichzeitig deduktiven wie auch induktiven Vorgehensweise des wechselseitigen Suchens und Findens, des Spekulierens und Vermutens, der Bestätigung gewisser Vermutungen, aber auch des Widerlegens und Entdeckens unvermuteter ‚neuer' Phänomene während der Raumerkundung auf (Abb. 4).[4]

Um strukturelle Ordnung in die vielfältigen Eindrücke der Erkundungen hineinzubringen, braucht es zunächst ein übergeordnetes und nachvollziehbares Erkundungsraster. Hier erfolgt dies entlang gerichteter Wegstrecken, die strukturelle Sequenzen, Kontinuitäten und Brüche erkennen lassen. Wir erleben die sukzessiven Eindrücke während des Spaziergangs wie ‚aufgereihte Perlen an einer Perlenschnur' – die Erzählung der Erlebnisse sucht nach einer logischen ‚narrativen Folge'.[5] Da sich diese häufig nicht einstellen mag, manipulieren wir unsere Erzählung. Ebenso sind wir befangen durch unser inneres ‚mentales Bild im Kopf', das den permanenten Abgleich mit den äußeren Raumrealitäten sucht – ein Vorgang, den Burckhardt ‚Subsumtion' nennt.[6] Um uns zu orientieren oder mentale Ordnung herzustellen, versuchen wir, die Raumrealitäten mit Vorwissen, Erfahrungen oder prägnanten medialen Bildern in Beziehung zu setzen, ‚hier ist es wie in ...!', wir bilden Analogien oder assoziieren ‚dies erinnert mich an ...!' Ein kognitiver aber auch kreativer Prozess, des Sich-ein-Bild-Machens, der Aufnahme, und des Bild-Redigierens setzt ein. Was sehe ich, was will ich sehen, was stört das Bild? Dies hat mit persönlichen Wertvorstellungen und Weltanschauungen zu tun. In Teilen entspringen diese einem mehr oder weniger kollektiven Bewusstsein jener Gruppen, denen wir angehören, seien es politische, berufliche oder generationsbedingte Vorstellungen, in anderen Teilen folgen sie ganz privaten Assoziationsmustern. André Corboz beschreibt diese Wahrnehmungs- und Deutungsprozesse zwischen Landschaft und Betrachter als kulturbedingte und kulturstiftende Interaktion.[7]

Neben der physischen Raumbegegnung beinhaltet die Erkundung und deren Wiedergabe eine prägnante seelisch-mentale Komponente, die bei selbstreflektiertem Bewusstsein dieser kognitiven Prozesse für kreative Interpretationen der vorgefundenen Räume produktiv eingesetzt werden kann, beispielsweise bei den Collagen. Das Sich-Einlassen bzw. Sich-Exponieren im Raum beinhaltet auch eine situative Komponente, die den Zufall von

5 | Fotosequenzen Raumkorridor Sarstedt-Braunschweig | Photo sequences space passage Sarstedt-Braunschweig

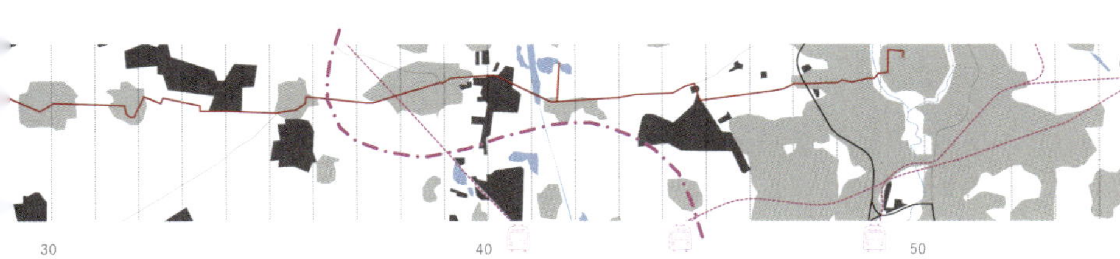
30
40
50
>0:30
< 0:30

The second graphic presentation has a much more complex structure and offers a range of different information and 'spatial notations' on a page (fig. 6). Contrary to the first illustration, the seventeen pictures of the photo sequence are deliberately chosen as quality-oriented, in order to convey 'typical' spatial impressions. Their arrangement as a photo strip is intended by all means to evoke associations with indicator strips or barcodes.

Route notes accompany the photo strip. Names and spatial references to the depicted places and objects are stated, spontaneous associations and atmospheric statements are made, and supposed speculative insights emerging locally are noted. In a transverse profile, all spatially distinctive structures are shown: topography, infrastructure, forest, conspicuous tree arrangements and striking or typical development and settlement types. In the line below, observed activities and types of usage are indicated by means of symbols. Below that there is a strip that shows the type of surface usage. The map section is similar to the first illustration for spatial surveying but adds to the three spatially-temporally defined zones a place name, driving times and means of transport to the nearest central core cities. A lot of information about significant features of the spatial corridor – with a view to the spatial structural conditions and 'capabilities' and the time-space location conditions relating to the staggered degrees of urbanity (three space-time zones) – can be viewed here at a glance.

These thoughts lead to 'spatial image' and to a definition by the city and regional sociologist Detlev Ipsen, who sees traces of social development concepts in spatial images (meaning image excerpts from the real physical space in photos): "To be able to intervene in conscious or unconscious developments of a landscape, one must understand them. Ideas or general principles of conscious renovation or innovative development start with the meaning content of a landscape. The theory of spatial images is intended to contribute to this. The theory of spatial images seeks to interpret the essence of space as a symbolic expression of social development concepts."[8]

SCENIC SPATIAL IMAGE The preparation of the transverse profile was through a manual sketch from memory. It became evident afterwards that this sketch had a much more narrative and atmospheric character than the transverse profile. As a 'narrative excerpt', it forms an independent artifact, a phenomenological perspective, combined with a mental memory picture and personal handwriting. Complemented by a brief explanatory text and selected atmospheric photos that point towards the distinctive character of the spatial corridor, an initial atmospheric spatial image emerges that steers towards a quite specific interpretational direction (fig. 7). Can a topographical logic

Begegnungen und Ereignissen bewusst einschließt und situative Entscheidungen unterwegs abfordert: Welcher Route folge ich? Welche Phänomene nehme ich auf? Wie nehme ich sie auf? Wonach entscheide ich? Wie reagiere ich auf Umleitungen? Wo gehe ich verloren? Wo fehlt Orientierung? Was sagt das über den Raum aus? Was sagt das über mich aus? Durch die persönliche Raumbegegnung erhält die Vermittlung von erworbenem Raumwissen eine gewisse ,Authentizität' und Nachvollziehbarkeit.

Die Erkundungen wurden mit dem Fahrrad innerhalb je eines Tages und innerhalb eines ca. 60 Kilometer langen und drei Kilometer breiten Raumkorridors von West nach Ost durchgeführt. Je Korridor sind ca. 600 Fotos und verschiedene Formen der Notizen entstanden. Neben der Erkundung der Raumstruktur wurden Indizien für eine urbane Lebensweise in ländlichen Teilräumen gesammelt und Versuche unternommen, deren ,mentale Verfassung' aufzuzeigen. Erkenntnisse und verschiedene Formate der Repräsentation werden am Beispiel einer zweiten Raumerkundung von Sarstedt nach Braunschweig dargestellt und diskutiert. Nach der Erkundung stellte sich die Frage: Nach welchen Kriterien und mit welcher Intention der Aussage lassen sich 600 Bilder sortieren bzw. grafisch verarbeiten?

Die erste Grafik bietet einen bildhaften Überblick des Raumkorridors in Fotosequenzen (Abb. 5). Einundfünfzig Bilder, je Kilometer ein Bild, meist Blick voraus, verschaffen einen ,entfernungskohärenten' Gesamteindruck. Fünf weitere Bilder, etwas größer und teilweise als Panoramen, wurden so ausgewählt, dass sie einen typischen Raumeindruck pro zehn Kilometer vermitteln. Ziel war es, den Raum zunächst zu erfassen und allmähliche Veränderungen der Landschaftsräume aufzuzeigen. Auf einer Karte wird die Wegstrecke mit Kilometerskala, Uhrzeiten und wesentlichen Raumstrukturen dargestellt.

Die zweite Grafik ist sehr viel komplexer aufgebaut und bietet viele unterschiedliche Informationen und ,Raumnotationen' auf einem Blatt an (Abb. 6). Im Gegensatz zur ersten Grafik sind die siebzehn Bilder der Fotosequenz bewusst qualitätsorientiert ausgewählt, um ,typische' Raumeindrücke zu vermitteln. Ihr Arrangement als Bildstreifen soll durchaus Assoziationen mit Indikatorstreifen oder Barcodes wecken. Streckennotizen begleiten den Bildstreifen. Namen und Raumbegriffe zu den abgebildeten Orten und Objekten werden genannt, spontane Assoziationen und atmosphärische Aussagen zu Stimmungen getroffen und vermeintliche, spekulative Erkenntnisse, die sich vor Ort ergeben haben, vermerkt. Im Querschnittsprofil werden alle räumlich prägnanten Strukturen gezeigt: Topografie, Infrastruktur, Waldkörper, auffällige Baumanordnungen und auffällige oder typische Bebauungs- und Siedlungstypen. In der Zeile darunter werden beobachtete Aktivitäten und Nutzungsarten durch Symbole angedeutet. Darunter befindet sich ein Streifen, der die Art der Flächennutzung anzeigt. Der Kartenausschnitt ähnelt dem der ersten Grafik zur Raumerkundung,

HOHER ZERSCHNEIDUNGSGRAD
TRANSITRAUM
ABGRENZUNG
PRIVAT!
VERKEHRSDRUCK
KONTRASTE
UNVERMITTELTES NEBENEINANDER
NICHT DORF NOCH STADT
INFRASTRUKTUREN PRÄGEND

ÜBERGANGSRAUM
STADTRAND HANNOVER SICHTBAR
AUSBREITUNG GEWERBE
EINZUGSRAUM PENDLER
WOHNSTATUS STÄDTISCH GEPRÄGT
VEREINSWESEN
LEICHT WELLIG
KLEINE GEHÖLZE
WEITE

PRÄGNANTE LINEARE ELEMENTE
A7 - RAUMGRENZE STADT / LAND
ÜBERLANDROUTEN
AGRARINDUSTRIE
WINDENERGIE
BIOGAS
GEREGELT
WEITE

BÖRDE
PRODUKTIONSLANDSCHAFT
AGRARINDUSTRIE
TRANSITRAUM
BUNDESSTRASSEN
EXPONIERT
WEITE

BÖRDE
PRODUKTIONSLANDSCHAFT
EXPONIERT
KAHL
HORIZONTE
KRAFTWERK = MONUMENT
PFLANZART STIMMUNGSPRÄGEND
EFH WÜSTEN AN DORFRÄNDERN
WEITE

XL-LANDSCHAFT
WINDENERGIE
BIOGAS
ENDLOSE
ACKERFLÄCHEN
EXPONIERT

SARSTEDT
H 0:11 HI 0:11 BS 0:51
RE RE- RE-ICE

HEISEDE
H 0:28 HI 0:32
STB-S STB-BUS

HOTTELN
H 0:43 HI 0:26
BUS-S BUS-S

ALGERMISSEN
H 0:29 HI 0:09
S-RE S

CLAUEN
H 1:07
BUS-RE

HOHENHAMELN
H 0:55 HI 0:22
BUS-RE BUS

ADENSTEDT
H HI

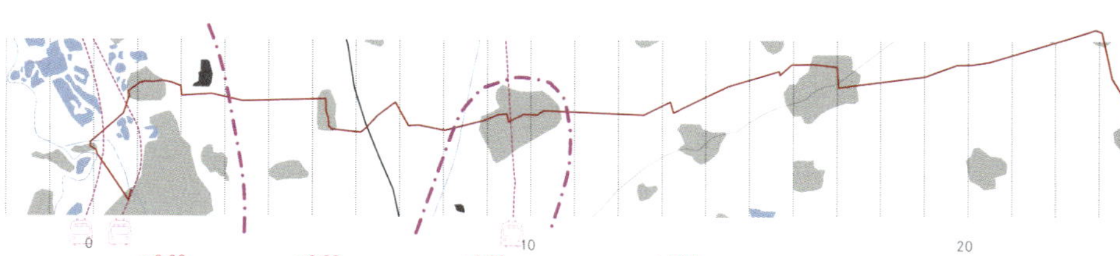

6 | Raumnotationen Sarstedt-Braunschweig | Space notations Sarstedt-Braunschweig

11 12 13 14 15 16 17

EM. BERGBAU
DRIGER SOZ. STATUS
NNERUNG
BEITERHÄUSER
STESSE
MBIOSE KLEINSTADT-LAND
CHT WELLIG

BÖRDE
PRODUKTIONSLANDSCHAFT
STAHLINDUSTRIE AM HORIZONT
WEITE
KIOSK ALS VERSORGER
SELBSTINITIATIVE
INFORMELLE AMBITION

BÖRDE
PRODUKTIONSLANDSCHAFT
WEITE
HALDE AM HORIZONT
KLEINE GEHÖLZE
KONTRASTREICHER
HOMOGEN ERSCHEINENDES DORF
HOHER STATUS

KANAL = GRENZE EINZUGSBE-
REICH STADT
TEICHIDYLLE
SPORTVEREINE
GARTENCENTER
DICHTER DURCHGANGSVER-
KEHR B1

KRUDER STADTRAND
KONTRAST LANDWIRTSCHAFT
DICHTER DURCHGANGSVERKEHR

STADTENTRÉE WESTPARK
KONTRAST LANDWIRTSCHAFT
NISCHENMILIEU

KERNSTADT

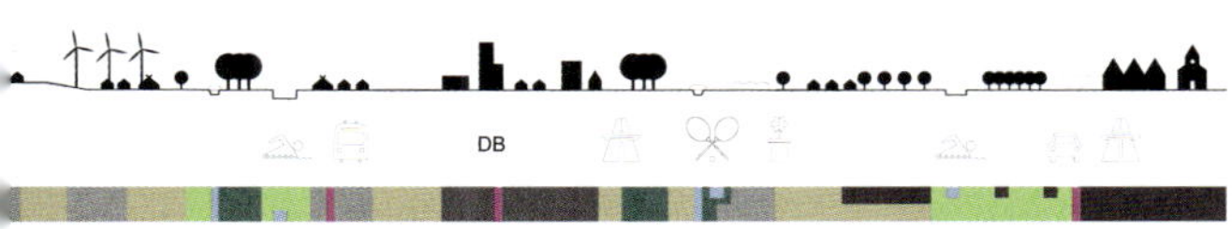

OBERG
H 0:51 BS 0:39
BUS-RE BUS-RE

MÜNSTEDT
H 0:48 BS 0:41
BUS-RE BUS-RE

BETTMAR
H 1:10 BS 0:37
BUS-RE BUS-RE

VECHELDE
H 0:35 BS 0:09
RE RE

DENSTORF
H 0:54 BS 0:26
BUS-RE BUS

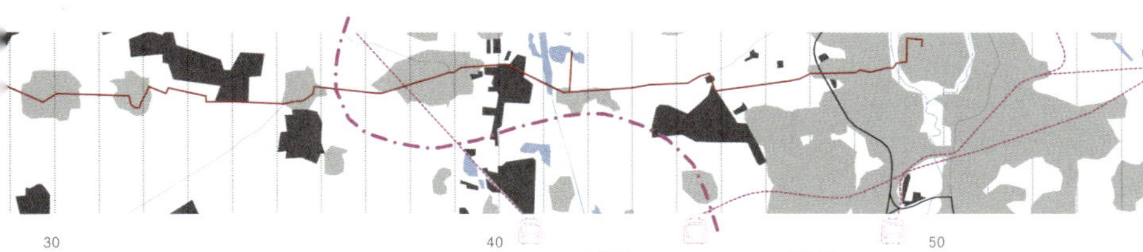

7 | Atmosphärisches Raumbild | Atmospheric spatial picture

be identified from the observation and inspection, can a consistent story be told? Does the 'narrative sequence' of the story still work, or do we come up against a diffuse and seemingly unconnected juxtaposition of objects and phenomena? Where? Why might that be? Do these contrasts offer a unique esthetic charm?

The second format, that of collage, opens up ways of thinking and possibilities. In an initial collage, found elements and structures along the route are arranged against a white background according to their location (fig. 8). Lifestyles and the 'mental state' of the area are illustrated here. A second collage appears to have a more comprehensive and independent composition (fig. 9). The picture title indicates, with an ironic tone, a distinctive feature of the area. All distinctive spatial features are presented as movable pieces of scenery, with graphic additions, creating peripheral formations at the top edge of the picture, in the 'north', by means of urban silhouettes, and at the bottom edge of the picture in the 'south' through industrial relics and topographical elements. Framing and atmospheric density characterize this collage and enable a clear distinction of the three spatial corridors as a direct comparison (fig. 9-11).

A further dimension of the collage is the showing of possible futures in scenarios that make an atmospheric statement about ways of life and programs, but which remain only vaguely located (fig. 12). This offers the advantage of stimulating possibilities for an open discussion, without triggering areas of conflict through concrete assignation. Various conceivable programming and ways of life can be shown comparatively in a series. Collages have an esthetic and emotional effect. They provoke a more intensive involvement from the viewer than plans and open up room for interpretation. There is often a recognition of the situation, but measurable consequences of the intervention like in planning suggestions are deliberately avoided. Collages are bound up with notions of value and therefore address questions about the identity of spaces, offering at the same time a quick and direct means of illustrating and juxtaposing.

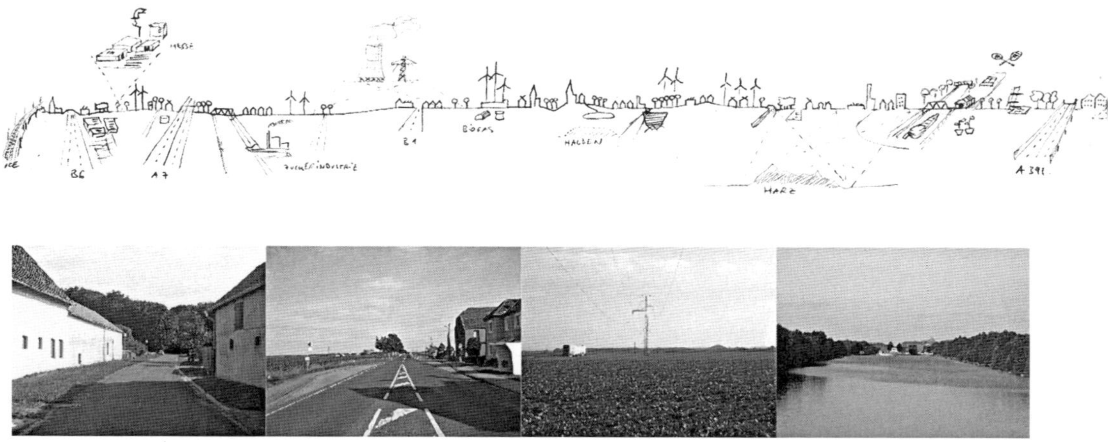

7 | Atmosphärisches Raumbild | Atmospheric spatial picture

ergänzt aber die drei raum-zeitlich definierten Raumzonen um Ortsnamen, Fahrzeiten und Verkehrsmittel zu den nächsten zentralen Kernstädten. Viele Informationen zu wesentlichen Eigenschaften des Raumkorridors – mit Blick auf die raumstrukturellen Bedingungen und Begabungen und zu den raum-zeitlichen Lagebedingungen bezogen auf die gestaffelten Urbanitätsgerade (drei Raum-Zeit-Zonen) – sind hier auf einen Blick erfassbar.

Diese Gedanken leiten über zu ‚Raumbild' und zu einer Definition durch den Stadt- und Regionalsoziologen Detlev Ipsen, der in Raumbildern (gemeint sind Bildausschnitte des realen physischen Raums in Fotos) Spuren gesellschaftlicher Entwicklungskonzepte sieht: „Um bei bewussten oder unbewussten Entwicklungen einer Landschaft eingreifen zu können, muss man sie verstehen. Ideen oder gar Leitbilder bewusster Renovierung oder innovativer Entwicklung setzen an dem Bedeutungsgehalt einer Landschaft an. Dazu soll die Theorie der Raumbilder einen Beitrag leisten. Die Theorie der Raumbilder versucht die Gestalt des Raumes als symbolischen Ausdruck gesellschaftlicher Entwicklungskonzepte zu interpretieren."[8]

SZENISCHES RAUMBILD Die Vorbereitung des Querschnittprofils erfolgte über eine Handzeichnung aus dem Gedächtnis. Nachträglich fiel auf, dass diese Zeichnung einen sehr viel erzählenderen und atmosphärischeren Charakter hatte als das Querschnittsprofil. Als ‚narrativer Schnitt' bildet es ein eigenständiges Artefakt, eine phänomenologische Betrachtungsweise verknüpft mit einem mentalen Erinnerungsbild und einer persönlichen Handschrift. Ergänzt um einen kurzen erläuternden Text und ausgewählte atmosphärische Fotos, die auf einen prägenden Charakter des Raumkorridors zugespitzt sind, entsteht ein erstes atmosphärisches Raumbild, das in eine ganz bestimmte Richtung der Deutung lenkt (Abb. 7). Lässt sich aus der Betrachtung und Begehung eine Topo-Logik erkennen, eine konsistente Geschichte erzählen – funktioniert noch die ‚narrative Folge' der Erzählung oder stoßen wir auf ein diffuses und scheinbar zusammenhangloses Nebeneinander von Objekten und Phänomenen? Wo? Warum möglicherweise? Bieten diese Kontraste einen eigenen ästhetischen Reiz?

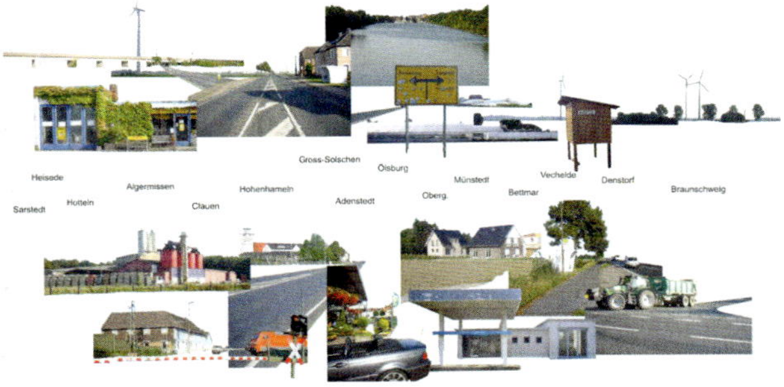

8 | Lebensraum: Collage ‚Ist' | Habitat: Collage 'is-state'

9 | Super.Productive

STRUCTURAL SPATIAL IMAGE The structural spatial image pursues the aim of conveying new spatial concepts within complex physical spatial realities. Spatial concepts can be readings and interpretations of existing structures – with 'concept' here as a specific view of the existing – but they can also be projections of new ideas onto existing structures – with 'concept' in this case as a basis for a new spatial understanding and new spatial designs, as shown on fig. 1 and 2. An application example for the region 'Cologne to the right of the Rhine' from Leverkusen to Siegburg shows four structurally linked landscape units and five identifiable different settlement areas (fig. 13 and 14). 'Narrative' titles convey special qualities of the individual areas and bring them into an overall discussion about specific capabilities and a possible task distribution within a cooperative planning procedure. In a further step, the individual areas were examined structurally in depth. Collages show possible future programs and ways of life (fig. 12).

CONCRETE SPATIAL QUALITIES The methods presented here contribute to the development of awareness and communication about specific spatial qualities. They offer the basis for a quality-oriented, esthetically motivated planning and support the required qualified communication processes in which various involved parties discuss a new overall spatial orientation. Possible objectives, needs for action and strategies can be discussed descriptively and possible or necessary areas of intervention can be identified.

Walks as concrete spatial encounters should become an immanent part of planning processes as 'in situ knowledge generation'. It is astounding how much information and statements with different focuses can be generated from three day surveys with 600 photos each. The explorations also offer a suitable starting position for further information gathering through in-depth research into found phenomena, as well as surveys and the inclusion of local protagonists. A new aspect of the presented methods is the

10 | Super.Green

11 | Super.Rural

Das zweite Format, das der Collage, eröffnet Denk- und Möglichkeitsräume. In einer ersten Collage werden vorgefundene Elemente und Strukturen entlang der Wegstrecke gemäß ihrer Lage im Raum vor weißem Grund angeordnet (Abb. 8). Lebenswelten und ‚mentale Verfassung' des Raums werden hier illustriert. Eine zweite Collage erscheint allumfassender und eigenständiger komponiert (Abb. 9). Der Bildtitel verweist mit ironischem Ton auf ein prägnantes Wesensmerkmal des Raums. Alle raumprägnanten Merkmale kommen als Versatzstücke vor, werden grafisch ergänzt und schaffen Randausbildungen am oberen Bildrand, im ‚Norden', mittels Stadtsilhouetten und am unteren Bildrand im ‚Süden' durch Industrierelikte und topografische Elemente. Rahmung und atmosphärische Dichte kennzeichnen diese Collage und ermöglichen eine klare Unterscheidung der drei Raumkorridore im unmittelbaren Vergleich (Abb. 9-11). Eine weitere Dimension der Collage ist das Aufzeigen möglicher Zukünfte in Szenarien, die atmosphärische Aussagen zu Lebenswelten und Programmen treffen, jedoch unscharf in der Verortung bleiben (Abb. 12). Dies bietet den Vorteil, Möglichkeitsräume für eine offene Diskussion anzuregen, ohne bereits durch konkrete Zuweisung Gebietskonflikte auszulösen. Verschiedene denkbare Programmierungen und Lebenswelten können in Serie vergleichbar aufgezeigt werden. Collagen berühren ästhetisch und emotional. Sie lösen eine intensivere Einlassung beim Betrachter aus, als Planungen dies tun, und eröffnen Interpretationsspielräume. Ein Wiedererkennen der Situation ist oft gegeben, messbare Konsequenzen des Intervenierens wie in Planungsvorschlägen sind aber bewusst ausgelassen. Collagen sind verbunden mit Wertvorstellungen, adressieren somit Fragen zur Identität von Räumen und bieten gleichzeitig ein schnelles und unmittelbares Medium des Zeigens und Gegenüberstellens.

STRUKTURELLES RAUMBILD Das strukturelle Raumbild verfolgt das Ziel, neue Raumkonzepte innerhalb komplexer physischer Raumrealitäten anschaulich zu vermitteln. Raumkonzepte können Lesarten und Interpretationen vorhandener Strukturen sein – ‚Konzept' hier als spezifische Auffassung von Bestehendem – sie

12 | Lebensraum: Collage ‚Kann' | Habitat: Collage 'Can'

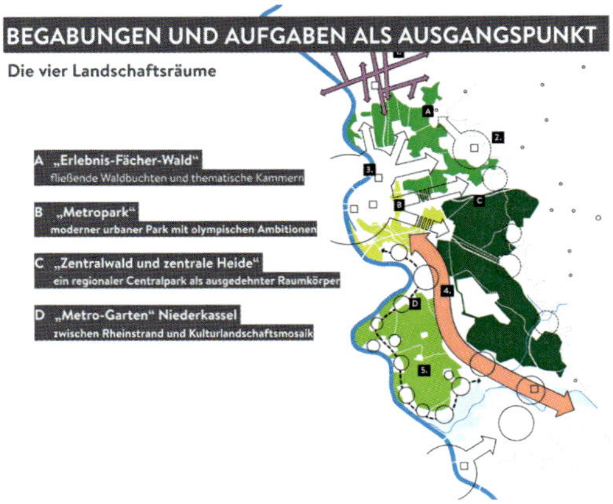

13 | Köln rechtsrheinisch: Landschaftsräume | Cologne Rhine right: Landforms

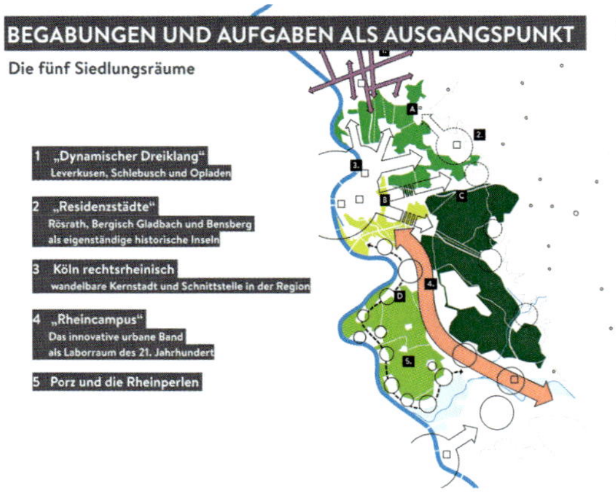

14 | Köln rechtsrheinisch: Siedlungsräume | Cologne Rhine right: Settlement areas

können aber auch Projektionen neuer Ideen auf bestehende Strukturen sein – ‚Konzept' hier als Grundlage für ein neues Raumverständnis und neue Raumentwürfe, wie es die Abb. 1 und 2 zeigen. Ein Anwendungsbeispiel für die Region ‚Köln rechtsrheinisch' von Leverkusen bis Siegburg zeigt vier strukturell sinnvoll zusammengehörige Landschaftseinheiten und fünf identifizierbare unterschiedliche Siedlungsräume auf (Abb. 13 und 14). ‚Narrative' Titel vermitteln besondere Qualitäten der Teilräume und bringen diese in eine gesamträumliche Diskussion über spezifische Begabungen und mögliche Aufgabenteilung innerhalb eines kooperativen Planungsverfahrens ein. In einem weiteren Schritt wurden die Teilräume vertieft strukturell untersucht. Collagen zeigen mögliche zukünftige Programme und Lebenswelten auf (Abb. 12).

KONKRETE RÄUMLICHE QUALITÄTEN Die hier dargestellten Methoden tragen zur Bewusstseinsbildung und Verständigung über konkrete räumliche Qualitäten bei. Sie bieten die Basis für eine qualitätsorientierte, ästhetisch motivierte Planung und unterstützen die hierzu erforderlichen qualifizierten Kommunikationsprozesse, in denen sich unterschiedliche Akteure über eine neue gesamträumliche Ausrichtung verständigen. Mögliche Ziele, Handlungsbedarfe und Strategien lassen sich anschaulich diskutieren und mögliche oder erforderliche Interventionsbereiche identifizieren.

Spaziergänge als konkrete Raumbegegnungen sollten als ‚in situ Wissensgenerierung' immanenter Teil von Planungsprozessen werden. Es ist erstaunlich, wie viele Informationen und unterschiedlich fokussierte Aussagen sich aus drei Tageserkundungen mit jeweils 600 Bildern generieren lassen. Ebenso bieten die Erkundungen auch eine geeignete Ausgangslage für weiteren Informationsgewinn durch vertiefte Recherche vorgefundener Phänomene, Befragungen und das Einbeziehen lokaler Akteure. Neu bei den dargestellten Methoden ist der Transfer originär städtebaulicher Methoden der raumstrukturellen Betrachtung auf größere Räume. Räumliche Qualitäten werden auf vielfältige Weise in regionalen Dimensionen aufgezeigt, wie es übliche Planungsinstrumente, die sich meist auf funktionale Fragestellungen oder Zonenzuweisungen beschränken, nicht vermitteln können.

Raumerkundung und Raumbild sind Teil eines ‚Entwerfens als Erkenntnis generierender und iterativer Prozess'. Dabei stellen die aufgezeigten Methoden den Standardisierungs- und Normierungstendenzen in der Planung ein vertieftes Nachdenken über konkrete Kontexte und Qualitäten gegenüber. Diese raumästhetische und experimentelle Methodik ist Teil eines reflexiven, gleichzeitig deduktiven wie auch induktiven Prozesses der Wissensgenerierung mit einer Dynamik durch alle Maßstäbe hindurch. Im Transfer – beispielsweise durch Musterkennung und Übertragung auf andere Räume – lässt sich aus dieser sehr konkreten qualitativen Betrachtung auch allgemeines methodisches oder raumtypologisches Wissen generieren.

application of original urban development methods of spatial structure observation to wider areas. Spatial qualities are shown in a variety of ways in regional dimensions, in a way that conventional planning tools, which are usually limited to functional aspects or zone assignations, cannot convey.

Spatial surveys and spatial image are part of a 'designing as a knowledge-generating and iterative process'. The presented methods counter the standardization and normalization tendencies in planning with more in-depth thoughts about concrete contexts and qualities. This spatial esthetic and experimental methodology is part of a reflexive, both deductive and inductive process of knowledge generation with a dynamic on all scales. When applied – for example through pattern recognition and transfer to other areas – it is also possible to generate general methodological or spatial typology knowledge from this very concrete qualitative observation.

1 Zur Charakterisierung mitteleuropäischer Territorien vgl. | For the characterization of Central European territories cf. André Corboz, Die Kunst, Stadt und Land zum Sprechen zu bringen, Bauwelt Fundamente 123, Basel u.a.: Birkhäuser 2001, 146 **2** Zu teilräumlichen ‚Begabungen' vgl. | On area 'advantages' cf. Thomas Sieverts, Zwischenstadt, Bauwelt Fundamente 118, Braunschweig u.a.: Vieweg 1997, 51-55; 74 **3** Zu ‚umherschweifender Neugier' und ‚Unbetroffenheit des Betrachters' vgl. | On 'sweeping curiosity' and 'unaffectedness of the viewer' cf. Lucius Burckhardt, Warum ist Landschaft schön? Die Spaziergangwissenschaft, Herausgeber: Markus Ritter/Martin Schmitz, Berlin: Verlag Martin Schmitz 2006, 110-111 **4** Zu ‚Wahrnehmungszyklus' vgl. | On 'perception cycle' cf. Ulrich Neisser, Kognition und Wirklichkeit: Prinzipien und Implikationen der kognitiven Psychologie, Stuttgart, 1979, 19 **5** Zu Eindrücken eines Spaziergangs ‚aufgereiht wie Perlen an einer Perlenschnur' vgl. | On impressions of a walk 'lined up like pearls on a necklace' cf. op.cit. (Anm. 3 | note 3), 260; zur ‚narrativen Folge' vgl. | on 'narrative sequence' cf. ibid., 103-106 **6** Zu Landschaft als ‚mentales Bild im Kopf' vgl. | On landscape as a 'mental image in the head' cf. ibid., 82-83; zu ‚Subsumtion' vgl. | on 'subsumption' cf. ibid., 257-259 **7** op.cit. (Anm. 1 | note 1), 160 **8** Detlev Ipsen, Ort und Landschaft, Wiesbaden: VS Verlag für Sozialwissenschaften 2006, 92

„Wenn es so etwas gibt wie ein Repertoire möglicher Aktionen zwischen dem, dass man Veränderungen in der Welt herbeiführt oder sie lässt wie sie ist, ist der Architekt immer auf der Seite der Veränderung." | 'If there is a repertoire of possible action between making changes in the world and leaving it as it is, the architect is always on the side of the change.'

Rem Koolhaas

TRANSFORMATION
TRANSFORMATION

Transformation processes and the active shaping of the future play a central role as research subjects in a wide variety of disciplines.[1] The exploratory imagination and knowledge production of designing and planning can become constructive and provide speculative initiatives if transformation processes in spatial design and a wider social effectiveness are explicitly striven for. One can therefore refer for example to social, cultural and ecological realities to make their potential and otherness visible and discussible. The examinations integrate both analytical-methodological and practical-creative procedures in a special way in relation to perception and action options in the flow of past and future. The close connection between modification and construction comes to the fore as a significant characteristic of transformational processes, either consecutively or synchronously, and can also include an instrumental change.[2] The development of conceptual frameworks that seek to extend the architectural and urbanistic knowledge repertoire in consideration of existential and incidental aspects of everyday cultural associations, in order to shape the human habitat in a more humane and sustainable manner, forms an exemplary case of a transformational process structure. The discourses and designs generate ideas or knowledge to produce alternative concepts and possibilities — also in the knowledge of the relativity of cultures and the unavailability of historical developments. Exemplary approaches can contribute here within the horizon of the living environment to enriching knowledge of how the close relationships between design and research can be newly constituted.[3]

Transformationsprozesse und eine aktive Zukunftsgestaltung spielen in verschiedensten Disziplinen als Forschungsthemen eine zentrale Rolle. Die forschende Imagination und Wissensproduktion von Entwerfen und Planen kann konstruktiv und spekulativ initiierend wirksam werden, wenn explizit Wandlungsprozesse in der räumlichen Gestaltung und eine weitere gesellschaftliche Wirksamkeit angestrebt werden.[1] So können beispielsweise soziale, kulturelle und ökologische Realitäten befragt werden, um deren Potentiale und Alterität sichtbar und diskutierbar zu machen. Dabei integrieren die Untersuchungen sowohl analytisch-methodische wie auch praktisch-gestalterische Verfahren in besonderer Weise in Bezug zu Wahrnehmungs- und Handlungsoptionen im Fluss von Vergangenheit und Zukunft. Als signifikantes Merkmal transformatorischer Prozesse tritt die enge Verbindung von Modifikation und Konstruktion hervor, die nacheinander erfolgen oder auch synchron verlaufen und ebenfalls einen instrumentellen Wandel einbeziehen kann.[2] Das Entwickeln von konzeptuellen Rahmungen, die das architektonische und urbanistische Wissensrepertoire im Blick auf existentielle und beiläufige Aspekte alltagskultureller Zusammenhänge zu erweitern suchen, um das menschliche Habitat humaner und nachhaltiger zu gestalten, bildet ein exemplarisches Beispiel für transformatorische Prozessgestalt. Die Diskurse und Entwürfe generieren Ideen oder Wissen, um alternative Konzepte und Möglichkeiten zu erzeugen — auch in dem Wissen um die Relativität von Kulturen und die Unverfügbarkeit historischer Entwicklungen. Exemplarische Annäherungen können hier dazu beitragen, im Horizont der Lebenswelt, das Wissen, wie die engen Relationen von Entwerfen und Forschen neu konstituiert werden können, zu bereichern.[3]

The contribution by Tom Avermaete illuminates and updates the view of the so-called grid that was designed and discussed as a methodological analysis, design, communication and mediation tool for urban projects from 1949 at the CIAM. Based on the example of the architecture and urban development by Candilis Josic Woods, it shows how the analytical-conceptual level preceding the design process guides the ensuing architectural or planning suggestions, by selecting and organizing the architectural and urban spatial elements in such a way that they are oriented towards the wider idea.[4] All further design decisions are made against this background. The course of the process is structured by these priorities, which help to limit individual phases in time and to present them in a way that not only enables their discussion also in extradisciplinary contexts, but also qualifies their transferability.

The contribution by Giorgia Aquilar may spur discussions about how urban structural-spatial and cultural heritage can be transformed dynamically through contemporary interventions. Based on the example of the currently controversially discussed developments at the Steinhof in Vienna, an ensemble including a memorial to Nazi medicine, it takes the given discourse levels apart to reformulate them conceptually. With the concept of 'afterwardsness', it develops notions for architectural interventions and extensions with designs in which the present articulates itself in such a way that at the same time the retroactive appropriation and emphasis of various historical layers is created, in the sense of a hybrid, innovatively formed and documentary structural-spatial version that can have the effect of forging an identity in the 21st century and beyond.[5] With an interpretation of the power of action as a connection between the material world, institutions and human protagonists, it presents at the same time a discourse and design concept that transforms and can have a transforming effect.

Der Beitrag von Tom Avermaete erhellt und aktualisiert den Blick auf das sogenannte Grid, das als methodisches Analyse-, Entwurfs-, Kommunikations- und Vermittlungswerkzeug für urbane Projekte ab 1949 in der CIAM entworfen und diskutiert wurde. Am Beispiel der Architektur und des Städtebaus von Candilis Josic Woods wird verdeutlicht, wie die dem Entwurfsgeschehen vorgängige analytisch-konzeptuelle Ebene die nachfolgenden architektonischen oder planerischen Vorschläge leitete, indem die architektonischen und stadträumlichen Elemente so ausgesucht und organisiert wurden, dass sie an der größeren Idee ausgerichtet sind.[4] Alle weiteren Entwurfsentscheidungen erfolgten vor dieser Folie. Der Prozessverlauf wird dadurch strukturiert, dass diese Prioritäten helfen, einzelne Phasen zeitlich zu limitieren und in einer Weise zu präsentieren, die nicht nur deren Diskussion auch in fachfremden Kontexten ermöglichte, sondern auch ihre Transferfähigkeit qualifizierte.

Der Beitrag von Giorgia Aquilar möchte Diskurse darüber anfachen, wie urbanes baulich-räumliches und kulturelles Erbe durch zeitgenössische Interventionen dynamisch transformiert werden kann. Am Beispiel der aktuell kontrovers diskutierten Entwicklungen am Steinhof in Wien, dessen Ensemble u.a. eine Gedenkstätte für NS-Medizin beinhaltet, nimmt sie die gegebenen Diskursebenen auseinander, um sie begrifflich neu zu fassen. Mit dem Konzept der ‚Nachträglichkeit' entwickelt sie Vorstellungen für architektonische Interventionen und Erweiterungen mit Entwürfen, in denen sich Gegenwärtigkeit so artikuliert, dass gleichzeitig die retroaktive Aneignung und Betonung diverser historischer Schichtungen im Sinne hybride gekoppelter, forminnovativer und dokumentarischer baulich-räumlicher Fassung erzeugt wird, die im 21. Jahrhundert und darüber hinaus identitätsbildende Wirkung entfalten kann.[5] Mit dieser Deutung von Handlungsmacht als Verbindung von materieller Welt, Institutionen und menschlichen Akteuren präsentiert sie gleichzeitig ein Diskurs- und Entwurfskonzept, das transformiert und transformierend wirksam werden kann.

In light of the question of how urban planning interventions and design strategies can increase their success through the active inclusion of heterogenous experts from the real world and the promotion of social interaction, Isabel Finkenberger presents an example of explorative and experimental practice, an artistic-performative urban development project. The process in several stages with an open outcome comprised urban planning research, observations and surveys, theatrically designed events, conferences and workshops, as well as photo reports and explorative tests in staged real situations. It was accompanied and elaborated on in reflections about the assumptions, actions and results of the process as resources for future action. Throwing up questions about integration, poverty etc. in this manner can promote public interest in urban design and incorporate the interested public in the conceptual design of possible transformations of their urban districts. Architects and urbanists can then play an additional role in the commitment to values also based on social and political factors, instead of primarily on profit.[6] Over the course of the process, new tools and strategies are developed, as well as a vocabulary to communicate in various given situations and to convey the concerns of the general public. In addition, based on the pilot project, there is a sounding out of how knowledge production can be made intersubjective, comprehensible, criticizable and therefore revisable and compatible for further designs and research considerations.

Vor dem Hintergrund der Frage, wie stadtplanerische Interventionen und entwerferische Strategien in ihrem Erfolg durch den aktiven Einbezug heterogener Expert/inn/en aus der Wirklichkeit und die Förderung sozialer Interaktion gesteigert werden können, stellt Isabel Finkenberger ein Beispiel explorativer und experimenteller Praxis vor – ein künstlerisch-performatives Stadtentwicklungsprojekt. Der mehrstufige, ergebnisoffen gehaltene Prozess umfasste stadtplanerische Recherchen, Beobachtungen und Befragungen, theatral gestaltete Events, Konferenzen und Workshops sowie Fotoberichte und explorative Tests in inszenierten Realsituationen. Er wurde begleitet und fortgesetzt in Reflexionen zu den Annahmen, Aktionen und Resultaten des Prozesses als Ressourcen für zukünftiges Handeln. Fragen nach Integration, Armut etc. in dieser Weise aufzuwerfen kann das öffentliche Interesse für die Stadtgestaltung fördern und interessiertes Publikum in den konzeptuellen Entwurf von Möglichkeiten der Transformation ihrer Stadtbereiche einbeziehen. Dann auch können Architekturschaffende und Urbanisten zusätzlich eine Rolle spielen im Einsatz für Werte, die auch auf sozialen und politischen Faktoren beruhen, anstatt vorrangig auf Profit.[6] Im Verlauf des Prozesses werden neue Instrumente und Strategien entwickelt und zudem ein Vokabular, um in verschiedenen vorgefunden Situationen zu kommunizieren und die Anliegen der allgemeinen Öffentlichkeit zu vermitteln. Darüber hinaus wird ausgehend von dem Pilotprojekt ausgelotet, wie Wissensproduktion intersubjektiv nachvollziehbar, kritisierbar und damit revidierbar sowie anschlussfähig gemacht werden kann für weitere Entwürfe und Forschungsfragen. MB

1 Vgl. | Cf. Raj Kollmorgen/Wolfgang Merke/Hans-Jürgen Wagener, Zur Einführung, in: ids. (eds.) Handbuch Transformationsforschung, Wiesbaden: Springer VS 2015, 11-27 **2** Vgl. | Cf. Lutz Bergermann/Martin Dönike et al, Transformation. Ein Konzept zur Erforschung kulturellen Wandels, in: Hartmut Böhme (ed.), Transformation. Ein Konzept zur Erforschung kulturellen Wandels, München: Wilhelm Fink 2012, 39–55 **3** Uwe Schneidewind, Transformative Wissenschaft. Motor für gute Wissenschaft und lebendige Demokratie, in: GAIA 24 (2015)/2, 88–91 **4** Zu konzeptuellen Entwurfsansätzen vgl. | On concept-based design see Caroline Stapenhorst, Concept. A dialogical instrument in architectural design, Berlin: Jovis 2016, passim **5** Zu historisch nuancierter Gegenwärtigkeit vgl. | On historically nuanced presentness see Hartmut Böhme, Einladung zur Transformation, in: id. (ed.), Transformation. Ein Konzept zur Erforschung kulturellen Wandels, München: Wilhelm Fink 2012, 7-38, 9 und | and 16; Jorge Otero-Pailos Preservation. The potential of not-me creations, in: Thordis Arrhenius/Erik Fenstad Langdalen/id. (eds.), Experimental preservation, Zürich: Lars Müller 2016, 11-39 **6** Vgl. hierzu auch | Cf. on this subject also Sarah Nichols, Reforming architecture, in: Marc Angélil/id. (eds.), Reform! Essays on the political economy of urban form, Berlin: Ruby Press 2015, 7-20, 15-18

THE VIEW FROM THE GRID

CIAM and the framing of architecture as process

Tom Avermaete

"The Grid provides both a tool for thinking and a tool for transmitting thought."[1] The CIAM Grid remains until today one of the most remarkable tools of the modern movement in architecture. Introduced for the first time by Le Corbusier on the occasion of the 4th meeting of the Congres Internationaux d'Architecture Moderne (CIAM) at Bridgwater (UK) in 1947, it was considered as the methodological equivalent of what is generally considered to be CIAM's most important document: The Athens Charter. Consequently, the Grid was officially published in 1948 in L'Architecture d'Aujourd'hui as the 'Application pratique de la Charte d'Athènes.'[2] In this article, the Grid is primarily presented as a sophisticated system for graphically organizing information on town planning projects. Shaped as a matrix composed of basic cells (panels) of 21x31 cm, its columns represent nine analytical categories: environment, occupation of the land, constructed volume, equipment, ethical and aesthetic problems, economic and social influences, legislation, finance and stages of realization. The rows encompass the four urban design themes around which CIAM had structured its thoughts since the first congresses: living (green), work (red), cultivation of body and spirit (blue) and circulation (yellow) (fig. 1).

DER BLICK DES GRIDS

CIAM und die Rahmung der Architektur als Prozess

Tom Avermaete

„Das Grid ist ein Werkzeug sowohl für das Denken, als auch ein Werkzeug für das Übermitteln von Gedanken."[1] Das CIAM-Grid besteht bis heute als eines der bemerkenswertesten Werkzeuge der architektonischen Moderne. 1947 zum ersten Mal vorgestellt von Le Corbusier anlässlich der 4. Zusammenkunft zum Congres Internationaux d'Architecture Moderne (CIAM) in Bridgewater (Großbritannien), war es gedacht als methodologisches Äquivalent zum wohl wichtigsten Dokument des CIAM: Der Charta von Athen. In der Folge wurde das Grid 1948 in ‚L'Architecture d'Aujourd'hui' als ‚praktische Anwendung der Charta von Athen' offiziell publiziert.[2] In diesem Artikel wird das Raster in erster Linie als durchdachtes System grafischer Organisation von Informationen innerhalb stadtplanerischer Projekte dargelegt. Als Matrix einfacher 21x23 cm großer Zellen, deren Spalten neun analytische Kategorien repräsentieren: Umgebung, Inanspruchnahme von Land, gebautes Volumen, Ausstattung, ethische und ästhetische Probleme, ökonomische und soziale Einflüsse, Gesetzgebung, Finanzen und Realisierungsabschnitte. Die Zeilen umfassen die vier Gestaltungsthemen, welche die Fragestellungen des CIAMs seit seiner ersten Zusammenkunft strukturierten: Leben (grün), Arbeiten (rot), Pflege körperlicher und geistiger Gesundheit (blau), sowie Erschließung (gelb) (Abb. 1).

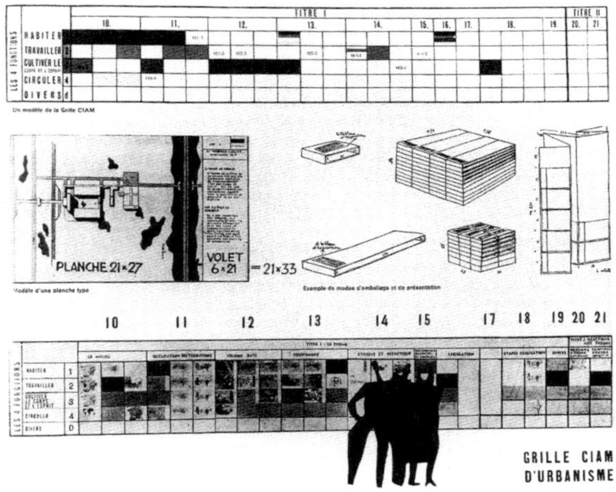

1 | Das CIAM Grid als ausgefeiltes System zur grafischen Informationsanordnung | The CIAM Grid as sophisticated system for graphically organizing information, publ. in l'Architecture d'Aujourd'hui 1948

In this text, I want to maintain that the CIAM Grid reached far beyond a harmless way of organizing information on urban design projects, and represents a fundamental epistemological shift in the modern movement's approach to architecture. The Grid, I argue, functioned as a tool to move from a more absolute understanding of architecture that was based on fixed norms and forms, towards an understanding of the built environment as the frame, substance and result of complex processes that had to be carefully investigated, measured and controlled by architects. As Le Corbusier rightly remarked concerning the CIAM Grid: "You are here in the presence of an attempt to make town planning a present of a measuring rod – indeed a 'metrology' (science of measurement)!"[3]

THE ANALYSIS OF THE REAL The Grid that Le Corbusier presented in 1947 was the culmination point of a methodology that had been elaborated by CIAM since the first CIRPAC meeting (Basel, 1929) and accepted at the subsequent second CIAM congress (Frankfurt, 1929). The well-known exhibition 'The Minimum Dwelling Unit', held on the occasion of the CIAM-meeting in Frankfurt in 1929, visualized this methodology for the first time. The most striking feature of the exhibition, organized with the intention of presenting the achievements of the Modern Movement in the realm of housing in different countries, is that it did not rely on traditional architectural presentation techniques such as perspectives, renderings and elevations. Instead, the public in Frankfurt was confronted with more than two hundred planimetric tracings of existing dwelling units. Though the Frankfurt exhibition relied exclusively on planimetrics to represent architecture, the objective of its composers was not to question architectural representation as such. Rather, the CIAM members intended, with their new presentation method, to visualize an approach to architecture that no longer took preset aesthetical norms as its basis. The exhibition panels with their detailed tracings of floor area and cubage were believed to illustrate that the careful measuring of the actual use of space could be a fruitful point of departure for architecture.

In diesem Text soll behauptet werden, dass das CIAM-Raster weitaus mehr repräsentierte, als eine einfache Art der Organisation von Informationen innerhalb städtebaulicher Projekte, sondern eine fundamentale epistemologische Veränderung in der Haltung der modernen Architekturbewegung darstellte. Das Raster, ist zu argumentieren, war ein Werkzeug um von einem tendenziellen Verständnis von Architektur, basierend auf Normen und Formen, zu einem Verständnis der gebauten Umgebung als Rahmung, Substanz und Ergebnis komplexer Prozesse zu gelangen, welche präzise von Architekten untersucht, gemessen und kontrolliert werden mussten. Wie von Le Corbusier bezüglich des CIAM-Grids folgerichtig bemerkt: „Sie sind anwesend bei dem Vorhaben, Stadtplanung zu einem Moment des Messstabes zu machen – geradezu einer ‚métrologie' (Wissenschaft der Vermessung)."[3]

D I E A N A L Y S E D E S R E A L E N Das Grid, das Le Corbusier 1947 vorgestellt hatte, war der vorläufige Höhepunkt einer Methodologie, die von den CIAM seit dem ersten CIRPAC-Treffen (Basel, 1929) diskutiert und im nachfolgenden zweiten Treffen der CIAM (Frankfurt, 1929) schließlich anerkannt wurde. Die wohlbekannte Ausstellung ‚Die Wohnung für das Existenzminimum' anlässlich des CIAM in Frankfurt 1929 stellte diese Methodologie zum ersten Mal visuell dar. Das auffälligste Merkmal der Ausstellung, welche der Präsentation der Errungenschaften der Architekturmoderne im Bereich des Wohnens in verschiedenen Ländern diente, war, dass sie nicht auf traditionelle Präsentationstechniken wie Perspektiven, Ansichten und Schnitten zurückgriff. Stattdessen war die Öffentlichkeit in Frankfurt mit mehr als zweihundert planimetrischen Zeichnungen bestehender Wohneinheiten konfrontiert. Obwohl die Frankfurter Ausstellung ausschließlich auf diesen planimetrischen Darstellungen von Architektur beruhte, war das Ziel ihrer Kurateure nicht die Infragestellung architektonischer Darstellungen als solche. Vielmehr versuchten die CIAM-Mitglieder mit ihrer neuen Präsentationsmethode einen Architekturansatz zu verbildlichen, welcher nicht länger aus ästhetischen Normen hervorgehen sollte. Die detaillierten Zeichnungen von Bodenflächen und Kubaturen auf den Ausstellungstafeln sollten illustrieren, wie ein sorgfältiges Kartografieren des tatsächlichen Flächenbedarfs als ergiebige Ausgangslage der Architektur dienen konnte.

Dieses spezifische Verständnis architektonischen Wissens wurde mit dem CIAM-Raster 1947 weiter ausgearbeitet. Dessen Form und Kategorien beinhalteten einen Zugang zur Architektur, in welchem Wissen nicht länger tautologisch oder absolut, sondern analytisch war – und somit in Relation zu einer bestimmten Rahmung stand. Das Raster veranschaulichte einen Zugang zur Architektur, der auf Wissen beruhte, das auf Objekten, Prozessen und Strukturen der realen Welt basierte. Bei genauerer Betrachtung des Gründungsmanifestes (La Sarraz, 1928) zeigt sich, dass die Suche nach einer Alternative zu architektonischen und städtebaulichen Ansätzen, welche auf Normen und Standards basierte, schon immer ein Teil des CIAM-Programmes war: „Stadtbau kann niemals durch ästhetische Überlegungen bestimmt werden, sondern ausschließlich durch funktionelle

This particular understanding of architectural knowledge was further elaborated within the 1947 CIAM Grid. Its form and categories embodied an approach to architecture in which knowledge was no longer characterized as tautological or absolute, but as analytic – and thus relative to a certain framework. The Grid exemplified an approach to architecture that was grounded in knowledge concerning the objects, processes and structures of the real world. A close reading of the inaugural declaration (La Sarraz, 1928) reveals that it was always part of CIAM's program to offer an alternative to architectural and urban design approaches that were based on preset norms or standards: "Urbanization cannot be conditioned by the pretensions of a pre-existent aestheticism: its essence is a functional order."[4] Hence, the development of CIAM between 1928 and 1947 can be understood as the installation of an epistemological transition from absolute values towards the analysis of empirical facts: "As it developed, it did not seek the rigor of a Cartesian demonstration, but rather the rhythm of life, with its meanderings, its constant questioning, its need for certitudes and its constant calls for experimentation and for the virtue of the 'concrete case'."[5]

C I A M I X : T O W A R D S T H E E V E R Y D A Y The actual epistemological turn towards real processes and practices was most convincingly elaborated in two presentations for CIAM IX (Aix-en-Provence, 1953) by future Team 10 contributors: the 'Habitat du plus grand nombre Grid' or GAMMA Grid by the GAMMA group of Georges Candilis and Shadrach Woods and Alison and Peter Smithson's Urban Re-Identification Grid or UR Grid.[6] The two Grids evoked a lot of upheaval among the participants of CIAM IX. Retrospectively, it seems that the reason for these vivid reactions was not the layout of the Grids, which as Alison Smithson recalls virtually conformed to the standard Grid, but rather their actual content.[7]

The GAMMA Grid was a large matrix that started off with photographs of the everyday dwelling conditions in a North African bidonville and descriptions of the demographic forces that gave rise to them (fig. 2). In the following columns of the Grid, the dwelling practices within the bidonville were compared to photographic investigations of indigenous dwelling conditions in villages and towns. Further on in the Grid there were panels with GAMMA's 8x8m grid housing projects for settlements in Morocco and a set of three new housing blocks designed by Georges Candilis, Shadrach Woods and Victor Bodiansky for the Carrieres Centrales settlement in Casablanca (Morocco). In a similar way, the UR Grid maintained the form of the CIAM Grille, while simultaneously making two important adjustments to it: a change of categories and the introduction of representations of

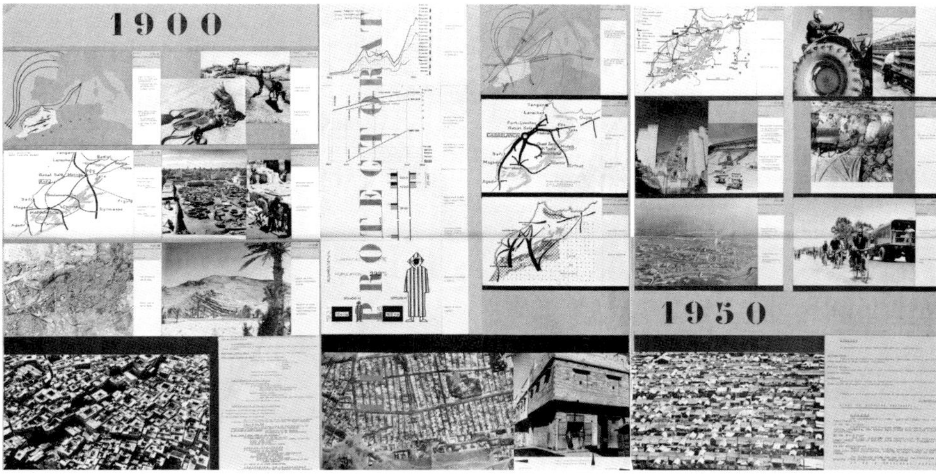

2 | Candilis, Woods, GAMMA group: GAMMA Grid (Ausschnitt | section), CIAM IX, Aix-en-Provence 1953

Folgerungen."[4] Insofern kann die Entwicklung des CIAM zwischen 1928 und 1947 als Beginn eines epistemologischen Übergangs von einer absoluten Wertevorstellung hin zu einer Analyse empirischer Fakten verstanden werden: „In seinem Entstehen suchte er nicht die Strenge kartesischer Vorführung, sondern den Rhythmus des Lebens, mit seinem Mäandern, seiner konstanten Hinterfragung, seinem Bedürfnis von Eindeutigkeiten und dem unablässigen Drang des Experimentierens, sowie der Tugend des ‚konkreten Falls'."[5]

CIAM IX: HIN ZUM ALLTÄGLICHEN Die eigentliche epistemologische Wende hin zu realen Prozessen und Praktiken verdeutlichte sich überzeugend anlässlich des CIAM IX (Aix-en-Provence, 1953) in zwei Präsentationen späterer Team-10-Mitglieder: dem ‚Habitat du plus grand nombre Grid' oder GAMMA-Grid, der GAMMA-Gruppierung von Georges Candilis und Shadrach Woods sowie Alison und Peter Smithsons Urban Re-Identification Grid, oder UR-Grid.[6] Beide Grids sorgten für Aufruhr unter den Teilnehmern des CIAM IX. Rückblickend scheint es, dass der Grund für diese Reaktion weniger das Layout des Grids selbst, welches Alison Smithson als nahezu identisch mit dem des Standard-Grids erinnerte, sondern dessen eigentlicher Inhalt war.[7]

Das GAMMA-Grid war eine große Matrix, welche mit Fotografien alltäglicher Wohnsituationen in einer nordafrikanischen Bidonville begann sowie mit Beschreibungen demografischer Einflüsse, die zu ihrer Entstehung geführt hatten (Abb. 2). In den weiteren Spalten des Grids wurden diese Wohnpraktiken fotografischen Untersuchungen indigener Wohnsituationen in Dörfern und Städten gegenübergestellt. Des Weiteren zeigte das Grid GAMMAs 8x8 Wohnungsprojekte für Siedlungen in Marokko und drei Wohnblöcke von Georges Candilis, Shadrach Woods und Victor Bodiansky für die Carrieres Centrales-Siedlung in Casablanca (Marokko). Auf ähnliche Art und Weise behielt das UR-Grid das Format des CIAM-Grids bei, nahm jedoch zwei essentielle Anpassungen vor: Eine Veränderung der Kategorien sowie die Einführung von Darstellungen alltäglicher Realität (Abb. 3). Auf der linken Seite des Rasters zeigten neue Kategorien wie ‚Haus', ‚Straße' und ‚Relationen' Fotografien alltäglicher

3 | Alison & Peter Smithson: Urban Re-Identification (UR) Grid, CIAM IX, Aix-en-Provence 1953

everyday reality (fig. 3). In the left part of the Grid new categories such as 'house', 'street' and 'relationship' head photographs taken by Nigel Henderson of everyday scenes of children playing in the working-class and immigrant London neighborhood of Bethnal Green. For the material on the right-hand side of the Grid the Smithsons relied mainly on their submission for the Golden Lane Housing Competition of the previous year. This project for a neighborhood in Coventry consisted of a network of ten-story housing blocks with internal streets (streets-in-the-air), which consider the specific topography of the bombed competition site as structuring context.

These two Grids can be regarded as encapsulating a different way of approaching the built environment. In both cases this new approach was informed by the methodologies and perspectives of contemporary anthropological and sociological research. Two important direct influences are worth mentioning. The photographs by Nigel Henderson in the UR Grid were highly informed by the anthropological investigations of his wife, Judith Henderson. As an anthropologist, she was in charge of the sociologist J. L. Peterson's research project 'Discover Your Neighbor'.[8] In contrast to the statistical 'Mass Observation' project begun in 1937, this research used case studies to explore the sociological effects of spatial parameters on the working class.[9] Judith Henderson observed and recorded the lives of neighboring families. This ordinary and participatory perspective was of decisive influence on the work of Nigel Henderson. In his photographs, streets figure as sites of everyday practices; as places of meeting, communication, anonymity and equality. It was especially this aspect that fascinated the Smithsons and that influenced their approach to the built environment.

Likewise, Candilis and Woods s GAMMA Grid was highly informed by the anthropological research that was going on at the Service de l'Urbanisme in Casablanca, Morocco. After the Second World War, these urban services of the French protectorate initiated large programs for the investigation of indigenous dwelling patterns in towns and villages.

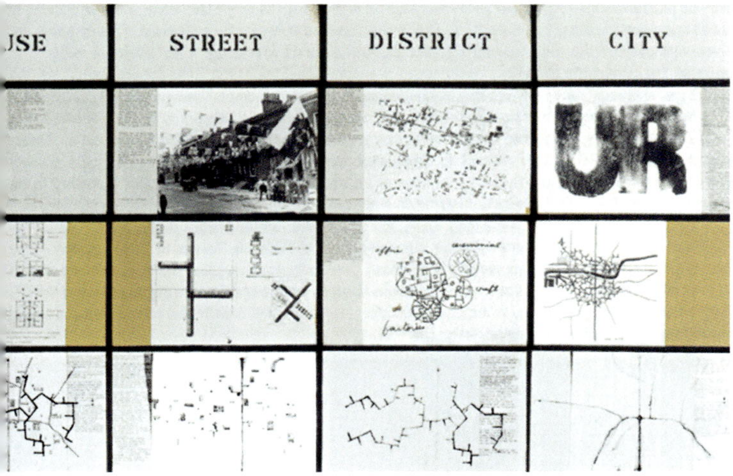

Szenen spielender Kinder des Arbeiter- und Immigrantenviertels Bethnal Green von Nigel Henderson. Das Material der rechten Seite des Grids der Smithsons verließ sich hauptsächlich auf die Beiträge der Golden Lane Housing Competition des Vorjahres. Diese Planung eines Stadtteils in Coventry bestand aus einem Netzwerk zehnstöckiger Häuserblöcke mit internen Straßen (streets-in-the-air), welche die spezifische Topografie des zerbombten Wettbewerbsgeländes als strukturierenden Kontext berücksichtigten.

Diese beiden Grids können als Zusammenfassung einer anderen Art des Zugangs zur gebauten Umgebung gesehen werden. In beiden Fällen war dieser neue Zugang geprägt von Methoden und Perspektiven zeitgenössischer anthropologischer Forschung. Zwei wichtige direkte Einflüsse sind hierbei zu nennen: Die Fotografien von Nigel Henderson im UR Grid waren stark beeinflusst von den anthropologischen Untersuchungen seiner Frau Judith Henderson. Als Anthropologin war sie verantwortlich für das Forschungsprojekt ‚Discover Your Neighbor' des Soziologen J. L. Peterson.[8] Im Unterschied zum ‚Mass Observation Project' von 1937 nutzte dieses Forschungsprojekt Fallbeispiele, um soziologische Effekte räumlicher Parameter auf die Arbeiterklasse zu beleuchten.[9] Judith Henderson beobachtete und zeichnete hierzu den Alltag in Nachbarschaft lebender Familien auf. Diese alltägliche und partizipatorische Sicht nahm einen entscheidenden Einfluss auf die Arbeit Nigel Hendersons und seine Fotografien der Straßen als Orte alltäglichen Lebens; als Orte des Treffens, der Kommunikation, Anonymität und Gleichheit. Es war insbesondere dieser Aspekt, welcher die Smithsons faszinierte und ihre Haltung zur gebauten Umwelt beeinflusste.

Zugleich war das GAMMA-Grid von Candilis und Woods stark beeinflusst von der anthropologischen Forschung des Service de l'Urbanisme in Casablanca, Marokko. Nach dem Zweiten Weltkrieg initiierten diese Stadtplanungsdienste des französischen Protektorats weitgehende Programme zur Untersuchung einheimischer städtischer und ländlicher Siedlungsstrukturen. 1947 begründete der Service de l'Urbanisme eine Forschungsmethode zur Untersuchung von Wohnbedingungen in ländlichen Gebieten. Diese Methode bestand

In 1947 the Service de l'Urbanisme set up a research methodology to investigate dwelling conditions in rural areas. This methodology consisted primarily of a mobile unit or atelier ambulant – consisting of an engineer, an urban designer, a topographer and two draughtsmen – that literally travelled through the country to investigate dwelling culture in a truly ethnological manner.[10] The atelier ambulant can be considered as the exponent of a different attitude towards architectural and urban design. If in the pre-war period the studio had been the point of departure for the master-architect, in the post-war period the everyday reality of the terrain was the field of initial action for the architect-ethnologist.

The most interesting aspect of the investigations by the Service de l'Urbanisme is that they did not remain limited to the terrain of traditional rural environments. The everyday urban spaces of the bidonville or shantytown of Casablanca were investigated in a similar ethnological fashion through tracings and photographs. Once again, the aim of these investigations was the delineation of noticeable recurrent or structural characteristics. The Service de l'Urbanisme pursued their study of the bidonville in order to get a grip on the housing problems that emerged due to the enormous economical influx from the Moroccan countryside towards urban centers such as Casablanca. It is the merit of the GAMMA architects that they presented this at one of the High Masses of the Modern Movement in architecture – CIAM IX at Aix-en-Provence in 1953, thereby raising the status of the study material to important lessons about the practices of dwelling and building for the realm of modern architecture. Moreover, in the GAMMA Grid the GAMMA architects illustrated for their fellow CIAM members how their investigations of the forms and practices of the bidonville had informed the design of new housing developments.

AN EPISTEMOLOGICAL SHIFT "The structure of the city lies not in its geometry but in the human activities within it."[11] The most significant aspect of both the UR Grid and the GAMMA Grid is that the entities of the house, street and neighborhood are not only depicted as physical elements but also – and more importantly – as social practices. In the left part of the UR Grid, Alison and Peter Smithson portrayed the house and the street through the activities of gathering on the pavement, playing on the street and meeting at the doorstep. At closer inspection, a similar approach underlies the 'Habitat du plus grand nombre Grid'. The bidonville of Casablanca is portrayed almost exclusively through the social practices of its inhabitants. The Grid shows a combination of meticulous tracings and photographs of the everyday practices of

hauptsächlich aus einer mobilen Einheit (‚atelier ambulant') – zusammengesetzt aus einer/m Ingenieur/in, einer/m Stadtplaner/in, einer/m Topografen/in und zwei Zeichnern/innen – welche das Land durchreisten, um Wohnkultur auf einer ethnologischen Art und Weise zu betrachten.[10] Das atelier ambulant kann dabei als Vertreter einer alternativen Haltung zu Architektur und Stadtplanung gesehen werden. War in der Vorkriegszeit das Studio Ausgangspunkt des Architekten, stellte in der Nachkriegszeit die Alltagsrealität des Terrains das Feld erster Handlungen des Architekturethnologen dar.

Der interessanteste Aspekt der Untersuchungen des Service de l'Urbanisme war, dass diese sich nicht auf den Bereich traditioneller ländlicher Umgebungen beschränkten. Die alltäglichen urbanen Räume der Bidonvilles oder Shantytowns von Casablanca wurden auf ähnliche ethnologische Art mittels Zeichnungen und Fotografien untersucht. Abermals war das Ziel dieser Untersuchungen die Abgrenzung wiederholender oder strukturierender Charakteristika. Der Service de l'Urbanisme führte diese Studien der Bidonville durch, um die durch die enorme, ökonomisch bedingte Landflucht aus den marokkanischen Landregionen in Städte wie Casablanca entstandenen Probleme in den Griff zu bekommen. Dies ist der Verdienst der GAMMA-Architekten – CIAM IX in Aix-en-Provence 1953 erhob das Studienmaterial zur wertvollen Lektion über die Praktiken des Wohnens und Bauens für den Bereich der modernen Architektur. Mehr noch illustrierte das GAMMA-Grid der GAMMA-Architekten den anderen CIAM-Mitgliedern, in wie weit ihre Untersuchungen der Formen und Praktiken der Bidonville die Gestaltung neuer Wohnbauten beeinflusst hatte.

EIN EPISTEMOLOGISCHER WECHSEL „Die Struktur der Stadt findet sich nicht in ihrer Geometrie, sondern in den menschlichen Aktivitäten innerhalb dieser."[11] Der auffälligste Aspekt sowohl des UR- als auch des GAMMA-Grids ist, dass die Instanzen von Haus, Straße und Nachbarschaft nicht als bloße physische Elemente, sondern auch – und wichtigerweise – als soziale Praktiken dargestellt sind. Im linken Teil des UR-Grids porträtierten Alison und Peter Smithson das Haus und die Straße mittels der Aktivitäten des Versammelns auf dem Bürgersteig, Spielens auf der Straße und Treffens vor der Haustür. Bei näherer Betrachtung unterliegt dem Grid des ‚Habitat du plus grand nombre' ein ähnlicher Ansatz. Das Bidonville Casablancas ist fast ausschließlich mittels der sozialen Praktiken seiner Bewohner veranschaulicht. Das Grid zeigt eine Kombination genauer Zeichnungen und Fotografien alltäglicher Handlungen des Wohnens und Bauens innerhalb des Slums und kommentiert diese textlich. Mit dem Fokus auf Handlungen des Wirtschaftlichen, des Religiösen und des Wohnens wird das Bidonville als dichtes Netz sozialer Praktiken dargestellt (Abb. 4-6).

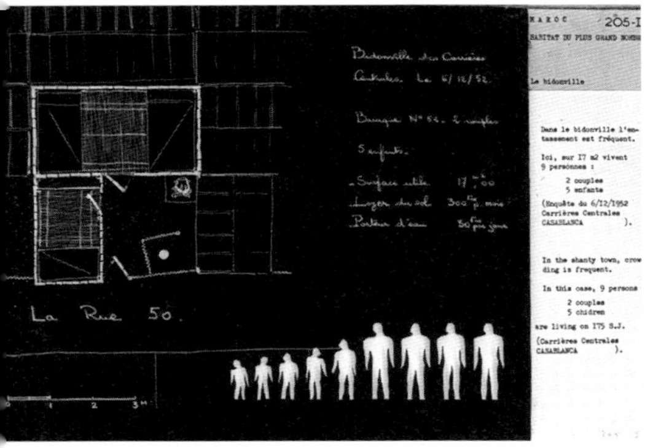

4 | GAMMA Grid-Tafeln: ‚Hütte' | GAMMA Grid panels: 'shack'

5 | ‚Kollektives Leben im Bidonville' | 'Collective life in the bidonville'

dwelling and building within the slum neighborhood, supplied with textual comments. Focusing alternatively on commercial, religious and dwelling activities, the bidonville is represented in this manner as a rich fabric of social practices (fig. 4-6).

This understanding of the built environment through the lens of social practice, through an idea of collectively held signifying practices, is the essence of the epistemological transition that Team 10 caused within CIAM. It would strongly influence Candilis-Josic-Woods' general attitude towards the built environment. Throughout its existence, the partnership approached architectural and urban projects through social practices and more particularly through their spatial characteristics and thus through spatial practices. Shadrach Woods phrased this attitude retrospectively as follows: "We are at the point now of realizing that the city is not simply a tool and manifestation of capitalism, but also an environment, an ecological entity. ... The citizen begins to appropriate to himself the space of the city, and to realize that he and his activities and aspirations form the built environment."[12]

Already in the panels of the 1953 UR Grid by Alison and Peter Smithson and the GAMMA Grid by Candilis and Woods, it becomes apparent that the epistemological switch to the everyday was understood, by the future Team 10 members, as a re-situating of architectural meaning in the cultural reality of everyday spatial practices. Both Grids suggest not only a way of thinking about urbanism and architecture that stays closer to the grain of everyday experience than had been customary within CIAM, they also bypass the categories and rubrics under which architectural and urban culture were to be found until then and through which man organizes his relations with nature and with others.
Within the work of Candilis-Josic-Woods, spatial practices are likewise thought to be products of a conjuncture. The practices of dwelling and building were not considered autonomous expressions, but rather specific instances of a larger system of cultural and societal dispositions. As Georges Candilis explained, spatial practice "can't be taken to be an isolated act, any more than the design of an object, the building of a house, the

6 | ‚Religiöse Praktiken' | 'Religious practices'

7 | ‚Vgl. Atlasgebirge - Casablanca' | 'Atlas Mountains - Casablanca comparison'

Dieses Verständnis gebauter Umgebung durch den Blickwinkel sozialer Praxis und durch eine Vorstellung kollektiver Bedeutungssysteme ist die Essenz jenes epistemologischen Übergangs, welchen Team 10 innerhalb des CIAM anstieß. Es sollte Candilis-Josic-Woods' allgemeine Haltung gegenüber der gebauten Umwelt stark beeinflussen. Im Verlauf ihrer Existenz näherte sich diese Partnerschaft architektonischen und städtebaulichen Projekten mittels sozialer Praktiken und, spezifischer, deren räumlicher Charakteristika und somit räumlicher Praktiken. Shadrach Woods beschrieb diese Haltung wie folgt: „Wir sind an einem Punkt angelangt, an dem wir realisieren, dass die Stadt nicht bloß Werkzeug und Manifestation des Kapitalismus ist, sondern auch eine Umgebung, eine ökologische Einheit. [...] Der Bürger beginnt, sich dem Raum der Stadt zugehörig zu fühlen und zu realisieren, dass er und seine Aktivitäten und Sehnsüchte die gebaute Umgebung formen."[12]

Bereits in den Präsentationstafeln des UR-Grids von Alison und Peter Smithson von 1957 als auch in dem GAMMA-Grid von Candilis und Woods, wird deutlich dass der epistemologische Wechsel hin zum Alltäglichen von den zukünftigen Team-10-Mitgliedern als eine neue Verortung architektonischer Bedeutung innerhalb alltäglicher räumlicher Praktiken verstanden wurde. Beide Grids schlagen nicht nur ein Art der Auseinandersetzung mit Urbanismus und Architektur vor, welche näher am Maßstab alltäglicher Wahrnehmung bleibt, als es bis dahin innerhalb des CIAM üblich war, sondern umgehen hierbei Kategorien und Rubriken, unter welchen architektonische und urbane Kultur bis dahin zu finden waren, und durch welche der Mensch sein Verhältnis zur Natur und zu anderen einordnete.

Innerhalb der Arbeit von Candilis-Josic-Woods werden räumliche Praktiken auf ähnliche Art und Weise als Produkte des Zusammentreffens gedacht. Die Praktiken des Wohnens und Bauens wurden nicht nur als autonome Ausdrucksweisen betrachtet, sondern als spezifische Instanzen innerhalb eines größeren Systems kultureller und sozialer Anordnungen. Wie George Candilis erläutert, kann räumliches Handeln „nicht weniger als isolierte Handlung betrachtet werden, als die Gestaltung eines Objekts, das Bauen eines Hauses, die Untersuchung einer Nachbarschaft oder die Planung einer Stadt. Ihr Tätigkeitsfeld

study of a neighborhood or the planning of a city can be. Its field of action merges with the life of the collective."[13] Candilis considered spatial practices as part of a system of collectively-held cultural dispositions, incorporated by the individual through education and experience. In the GAMMA Grid this particular understanding is operative. Images and texts suggest that the spatial practices that were proper to the everyday life of the villages in the Atlas Mountains reappear in the completely dissimilar environment of the bidonville of Casablanca (fig. 7). Moreover, the GAMMA architects held that since the spatial practices of dwelling and building had a certain perenniality, it was possible to transpose them to new environments. The literal transport of nouallas (traditional houses) to the urban grids of the Service de l'Urbanisme is probably the best example of this.

However, spatial practices were not considered static. As culture changes, the cultural dispositions change and thus practices are in evolution. It is from this perspective that the multiple references to change, growth and mobility within the work of Candilis, Josic and Woods should be understood. These are not abstract theoretical concepts, but rather consequent results of situating the essence of architecture within the cultural practices of dwelling and building. As Candilis remarked, these are attempts to think of the architecture of the dwelling environment as "integrated into the social and collective milieu, whose mobility and growth are in permanent flux. The outside social milieu constantly influences people's housing. The collective reality penetrates, transforms, changes and characterises family space."[14]

Moreover, Candilis held that the relation between the wider system of cultural dispositions and specific practices is janus-faced. Practices are determined by a larger cultural framework, which – in its turn – is the result of social practices. It is in this field of tension that the partnership situated its understanding of the practices of dwelling and building and thus of the built environment. As Georges Candilis underlined, this demanded "a new attitude. And that this attitude in the architectural domain not only showed itself through forms, but above all through content, which is to say in the manifestation of the interior life of a human community."[15] The CIAM Grid was the tool 'par excellence' to obtain such a new attitude: it introduced into the CIAM debates the perspective that the built environment is not simply a physical support, but simultaneously the frame, the substance and the result of spatial processes and practices.

vermischt sich mit dem kollektiven Leben."[13] Candilis betrachtete räumliche Praxis als Teil einer kollektiven Anordnung, welche vom Individuum durch Bildung und Erfahrung einverleibt ist. Im GAMMA-Grid ist diese Betrachtung handlungsweisend. Bilder und Texte suggerieren, dass die räumlichen Praktiken, welche zum alltäglichen Leben in den Dörfern des Atlasgebirges passten, ebenso in den gänzlich unterschiedlichen Umgebungen der Bidonvilles Casablancas wiederzufinden waren (Abb. 7). Darüber hinaus gingen die GAMMA-Architekten davon aus, dass diese Kontinuität der Praktiken des Wohnen und Bauens eine Anwendung auf weitere Kontexte ermöglichte. Die Übertragung der Nouallas (traditioneller Haustypus) auf das urbane Raster des Service de l'Urbanisme ist vermutlich das beste Beispiel hierfür.

Nichtsdestotrotz wurden räumliche Praktiken nicht als statisch gesehen. Verändert sich Kultur, so verändern sich kulturelle Dispositionen, wodurch sich letztlich Praktiken selbst in konstanter Evolution befinden. Aus dieser Perspektive sollten unterschiedliche Referenzen bezüglich Veränderung, Wachstum und Mobilität innerhalb der Arbeit Candilis-Josic-Woods' verstanden werden. Diese sind keine abstrakten theoretischen Konzepte, sondern schlüssige Ergebnisse der Verortung von Architektur innerhalb kultureller Praktiken des Wohnens und Bauens. Wie Candilis bemerkte, sind dies Versuche, Architektur des Wohnens „integriert in das soziale und gemeinschaftliche Milieu, dessen Mobilität und Wachstum in permanenter Veränderung sind", zu beleuchten. „Das umgebende soziale Milieu beeinflusst ständig das Wohnen der Menschen. Die gemeinschaftliche Realität durchstößt, transformiert, verändert und charakterisiert den familiären Raum."[14]

Ferner sah Candilis die Relation zwischen einem breitgefächerten System kultureller Voraussetzungen und spezifischen Praktiken zweischneidig. Praktiken sind von einem größeren kulturellen Kontext determiniert, welcher umgekehrt das Ergebnis sozialer Praktiken ist. Es ist dieses Spannungsfeld, in welchem die Zusammenarbeit von Candilis, Josics und Woods ihr Verständnis einer Praxis des Wohnens und Bauens und damit der gebauten Umgebung verortet. Wie Georges Candilis betonte, bedurfte dieses einer „neuen Haltung. Und dass diese Haltung im architektonischen Feld sich nicht nur durch Formen, sondern vor allem durch Inhalt zeigte, das heißt in der Manifestation des internen Lebens einer menschlichen Gesellschaft."[15] Das CIAM-Grid war ein Werkzeug par excellence, um sich diese neue Haltung anzueignen: Es eröffnete innerhalb der Diskussionen des CIAM eine Perspektive, welche die gebaute Umgebung nicht ausschließlich zum physischen Tragwerk, sondern gleichermaßen zur Rahmung, zur Substanz und zum Ergebnis räumlicher Prozesse und Praktiken machte.

1 Le Corbusier, Description of the C.I.A.M. Grid, Bergamo 1949, in: Jacqueline Tyrwhitt/Jose-Luis Sert/Nathan Ernesto Rogers, The heart of the city, London: Humphries 1979, 171-176 **2** C.I.A.M., Grille C.I.A.M. d'urbanisme. Mise en application de la Charte d'Athènes', Boulogne: Editions L'Architecture d'Aujourd'hui 1948 **3** Le Corbusier, 'Description of the C.I.A.M. Grid, Bergamo 1949', in: Jacqueline Tyrwhitt/Jose-Luis Sert/Nathan Ernesto Rogers, The heart of the City, London: Humphries 1979, 174 **4** CIAM, Declaration of La Sarraz in: Eric Mumford, The C.I.A.M. Discourse on urbanism, Cambridge (Mass.): MIT Press 2002, 25 **5** Paul Emery, Les C.I.A.M. et la Charte d'Athènes, in: l'Architecture d'Aujourd'hui 43 (1971) 29 **6** Für eine Einführung zu beiden Grids siehe | For an introduction to both Grids see: Eric Mumford, The C.I.A.M. Discourse on Urbanism, Cambridge (Mass.): MIT Press 2002 **7** Alison Smithson, Team 10 Meetings, New York: Rizzoli 1991, 19 **8** Nigel Henderson, Autobiographical sketch, in: Nigel Henderson, Photographs of Bethnal Green, Nottingham: Midland Group 1978, 3-5 **9** Für eine Einführung zur Englischen Bewegung der ‚Mass-Observation' | For an introduction to the English mass-observation movement s. Dorothy Sheridan/ Brian Street/ David Bloome, Writing ourselves: Mass-Observation and literacy practice, Cresskill: Hampton Press 2000 **10** Zu dieser spezifischen Betrachtungsweise ländlicher Gebiete | For this specific approach to rural areas s. Etienne Mauret, Problèmes de l'équipement rural dans l'aménagement du territoire, in: L'Architecture d'Aujourd'hui 60 (1955) 42-45 **11** Shadrach Woods, Aesthetics and technology of preassembly, in: Progressive Architecture, (October 1964) 180 **12** Shadrach Woods, The man in the street. A polemic on urbanism, Harmondworth: Penguin Books 1975, 103 **13** Candilis, Georges, Un habitat pour l'homme d'aujourd'hui, nicht-publizierter Text in | unpublished text in: Les Archives d'Architecture du XXe siècle/Candilis, 5 **14** Ibid., 4 **15** Candilis, Bâtir la Vie, Paris: Stock 1977, 164

AFTERWARDSNESS AS DESIGN PROCESS

Giorgia Aquilar

"The past is preserved as the destruction of the past," claimed Horkheimer and Adorno in 'Dialectic of Enlightenment'.[1] Transposed to the design realm, this chiastic encounter constantly shapes the theories and practices of architectural interventions on pre-existing artifacts. Struggles between preservation and destruction trigger interrelated processes, where efforts to protect an alleged 'identity' clash with competing forms of 'alterity'. In the polarized space between the elements of this dyad, the notion of 'afterwardsness' emerges as a potential strategy for rethinking and engaging the binary relation between research and design as an open, on-going, and interconnected set of processes of translation, de-translation, re-translation.

ON ‹NACHTRÄGLICHKEIT› Drawn from the psychoanalytic field, the concept of 'Nachträglichkeit' was introduced by Sigmund Freud in the 1890s to describe the biphasic development and latency that shape the re-transcription of trauma through the retroactive attribution of new meaning.[2] In explicating this neologism, Freud speaks of a present in which traumatic events of the past gain alternative interpretations, at once transforming the original meaning and unfolding new effects in the future.[3]

NACHTRÄGLICHKEIT ALS GESTALTUNGSPROZESS

Giorgia Aquilar

„Heute aber setzt die Vergangenheit sich fort als Zerstörung der Vergangenheit." behaupten Horkheimer und Adorno in der ‚Dialektik der Aufklärung'.[1] Übertragen in das Feld der Gestaltung kann dieser chiastische Ansatz die Theorien und Praktiken architektonischer Eingriffe in bestehende Artefakte prägen. Kämpfe um Erhaltung und Zerstörung erzeugen dort in Wechselwirkung stehende Prozesse, wo Bemühungen des Bewahrens vermeintlicher ‚Identität' in Konflikt geraten mit dem Drang, bestimmte Formen der ‚Andersartigkeit' zu schaffen. Im polarisierten Raum zwischen den Elementen dieser Dualität erscheint die Idee der ‚Nachträglichkeit' als potentielle Strategie zur Gestaltung von Nachbildern verlorener oder bedrohter urbaner Bereiche; als ein binäres Verhältnis zwischen Forschung und Gestaltung und als eine offene, fortwährende und in Wechselwirkung stehende Reihe von Prozessen der Übertragung, Verfremdung und Rückübertragung.

N A C H T R Ä G L I C H K E I T   Entnommen aus der Psychoanalyse wurde der deutsche Begriff der ‚Nachträglichkeit' von Sigmund Freud in den 1890er Jahren eingeführt, um die zweiphasige Entwicklung und Verzögerung der Umarbeitung von Traumata durch ein retroaktives Zuschreiben neuen Sinns zu bezeichnen.[2] In der Erklärung des Neologismus spricht Freud von einer Gegenwart, in welcher traumatische Geschehnisse der Vergangenheit mit der Zeit alternative Interpretationen ausbilden, die gleichzeitig die ursprüngliche Bedeutung verändern und neue Auswirkungen auf die Zukunft erzeugen.[3]

1 | Psychiatrisches Krankenhaus Steinhof, Wien | Steinhof Psychiatric Hospital, Vienna, Erwin Pendl 1907

Translated into French as 'après-coup', the complexity of 'Nachträglichkeit' cannot be fully rendered in English.[4] Among the different possible versions – from 'deferred' or 'delayed' action, to 'retroactivity' and 'belatedness' – maybe the neologism 'afterwardsness', chosen by Jean Laplanche, is the one which best expresses the paradoxical coexistence and simultaneity of opposite movements, transferrable to the dimension of architecture.[5] Incorporating the ambiguity of the two directions of temporality, the afterwardsness approach allows comparison of the two stages of trauma to the role of research and design in intervening in already modified urban artifacts and tissues: something is deposited in the architectural space, which is only activated later on, and the transformations which thereby occur only take on meaning through research that takes place retrospectively, and steer the design intervention to 'afterwards'. At the intersection of research strategy and design process, it may suggest a translation and transmission of the inherited built legacy which also admits removals, erasures, and subtractions, opening up new configurations in the second lives of urban objects and tissues.

SPECTERS OF MODERNITY In Freud's Vienna, the overlapping strata of time and space which constitute the former psychiatric asylum 'Am Steinhof', today the Otto-Wagner-Spital, may serve as a paradigmatic example of the complex and contradictory processes that determine the dynamics of afterwardsness (fig. 1). Overlooking the urban landscape of Vienna from the hill described by Massimo Cacciari as the place of encounter between obscure forces, the Steinhof embodies the challenges and potentialities of design as a second-stage return.[6] To follow the psychoanalytic discourse, it is 'second' in the sense of happening 'afterwards'.

Completed in 1907 – with its 60 pavilions built on a terraced slope along the edge of the Viennese woods, symmetrically composed around a central axis and tending towards the gold leaf cupola of Wagner's church of Saint Leopold as the focal point of the entire composition – the Steinhof's overall plan comprised an integrated whole, a 'white city' whose utopian ambitions envisioned a modern world[7] (fig. 2). Encountering these

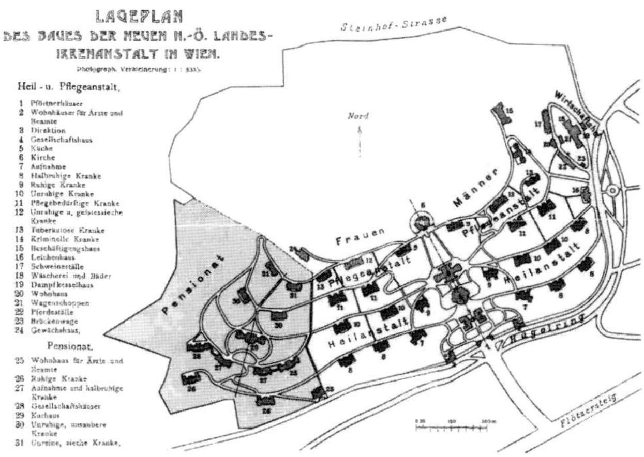

2 | Wagners Steinhof: Plan des Landesbauamts | Wagner's Steinhof: plan by the Landesbauamt

Im Französischen in ‚aprés-coup' übersetzt, kann die Komplexität des Begriffes nicht vollständig in das Englische übertragen werden.[4] Unter den verschiedenen Möglichkeiten – von ‚deferred' oder ‚delayed action' bis zu ‚retroactivity' und ‚belatedness' – ist der Neologismus ‚afterwardsness', gewählt von Jean Laplanche, derjenige, welcher die paradoxe Koexistenz und Gleichzeitigkeit gegenläufiger Bewegungen am besten zu beschreiben vermag und hierin übertragbar in die Dimensionen der Architektur scheint.[5] Wenn man die beiden zeitlichen Richtungen vereint, erlaubt ein Ansatz der Nachträglichkeit einen Vergleich der beiden Stufen des Traumas mit der Rolle von Forschung und Gestaltung beim Eingreifen in bereits veränderte Artefakte und Gewebe: Im architektonischen Raum ist etwas hinterlegt, das erst später aktiviert wird. Die Transformationen, welche dabei entstehen sollen, erhalten ihre Bedeutung erst durch eine retrospektive Forschung und steuern die gestalterischen Eingriffe ‚nachträglich'. An der Schnittstelle von Forschungsstrategie und Gestaltungsprozess ermöglicht der Begriff der Nachträglichkeit eine Übersetzung und Übertragung des ererbten baulichen Vermächtnisses, welches auch Entnahmen, Löschungen sowie Subtraktionen anerkennt und damit neue Konfigurationen im zweiten Leben von städtischen Objekten und Geweben eröffnet.

PHANTOME DER MODERNE Im Wien Freuds können die überlappenden Zeit- und Raumschichten der ehemaligen psychiatrische Anstalt ‚Am Steinhof', heute das Otto-Wagner-Spital, als paradigmatisches Beispiel für eine Erforschung der komplexen und widersprüchlichen Prozesse dienen, welche die Dynamik von Nachträglichkeit formen (Abb. 1). Die urbane Landschaft vom Hügel aus überblickend, den Massimo Cacciari als Zusammenkunft obskurer Kräfte beschrieb, verkörpert der Steinhof die Herausforderungen und Potentiale der Gestaltung einer zweiten Phase der Nutzung.[6] ‚Zweiten' ist hierbei gleichbedeutend mit ‚nachträglich' im psychoanalytischen Diskurs.

1907 fertiggestellt – samt seiner 60 Pavillons auf einem terrassierten Hang am Rande des Wienerwalds, symmetrisch um eine zentrale Achse angeordnet und sich zur goldenen Kuppel Wagners Kirche zum Heiligen Leopold als zentralen Punkt der Gesamtkomposition

buildings, the traces of trauma related to the original function of the hospital for mentally ill, and to the use of its structures under Nazi occupation, coexist and interweave with Wagner's vision of an ideal community (fig. 3).

Originally the largest institution of its kind in Europe, and today still functioning as Vienna's primary public psychiatric institution, the Steinhof is poised at the edge of a further 'après coup'. The forecasted establishment of a new branch of the Central European University on its grounds, the conversions of heritage-protected pavilions into housing and the addition of new residential units have triggered heated debates, spreading from citizens' initiatives to the international scene.[8] In the authorized heritage discourse, failed attempts to nominate the Otto-Wagner-Hospital for inclusion on the UNESCO World Heritage list have been followed by the publication of a 'Heritage Alert' by ICOMOS.[9] Despite the reduction of the originally planned new building units, the International Council on Monuments and Sites deems the new plans still out of keeping with the multifaceted significance of the site, calling for the complex to be maintained intact in its entirety, and asserting that "the new structures, that have regrettably already been built, serve as a reminder of a misguided concept and unsuccessful policy".[10]

Currently at center stage in controversial transformation projects and preservation battles – waged through petitions and architectural design competitions – the former asylum's second stage is still undetermined. Facing an undefined destiny, its "finite form", as Manfredo Tafuri puts it, may rediscover a forgotten essence as "the instrument, a material, a linguistic tool that could be manipulated".[11] To paraphrase Cacciari's 'Posthumous People' – those who haunt the landscape dominated by Wagner's church – what emerges is a posthumous architecture: not only a spectre of modernity, an afterimage of lost times and anticipation of worlds to come, but the very substance of afterwardsness, a persistence of the traumas undergone and relived within its walls in their re-emergence in the present, which serves both to repress and reinscribe originary events through the very act of erasure.[12] In this way, any repurposing of the site that fails to account adequately for afterwardsness both disavows the past and reaffirms it in its repression.

A PROCESS IN ‹ANA-› In a note to one of his 'Essays on Otherness', Laplanche writes: "For in between the primary intervention of the other and the creation of the other thing in me, there occurs a process called repression – an extremely complex process comprising at least two stages in mutual interaction, and leading to a veritable dislocation/reconfiguration of (explicit and implicit-enigmatic) experiential elements".[13] Without digging into the substance of this quotation, we may note the double movement of dislocation/reconfiguration here with regard to the role of prefixes in defining, dissolving and redefining architectural strategies.

ausrichtend – zielt die grundliegende Planung des Steinhofs auf die Erschaffung eines integrierten Ganzen ab, einer ‚weißen Stadt', deren utopische Ambitionen eine moderne Welt verkörpern sollten (Abb. 2).[7] In der Begegnung mit diesen Gebäuden koexistieren und – paradoxerweise – verflechten sich Wagners Absichten einer idealen Gemeinschaft mit den Spuren der Traumata sowohl bezüglich seiner ursprünglichen Funktion als Spital für Geisteskrankheiten als auch seiner Nutzung der Gebäude zur Zeit der Besatzung durch die Nationalsozialisten (Abb. 3).

Ursprünglich als größte Einrichtung ihrer Art Europas errichtet, und heute noch immer Wiens größte öffentliche Psychiatrie, ist der Steinhof gerade am Rande eines weiteren ‚après coups': In Folge der geplanten Gründung eines neuen Zweiges der Central European University haben die Umwandlung denkmalgeschützter Pavillons in Wohnhäuser und die Addition neuer Wohneinheiten auf dem Gelände heftige Debatten ausgelöst, die von Bürgerinitiativen auch auf die internationale Szene ausgeweitet wurden.[8] Auf den offiziellen Denkmalschutzdiskurs und die fehlgeschlagenen Versuche, das Otto-Wagner-Spital für eine Aufnahme in die Liste des UNESCO-Weltkulturerbes zu nominieren, folgte schließlich die Publikation eines ‚Heritage Alerts' von ICOMOS.[9] Trotz der Reduzierung der ursprünglich geplanten neuen Wohneinheiten sieht der International Council on Monuments and Sites die neue Planungsgrundlage noch immer im Widerspruch zur signifikanten Bedeutung des Gebiets und fordert, den Komplex in seiner Gesamtheit zu erhalten und „die neuen Strukturen, die bedauerlicherweise bereits gebaut wurden, als Mahnung an ein fehlgeleitetes Konzept und eine erfolglose Strategie zu belassen".[10]

Nun im Mittelpunkt kontroverser Transformationsprojekte und Konservierungskämpfe – geführt durch Petitionen und Architekturwettbewerbe – ist die zweite Nachnutzungsphase der ehemaligen Anstalt noch immer unbestimmt. Angesichts dieser ungewissen Zukunft kann seine „endliche Form" (Manfredo Tafuri zitierend), als eine vergessene Essenz und als ein „Instrument, ein Material, ein sprachliches Werkzeug, das manipuliert werden könnte", wiederentdeckt werden.[11] In Anlehnung an Massimo Cacciaris „posthume Menschen" – jene, die die von Wagners Kirche dominierte Landschaft heimsuchen – entsteht eine posthume Architektur: nicht nur ein Gespenst der Moderne, ein Nachbild der verlorenen Zeiten oder der Vorwegnahme kommender Welten, sondern als Substanz der Nachträglichkeit, ein Fortbestehen der Traumata, die in den Mauern in ihrer Wiederauferstehung in der Gegenwart erlitten und wiedererlebt werden könnten – und welche dazu beiträgt die ursprünglichen Ereignisse durch den Akt der Auslöschung sowohl zu verdrängen als auch neu einzuschreiben.[12] Auf diese Weise verleugnet jede Umnutzung des Ortes, die einer Nachträglichkeit keine Rechnung trägt, die Vergangenheit und bekräftigt ihre Unterdrückung.

The present condition of suspension of the Steinhof suggests design options that reappear in afterwardsness, and may allow us to anticipate what kind of (counter)artifacts may emerge from the dislocations and reconfigurations it triggers. If the negative side of the translation of the 'enigmatic message' – following Laplanche's interpretation of Freud – is the repression that produces dislocation, research into the architectural object may uncover the message and turn it into the seed of a reconfiguration. Otto Wagner claimed that for the Steinhof this process was inspired by both pragmatic realities and ideal essence, where the primacy of purpose ('Zweckmäßigkeit') encounters a truth-oriented architecture: truth of purpose and inner truth.[14] Today, as the shift in purpose may be read as a loss of 'Zweck', the inner truth of the Steinhof leads us back to its initial meaning as a document of co-authorship, the result of a plurality of forces and intentions.

This concerted process seems to mirror both the Italian texts of the 1980, which built upon Wagner's Steinhof: Cacciari's posthumous people having "too many alibis to be satisfied with simple truth", and Tafuri's "stasis-flux dialectic" that implies a "continual betrayal of form" in which "[t]ransformation and dissolution [...] are inseparable processes".[15] Intended not only in terms of the multiplicity of figures involved – both in the original design process and in the subsequent transformations via a design competition – this anti-authoritarian dimension also takes the form of a negotiation between meanings, a medium between different understandings (and misunderstandings), able to deal with a broad, changing and ambiguous body of knowledge, from asylum psychiatry to "self-consciously modern architecture".[16] To overcome the risk described by Tafuri in terms of a resistance to all analysis affecting "the work of the most recent commentators on 'posthumous' contaminations", a step forward might be suggested by Jean-François Lyotard.[17] In a 1985 issue of Casabella, referring to the Freudian principle of 'durcharbeiten' – 'perlaboration' or 'working through' – Lyotard suggests replacing 'post-' with 'ana-' and therefore reasoning in terms of anamnesis.[18] At the Otto-Wagner-Spital, reversing the temporal logic of the prefix 'post-' – which "threatens to leave behind the achievements of enlightenment" – means to move beyond the idea of a 'last' configuration.[19] A relic of doomed times, a dystopian simulacrum which has outlived the use it was originally conceived for, along with a multiplicity of misuses, the Steinhof may thus recall its "initial forgetting", and turn repetition into a radical anamnesis, a process of eternal losses and eternal returns.[20]

SUBTRACTION AS ‹CREATIVE INCREMENT›? Such an anamnesis, in terms of its implications for architectural design, requires not only the excavation of archival evidence, and the recollection of trauma, but of those acts of destruction inscribed in the attempt to impose a determinant meaning on the trauma as it plays out

PROZESS IN ‹ANA-› In einer Anmerkung in seinem Aufsatz ‚Essays on Otherness' schreibt Laplanche: „Denn zwischen der primären Intervention des Anderen und der Erschaffung des Anderen in mir findet ein Prozess statt, der Repression genannt wird – ein äußerst komplexer Prozess, der mindestens zwei Stufen gegenseitiger Interaktion umfasst und zu einer wahrhaftigen Dislokation/Rekonfiguration von (expliziten und implizit-enigmatischen) Erfahrungselementen führt".[13] Ohne dabei vollends in den Inhalt dieses Zitates einzusteigen, könnte es interessant sein, hier die Doppelbewegung der Dislokation/Rekonfiguration in Hinblick auf die Rolle der Präfixe im Bestimmen, Auflösen und Neudefinieren architektonischer Strategien hervorzuheben.

Der gegenwärtige Zustand der Stilllegung des Umnutzungsprozesses am Steinhof führt zu gestalterischen Möglichkeiten, die in einer Nachträglichkeit auftauchen und die uns antizipieren lassen, welche (Gegen-)Artefakte aus den Dislokationen und Rekonfigurationen, welche sie auslöst, entstehen könnten. Sofern die negative Seite der Übersetzung dieser ‚enigmatischen Nachricht' – Laplanches Interepretation Freuds folgend – die Unterdrückung ist, die diese Dislokation verursacht, kann durch eine Untersuchung des architektonischen Objekts diese Botschaft freigelegt werden und zum Keim einer Rekonfiguration werden. Otto Wagner behauptete, der Entstehungsprozess des Steinhofs sei von sowohl einer pragmatischen Realität als auch einer idealen Essenz inspiriert gewesen, in welchen das Primat des Nutzens (Zweckmäßigkeit) auf die Intention einer wahrheitsorientierten Architektur treffe; eine Wahrhaftigkeit des Zwecks und einer inneren Wahrheit.[14] Heute, während die sich verändernde Funktion als ein Verlust des ‚Zwecks' betrachtet werden kann, verweist die innere Wahrhaftigkeit des Steinhofs auf ihre ursprüngliche Bedeutung als Dokument einer Miturheberschaft, als Ergebnis pluraler Kräfte und Intentionen.

Dieser orchestrierte Prozess scheint sich in beiden italienischen Positionen, die auf Wagners Steinhof aufbauen, widerzuspiegeln: Cacciaris posthume Menschen, die „zu viele Alibis, um mit der einfachen Wahrheit zufrieden zu sein", hätten, und Tafuris „Stasis-Flux-Dialektik", die einen „kontinuierlichen Verrat der Form" impliziert, in welchem „[T]ransformation und Auflösung [...] untrennbare Prozesse sind".[15] Diese antiautoritäre Dimension ist nicht nur im Hinblick auf die Vielzahl der beteiligten Figuren gedacht – sowohl im ursprünglichen Gestaltungsprozess als auch in den nachfolgenden Transformationen, die in einigen Pavillons durch einen Gestaltungswettbewerb stattfanden –, sondern auch als Verhandlung zwischen Bedeutungen, als Medium zwischen verschiedenen Verständnissen (und Missverständnissen), die in der Lage ist, mit einem breiten, sich verändernden und mehrdeutigen Wissenskörper umzugehen, von der Anstaltspsychiatrie bis zur „selbstbewussten modernen Architektur"[16]. Um das von Tafuri beschriebene Risiko einer Resistenz gegen jegliche Analysen zu überwinden, welche „die Arbeit der jüngsten Kommentatoren zu ‚posthumen'

3-11 | Details zum heutigen Zustand des Steinhofs | Details of the Steinhof's current state, 2018

in the present. Subverting the binary opposition of erecting architecture and causing it to disappear, research can interrogate discrepancies between what seems to be demanded by the different processes involved to open up new territories where design may intervene.

One of the recurring dreams in the theories and practices of architecture is to spatialize the paradoxical interweaving between processes of identity creation and destruction. In some cases this intention is developed by explicitly expressing the subtractive dimension, such as in Diller and Scofidio's concretisation of synaptic laps in the re-enactment of 'The Memory Theater of Giulio Camillo', where the consequences of forgetting take the form of a suspension bridge made out of two discrete structural units that cantilever

Kontaminationen betreffen", könnte Jean-François Lyotards Denken einen weiteren Schritt nach vorn darstellen.[17] In einer Ausgabe von Casabella von 1985, die sich auf das Freudsche Prinzip des ‚Durcharbeitens' – oder auch ‚Perlaboration' – bezieht, schlägt Lyotard vor, ‚Post-' durch ‚Ana-' zu ersetzen und damit einen argumentativen Bezug zur Anamnese herzustellen.[18] Im Otto-Wagner-Spital bedeutet die Umkehrung der zeitlichen Logik des Präfixes ‚post-' – das „die Errungenschaften der Aufklärung hinter sich zu lassen droht" – über die Idee einer ‚letzten' Konfiguration hinauszugehen.[19] Als Relikt aus der Zeit des Untergangs, ein dystopisches Simulakrum, das den ursprünglich vorgesehenen Gebrauch und eine Vielzahl von Missbräuchen überlebt hat, kann der Steinhof so an sein „anfängliches Vergessen" erinnern und die Wiederholung in eine „radikale Anamnese" verwandeln, in einen Prozess ewigen Verlusts und ewiger Wiederkehr.[20]

SUBTRAKTION ALS ‹KREATIVES INKREMENT›? Eine solche Anamnese, in Bezug auf ihre Implikationen für die architektonische Gestaltung, erfordert nicht nur die Ausgrabung von Archivalien und die Erinnerung an Traumata, sondern auch jener Zerstörungshandlungen, die in dem Versuch eingeschrieben sind, dem Trauma, wie es sich in der Gegenwart abspielt, eine bestimmende Bedeutung aufzuerlegen. Indem die Forschung diese binäre Opposition der Erschaffung von Architektur unterläuft und sie verschwinden lässt, kann sie Diskrepanzen befragen zwischen dem, was von den verschiedenen beteiligten Prozessen verlangt wird, um neue Territorien der Gestaltung zu erschließen.

Einer der wiederkehrenden Träume in den Theorien und Praktiken der Architektur ist die Verräumlichung der paradoxen Verflechtung von Prozessen der Identitätsbildung und -zerstörung. In einigen Fällen wird diese Absicht dadurch entwickelt, dass die subtraktive Dimension explizit zum Ausdruck gebracht wird, wie in Dillers und Scofidios architektonischer Konkretisierung des Verfalls von Synapsen in der Reinszenierung des „The Memory Theatre of Giulio Camillo". In dieser nehmen die Folgen des Vergessens die Form einer Hängebrücke an, welche aus zwei einzelnen Struktureinheiten besteht, die einander entgegengesetzt sind, sich aber nie treffen.[21] In anderen Fällen können zerstörerische Ereignisse eine Umkehrung erfahren und in überbetonte Präsenzen übersetzt werden, wie es in Lebbeus Woods' Vergegenständlichung des Traumas geschieht. In diesem verwandeln sich die ‚Narben' des Krieges in veredelte Entitäten auf dem verwundeten städtischen Körper als Mittel zur Auslösung eines kreativen Heilungsprozesses.[22] So oder so, trotz des offensichtlich subtraktiven oder paradox additiven Charakters des Entwurfs, steht im Mittelpunkt der Interventionen der Architekten eine Abwesenheit: sei es die Abwesenheit eines Brückenteils, das damit den eigentlichen Zweck als Verbindungselement bedroht, oder die Abwesenheit von Materie eines bombardierten Gebäudes.

toward one another but never meet.[21] In other cases, the destructive events may undergo a subversion and be translated into hyper-accentuated presences, as happens in Lebbeus Woods' objectification of trauma, where the 'scars' of war turn into grafted entities onto the wounded urban body, as devices for triggering a creative healing process.[22] Either way, despite the evidently subtractive or paradoxically additive nature of the design act, what is at center stage in the architects' interventions is an absence: be it the absence of a bridge portion that thus threatens its very purpose as a connecting element, or the absence of matter on a bombed building.

It is worth recalling here Alfred North Whitehead's 'Process and Reality' and his notion of 'creative increment' – as the "novel entity diverse from any entity in the 'many' which it unifies".[23] The idea of 'advance' may be further challenged through Derrida's supplement: the substitution that comes about might also imply the replacing of a presence with an absence. In design terms, this creative (retro)action may also involve what Keller Easterling calls "the other half of a space-making repertoire": the paradoxical form of a subtraction that "offers a redoubled territory for design".[24]

AFTERIMAGE In this redoubled territory, dug out through a research process that resembles archeological excavations – following Freud's notorious comparison between the work of the analyst and the archeologist – design takes the form of a 'Nachbild', or 'afterimage'.[25] Composed of the same prefix 'nach-' as 'Nachträglichkeit', the idea of a 'Nachbild' of the Steinhof arises from the possibilities of subtraction: accepting some unavoidable and perhaps necessary amnesias and at the same time retaining the 'after-effects' of what went before, the notion of afterimage contains the ambiguity and instability of the image in which retrogressive and progressive action coexist, blur, and give light to a third entity in the superimposition. By working at the intersection of physical space and psychic time, a subversion of the common understanding of destruction thus turns into a means to redemption, and a device for design and research to generate 'critical spatial practices' – and perhaps critical design processes – able to intervene in currently suspended urban and architectural spaces.[26] In this way, perhaps the debates over the future of the Steinhof would be able to take account of its past by understanding it as present trauma, where the notion of afterwardsness may appear as a possible solution to the 'impasse' determined by the complex temporalities at stake: at once avoiding an appeal to the idea of an authentic origin that cannot be betrayed and to a retrospective projection that would turn into an endless re-enactment of the past.

An dieser Stelle lohnt sich ein Blick in Alfred North Whiteheads ‚Prozess und Realität' und seinen Begriff des ‚kreativen Zuwachses' – als das „neue Wesen, das sich von jedem Wesen in den ‚vielen', die es vereinigt, unterscheidet".[23] Als Herausforderung für eine durch Derrida herausgeforderte Idee des ‚Fortschritts' könnte die Substitution, die dabei zustande kommt, auch das Ersetzen einer Präsenz durch Abwesenheit bedeuten. Diese kreative (Retro-)Aktion erinnert in den Begrifflichkeiten der Gestaltung an das, was Keller Easterling „die andere Hälfte eines raumbildenden Repertoires" nennt: die paradoxe Form von Subtraktion, welche einen „verdoppelten Bereich der Gestaltung aufzeigt".[24]

N A C H B I L D In diesen verdoppelten Bereich, der durch einen Forschungsprozess freigelegt wurde, der archäologischen Ausgrabungen ähnelt – nach Freuds berüchtigtem Vergleich zwischen der Arbeit des Analytikers und des Archäologen –, wird das Design in Form eines ‚Nachbildes'[25] entworfen. Zusammengesetzt aus dem gleichen Präfix ‚nach-' wie Nachträglichkeit, ergibt sich die Idee eines ‚Nachbildes' des Steinhofes aus den Möglichkeiten der Subtraktion. Um einige unvermeidliche und vielleicht notwendige Amnesien zu akzeptieren und gleichzeitig die ‚Nachwirkungen' dessen, was vorher war, beizubehalten, enthält der Begriff des Nachbildes die Zweideutigkeit und Instabilität eines Bildes, in dem retrogressive und progressive Aktionen koexistieren, verschwimmen und eine dritte Art der Überlagerung erhellen. Indem sie an der Schnittstelle von physischem Raum und psychischer Zeit arbeitet, wird die Subversion eines gemeinsamen Verständnisses von Zerstörung zu einem Mittel der Erlösung und zu einem Werkzeug für Gestaltung und Forschung. Sie wird dies, um „kritische räumliche Praktiken" – und vielleicht kritischen Gestaltungsprozess – zu erzeugen, die in der Lage sind, in gegenwärtig außer Kraft gesetzte städtische und architektonische Räume einzugreifen.[26]

Auf diese Art und Weise könnten die Debatten über die Zukunft des Steinhofs dessen Vergangenheit als gegenwärtiges Trauma einbeziehen, sodass die Idee der Nachträglichkeit als ein möglicher Ausweg aus den Sackgassen komplexer, auf dem Spiel stehender Zeitlichkeiten gesehen werden kann: Solche Sackgassen führen zum Vermeiden eines Appells an die Idee eines authentischen Ursprungs, der nicht geleugnet werden kann, und einer retrospektiven Projektion, die sich in eine endlose Wiederholung der Vergangenheit verwandeln würde. Das Erforschen dieser verdeckten Historie, welche sich auf dem Gelände der ehemaligen Anstalt entfaltet, verweist auf das Vorhandensein einer Alternative zum Entweder-oder des Erlösenden und Unerlösten: Auf diese Weise kann ein neuer Anfang seine eigene Vorgeschichte überlappender Schichten von Bedeutung und Materie freilegen, allerdings nur dort, wo seine eigene räumliche Geschichte, seine Bedeutung und sein Material zerfallen.

R E S E A R C H   A N D   D E S I G N   The research into the covert history that unfolds on the grounds of the former asylum may suggest the existence of an alternative to the either/or binarism of the redemptive and the unredeemed: in this way, the new beginning may reveal its own prehistory of overlapped strata of meanings and matter, yet only at the point where its spatial history, meanings and matter fall apart. This would open a space for discussion of the dialectical relationship between 'research' – here meant as the activity of rediscovering pasts in present conditions – and 'design', understood in this context as the re-invention of a present through the reappraisal of the past, in line with Tafuri's final suggestion: "But one would be halting at 'the threshold' if, after listening attentively to the reverberations created by the Wagnerian abbreviations inside the forest, one were to refrain from preparing to cross the theatre by multiplying the pathways through it".[27] It is therefore precisely the tension between identity and alterity, memory and amnesia, the originary and originality, which offers the potential for reasoning in terms of processes of afterwardsness: at once an archiving process to be manipulated by research and a device for undoing, able to broaden the design protocol. In this way the process that might take place is meant in the etymological sense of 'processus', as the act of proceeding and having been advanced, taking the Latin root 'cedere' as 'letting something fall', and thus carrying the inherited built legacy towards new afterlives.

FORSCHEN UND GESTALTEN Dies könnte eine Diskussion eröffnen über die dialektische Beziehung zwischen dem ‚Forschen' – als der Grabungstätigkeit, die auf die Wiederentdeckung der Vergangenheit in der Gegenwart abzielt –, und dem ‚Gestalten' als der Neuerfindung einer Gegenwart durch die Manipulation der Vergangenheit. Dies spiegelt Tafuris abschließende Anregung wieder: „Aber man würde an der Schwelle stehen bleiben, wenn man, nachdem man den Nachhall der wagnerianischen Abkürzungen im Wald aufmerksam gehört hat, sich nicht darauf vorbereiten würde, das Theater zu überqueren, indem man die Wege durch den Wald vervielfacht."[27] Es ist also gerade die Spannung zwischen Identität und Alterität, Erinnerung und Amnesie, dem Ursprung und der Originalität, die das Potential zur Argumentation im Sinne einer Nachträglichkeit bietet. Es wäre gleichzeitig ein durch Forschung zu manipulierender Archivierungsprozess und ein Werkzeug des Rückgängigmachens, welches das Vorgehen im Gestalten und Entwerfen erweitern kann. Auf diese Weise ist der Prozess, der stattfinden kann, im etymologischen Sinne von ‚processus' gemeint; als der Akt des Fortschreitens und des Fortgeschrittenseins, der die lateinische Wurzel ‚cedere' im Sinne von ‚etwas aufgeben' in sich trägt und damit das gebaute Erbe zu neuem Nachleben trägt.

1 Max Horkheimer/Theodor W. Adorno, Dialectic of Enlightenment, London: Verso 1979, xv [Original: Dialektik der Aufklärung, hectographed manuscript 1944] **2** Das Deutsche Nomen Nachträglichkeit setzt sich aus dem Präfix ‚nach-' (auf ein späteres Handeln, Wiederholen oder Streben hinweisend und hierbei ähnlich dem englischen ‚after'), dem Verb ‚tragen' (welches vielseitig übersetzt, aber in erster Linie mit dem englischen ‚to carry' verglichen werden kann) sowie dem substantivierenden Suffix ‚-keit' (eine abstrakte Qualität des zugrundeliegenden Adjektivs bezeichnend, analog zum Englischen ‚-ness') zusammen | The German noun Nachträglichkeit is composed of the prefix 'nach-' (indicating a later action, a repetition, or a pursuit, and here comparable to the English 'after'), the verb 'tragen' (whose primary translation, in a multiplicity of transitive and intransitive meanings, is 'to carry') and the substantivizing suffix '-keit' (denoting an abstract quality of the adjectival root, analogously to the English '-ness'). **3** Freud beschreibt das Konzept der Nachträglichkeit ausführlich in seiner Studie über den ‚Wolfsmann' aus dem Jahr 1918. | Freud describes in detail the concept of Nachträglichkeit in his 1918 study of the 'Wolfman'. Vgl. | Cf. Sigmund Freud, Case histories II, London: Penguin 1991, 276-277; Unter den zahlreichen Texten, die sich mit dem freudschen Begriff befassen | Among the many texts interpreting the Freudian notion s. André Green, Time in psychoanalysis. Some contradictory aspects, London: Free Association Books 2001; Arnold Modell, Other times, other realities. Toward a theory of psychoanalytic treatment, Cambridge/London: Harvard University Press 1990; Alessandra Campo, Tardività. Freud dopo Lacan, Milan: Mimesis 2018 **4** Lacan greift dieses Konzept in seinem ‚Report of Rome' aus dem Jahr 1953 auf. Vgl. | Lacan retrieves this concept in his 'Report from Rome' of 1953. Cf. Jacques Lacan, Function and gield in speech and language, in: Bruce Firk (ed.), Écrits. Jacques Lacan, New York: Norton 2007, 197-268 **5** Vgl. | Cf. Jean Laplanche, Notes on Afterwardsness [1992], in: Essays on Otherness, New York/London: Routledge 1998, 260-65; Zu einer Übetragung der Idee der Nachträglichkeit in das Feld der Architektur | For the transposition of the notion of afterwardsness in the realm of architecture s. Jane Rendell, The architecture of psychoanalysis: Spaces of transition, London: IB Tauris 2017 **6** Massimo Cacciari, Posthumous people: Vienna at the turning point, Stanford: Stanford University Press 1996 [Original: Dallo Steinhof. Prospettive viennesi del primo Novecento, Milan: Adelphi 1980] **7** Vgl. | Cf. Ludwig Hevesi, Otto Wagners moderne Kirche, in: Altkunst-Neukunst, Wien 1894-1908, Vienna: Konegen 1909, und | and Peter Haiko/Harald Leupold-Löwenthal/Mara Reissberger, 'The White City'. The 'Steinhof' in Vienna: Architecture as a reflection of the attitude towards mental Illness, in: Sigmund Freud Haus Bulletin 5 (1981), 10-40 [Original: ‚Die weiße Stadt'. Der ‚Steinhof' in Wien; Architektur als Reflex der Einstellung zur Geisteskrankheit, in: Kritische Berichte 3/37 (1981), 3-37]. Für eine ausführliche Betrachtung dieses Aspekts, siehe | For a detailed exploration of this aspect see Leslie Topp, Otto Wagner and the Steinhof Psychiatric Hospital: Architecture as misunderstanding, in: The Art Bulletin 87/1 (2005), 130-156 **8** Die von George Soros gegründete CEU eröffnet ihren voraussichtlich dritten Standort nach Budapest und New York in Wien, zunächst ab 2019 in einer temporären Einrichtung und ab ca. 2022 ausgeweitet auf ungefähr ein Drittel des dann fertiggestellten Gesamtkomplexes. | Founded by George Soros, the CEU expects to open its third location in Vienna, after Budapest and New York, starting with a temporary setting in 2019 and then expanding to approximately one third of the whole complex from the time of its complete opening around 2022. **9** Zum UNESCO-Vorschlag | About the UNESCO proposals. Christian Schuhböck/Alliance for Nature, Otto-Wagner-Spital ‚Am Steinhof': ein potentielles UNESCO-Welterbe, Berndorf: Kral-Verlag 2013; Die Definition eines ‚offiziellen Denkmalschutzdiskurses' ist entliehen aus | The definition of 'authorised heritage discourse' is borrowed from Laurajane Smith, Uses of heritage, London/New York: Routledge 2006 **10** Letter from the ICOMOS International Heritage Advisory Board to the Mayor of the City of Vienna, 18.12.2015, in: http://www.icomos.at/images/News/20151231_Heritage-Alert/let_94_otto-wagnerspital_vienna_final20151218.pdf, 01.06.2018; Die ursprünglich geplanten 600 neuen Gebäudeteile im östlichen Teil des Gebietes wurden auf 440 reduziert, zuzüglich 100 weiterer Wohnungen, welche als Umnutzung geschützter Wohngebäude geplant waren. Eine 99-Jährige Verpachtung wurde im Januar 2018 zwischen der Stadt Wien und der Central European University in einem ‚Memorandum of Understanding' vereinbart. | The originally planned 600 new building units in the eastern part of the area have been reduced to 440, plus 100 additional apartments planned by conversion of usage of protected estate buildings. In January 2018, a 'Memorandum of Understanding' signed by the City of Vienna and the Central European University has established a 99-year lease. **11** Manfredo Tafuri, Am Steinhof. Centrality and 'surface' in Otto Wagner's Architecture, in: Lotus 29 (1980), 73 **12** Die englischen Übersetzung des Titels seines ‚Dallo Steinhofs' (‚Posthumous People') entleiht Cacciari Nietzsche: „Erst nach dem Tod werden wir ‚unser' Leben beginnen und lebendig werden, oh, sehr lebendig, wir posthumen Menschen!" Vgl.

| Cacciari takes the title of the English translation of his 'Dallo Steinhof' ('Posthumous People') from Nietzsche: "It is only after death that we will enter 'our' life and come alive, oh, very much alive, we posthumous people!" See Nietzsche, The gay science, 365, zitiert in | quoted in Massimo Cacciari, op. cit. (Anm. 6 | note 6) **13** Jean Laplanche, The Unfinished Copernican Revolution [1992], in: Essays on Otherness, New York/London: Routledge 1999, 71 (Anm. | note 37) **14** Leslie Topp, Architecture and Truth in Fin-de-Siècle Vienna, Cambridge/New York: Cambridge University Press 2004, 143 **15** Vgl. | Cf. Massimo Cacciari, op. cit. (Anm. 4 | note 4), and Manfredo Tafuri, op. cit. (Anm. 11 | note 11), 75, 77 **16** Leslie Topp identifiziert diese beiden als die „hauptsächlich in diesen Prozess involvierten Disziplinen bzw. Unterdisziplinen" | Leslie Topp identifies these two as "the main disciplines, or subdisciplines, involved in this process". Leslie Topp, Otto Wagner and the Steinhof Psychiatric Hospital, cit., 130; In Bezug auf die ursprünglichen Gestaltung schreibt Tafuri: „Es ist zwar plausibel anzunehmen, dass Wagner beratend in der Gestaltung der Grundrisse der Psychiatrie tätig war, dessen Ausführung jedoch außerhalb seines direkten Einflusses stand, obgleich der einfachen Gestaltung der gleichmäßig auf dem Hang verteilten Pavillons durchaus Wagners Aura anhaftet" | In relation to the original design, Tafuri writes: "Though it may be reasonable to suppose that Wagner was asked to act as a consultant in the layout of the psychiatric hospital, its construction lay outside his sphere of direct intervention, though the simplified form of the pavilions sloping regularly down the hillside seems to have Wagner's aura about it". Manfredo Tafuri, op. cit. (Anm. 11 | note 11), 79; Diesbezüglich identifiziert Caroline Jäger-Klein Carlo von Boog, Otto Wagner und Franz Berger als „Architekten der Anstalt". Vgl. | In this regard, Caroline Jäger-Klein identifies Carlo von Boog, Otto Wagner and Franz Berger as 'the architects of the institution'. Cf. Caroline Jäger-Klein, Der Architekten der Anstalt: Carlo von Boog, Otto Wagner und Franz Berger, in: Caroline Jäger-Klein/Sabine Plakolm Forsthuber (eds.), Die Stadt außerhalb. Zur Architektur der ehemaligen Niederösterreichischen Landes-Heil- und Pflegeanstalten für Geistes- und Nervenkranke Am Steinhof in Wien, Basel: Birkhäuser 2015, 107; Aus dem Wettbewerb von 1997 resultierte die Umgestaltung der Pavillons 3, 5 und 11 durch Ernst Beneder und Anja Fischer, des Pavillons 9 durch Runder/Prantl Architekten und des Pavillons 16 durch August Sarnitz. | For what concerns the current configuration, the design competition, launched in 1997, resulted in the transformation of pavilions 3, 5 and 11 by Ernst Beneder and Anja Fischer, pavilion 9 by Runser/Prantl Architekten, and pavilion 16 by August Sarnitz. **17** Manfredo Tafuri, op. cit. (Anm. 11 | note 11), 4 **18** Jean-François Lyotard, Repetition, Complexity, Anamnesis, in: Casabella 517 (1985), 44-45 **19** Ole W. Fischer, After-Image. A comparative rereading of postmodernism, in: Log 21 (2011), 109 **20** Zum ‚anfänglichen Vergessen' | About the 'initial forgetting' s. Jean-François Lyotard, Rewriting modernity, in: The inhuman: Reflections on time, Cambridge: Polity Press 1988, 25; Die Idee einer ‚radikalen Anamnese' betreffend schreibt Stanford Kwinter: „Durch (selektive) Erinnerung wird die Zukunft möglich, eine Zukunft, welche durch die Vergangenheit nicht gedacht werden konnte, und welche die Gegenwart nicht zu denken wagt" | For what concerns the notion of 'radical anamnesis', Sanford Kwinter writes: "Through (selective) memory the future becomes possible, a future that the past could not think and that the present-alone-dares not." Sanford Kwinter, Radical anamnesis (Mourning the future), in: Far from equilibrium: Essays on technology and design culture, Barcelona: Actar 2008, 142 **21** Vgl. | Cf. Edward Dimenberg, Diller Scofidio + Renfro, Architecture after images, Chicago/London: University of Chicago Press 2013, 32-34 **22** Lebbeus Woods, Beyond memory, 22.03.2012, https://lebbeuswoods.wordpress.com/2012/03/22/beyond-memory/, 01.06.2018 **23** Alfred North Whitehead, Process and reality. An essay in cosmology [1929], New York: The Free Press 1978, 2 **24** Keller Easterling, Take-Away, in: Perspecta 45 (2012) 157; Keller Easterling, Subtraction, Berlin: Sternberg Press 2014, 2 **25** Vgl. | Cf. Sigmund Freud, Constructions in analysis, in: James Strachey (ed. and trans.), The standard edition of the complete psychological works of Sigmund Freud, London: Hogarth Press and the Institute of Psycho-analysis 1964, 255-270 [Original: Konstruktionen in der Analyse. Internationale Zeitschrift für Psychoanalyse, 23, 1937, 459-469]. Vgl. hierzu auch | Cf. also on this subject also Sigmund Freud, Civilization and its discontents, London: Penguin 2002 [Original: Das Unbehagen in der Kultur, 1930] **26** Eingeführt von Jane Rendell zur Übertragung von kritischer Theorie in die Praxis, ist eine ‚kritische räumliche Praxis' als eine dreifache Art der Überschneidung zu sehen: Von Theorie und Praxis, von Öffentlichem und Privaten und von Kunst und Architektur. Vgl. | Introduced by Jane Rendell to transpose critical theory into practice, a 'critical spatial practice' stands at a three-way intersection: between theory and practice, public and private, and art and architecture. Cf. Jane Rendell, A Place Between Art, Architecture and Critical Theory, Tallinn: Proceedings to Place and Location 2003, 221-233 **27** Manfredo Tafuri, Am Steinhof. Centrality and 'Surface' in Otto Wagner's Architecture, in: Lotus 29 (1980), 89

RIDING THE THRESHOLD

Potential for new operational and planning practice

Isabel Maria Finkenberger

Projects are tasks within a certain time schedule that seek innovative answers to complex relationships. Especially in urban planning, they are embedded into constantly changing contexts, in some cases with strongly diverging dynamics, time constraints and constellations of involved parties. However, when do projects become determinants that have a targeted influence on ongoing processes and exert a catalytic effect on them? At what point does a project become a process that offers synaptic reference points and that reorders and develops content and building blocks? How can one create processes that integrate feedback loops as self-correction and celebrate dealing with uncertainty as a principle? And how can one anchor processes where, under what conditions, or possibly even institutionalize them?

'Stretching the boundaries' describes the discussion of questions of urban development, artistic practice and the institution of the theater based on the example of the pilot project of the German program 'Nationale Stadtentwicklungspolitik' (National Urban Development Policy) 'Seeing the city from the other side' – or 'Seeing the city from

SCHWELLENREITEN

Potenzial neuer Handlungs- und Planungspraxis

Isabel Maria Finkenberger

Projekte sind zeitlich befristete Aufgaben, die innovative Antworten auf komplexe Zusammenhänge suchen. Insbesondere in der Stadtplanung sind sie eingebettet in sich kontinuierlich verändernde Kontexte mit teilweise stark divergierenden Dynamiken, Zeitlichkeiten und Akteurskonstellationen. Wann aber werden Projekte zu Determinanten, die gezielt auf laufende Prozesse einwirken und darüber eine katalysatorische Wirkung entfalten? Ab wann wird ein Projekt zum Prozess, der synaptische Anknüpfungspunkte bietet und Inhalte und Bausteine neu sortiert und weiterdenkt? Wie kann man Prozesse entwerfen, die Rückkopplungsschleifen als Selbstkorrektive integrieren und den Umgang mit Unsicherheit als Prinzip zelebrieren? Und wie kann man Prozesse unter welchen Voraussetzungen wo verankern oder möglicherweise sogar institutionalisieren?

‚Schwellenreiten' beschreibt die Auseinandersetzung zwischen Fragen der Stadtentwicklung, künstlerischer Praxis und der Institution Theater am Beispiel des Pilotprojektes der nationalen Stadtentwicklungspolitik des Bundes ‚Die Stadt von der anderen Seite sehen' (Stadt sehen), das in den Spielzeiten 2015/16 und 2016/17 von der Theaterregisseurin Eva-Maria Baumeister und der Autorin als Stadtplanerin am Schauspiel Köln künstlerisch geleitet wurde – und welches das Ende einer mehrjährigen Auseinandersetzung des Schauspiels mit dessen Nachbarschaft Köln-Mülheim darstellte.

a different point of view' (Seeing the city), under the artistic direction of the theater director Eva-Maria Baumeister and the author as urban planner at the Schauspiel Köln (Cologne Theater) during the seasons 2015/16 and 2016/17. It represented the end of an engagement of the theater for several years with its neighborhood Cologne-Mülheim.

THE PROJECT The orientation of the Schauspiel Köln towards questions regarding neighborhood and urban development began in 2012 with the challenge of establishing an interim venue during the pending renovation of the opera and theater ensemble at Offenbachplatz in the city center of Cologne. The theater found its home in 2013 in the Carlswerk, a former industrial complex, that was still at the beginning of its conversion at the time, situated on the right side of the river Rhine, the so-called 'problem district' Mülheim and in the direct neighborhood of Keupstraße, which had gained sad notoriety through the nail bomb attack by the far-right terrorist group National Socialist Underground (NSU) in 2004.[1] Many current challenges to urban society are bundled in the district itself: post-industrial structural change and its accompanying loss of identity, heavily burdened and burdening mobility infrastructures and an extremely diverse population. At the same time, however, it is precisely this structural change and therefore the large spatial resources available that currently endow the district with a high transition dynamic and will change it lastingly in the forthcoming years.

The theater began its pioneering accomplishment with both an engagement with its new context on a theatrical level, as well as the establishment of the Carlsgarten as an oasis and gathering place for the whole neighborhood. It was also about gradually overturning the negative public perception of the district and its inhabitants due to the NSU attack. In order to drive the previous engagement and fruitful cooperation with the neighborhood a step forward, 'Seeing the city' was conceived as a cooperative project by the Schauspiel Köln and the Social Space Coordination Mülheim-Nord and Keupstraße. The interdisciplinary access was firmly inscribed and, apart from the previous theatrical, an urban planning perspective was integrated. The aim was to extend the focus of the Schauspiel Köln, at the time on Keupstraße and its themes, to the entire district and to deal with the immanent issues there. Especially the analytical view of the urban planning, but also establishing a relationship between the theater and the numerous other contexts and neighborhoods, was intended to embed the theatrical approach into a wider social and locally-related discourse.

SEEING THE CITY The interdisciplinary curated project was conceived as an 'urban-theatrical experimental setup'. Set out consciously as an open process without a predetermined construct of topics, structures, schedules or tools, 'Seeing the city'

D A S P R O J E K T Die Hinwendung des Schauspiel Köln zu Themen von Nachbarschaft und Stadtentwicklung begann 2012 mit der Herausforderung, einen Interimsstandort während der anstehenden Sanierung des Opern- und Schauspielensembles am Offenbachplatz zu etablieren. 2013 fand das Schauspiel sein Zuhause in dem damals erst am Beginn seiner Umnutzung stehenden Carlswerk, verortet im rechtsrheinischen, sogenannten ‚Problemstadtteil' Mülheim und in direkter Nachbarschaft zur Keupstraße, die durch das Nagelbombenattentat der rechtsterroristischen Gruppierung Nationalsozialistischer Untergrund (NSU) 2004 traurige Berühmtheit erlangt hatte. Im Stadtteil selbst bündeln sich viele aktuelle Herausforderungen an die Stadtgesellschaft: postindustrieller Strukturwandel und eine damit einhergehende verlustige Identität, stark belastete und belastende Mobilitätsinfrastrukturen und eine äußerst diverse Bevölkerung. Gleichzeitig sind es aber auch eben dieser Strukturwandel und die dadurch vorhandenen großen Flächenressourcen, die dem Stadtteil derzeit eine hohe Veränderungsdynamik bescheren und ihn in den kommenden Jahren nachhaltig verändern werden.

Das Schauspiel begann seine Pionierleistung mit sowohl einer Auseinandersetzung mit dem neuen Wirkungsort auf theatraler Ebene wie auch mit der Etablierung des Carlsgartens als Oase und Treffpunkt für die gesamte Nachbarschaft. Dabei ging es auch darum, die durch das NSU-Attentat verstärkte negative öffentliche Wahrnehmung des Stadtteils und seiner Bewohner zu triggern und diese nach und nach umzudeuten. Um die bisherige Beschäftigung und fruchtbare Zusammenarbeit mit der Nachbarschaft einen Schritt weiterzutreiben, wurde ‚Stadt sehen' als kooperatives Projekt vom Schauspiel Köln und der Sozialraumkoordination Mülheim-Nord und Keupstraße konzipiert. In dieses dezidiert eingeschrieben wurde der interdisziplinäre Zugang und – neben der bisherigen theatralen – eine stadtplanerische Perspektive integriert. Ziel war, den damaligen Fokus des Schauspiel Köln auf die Keupstraße und deren Themen auf den ganzen Stadtteil auszuweiten und die dort immanenten Fragestellungen zu bearbeiten. Insbesondere der analytische Blick der Stadtplanung, aber auch das In-Beziehung-Setzen des Schauspiels zu den zahlreichen anderen Kontexten und Nachbarschaften sollte den theatralen Ansatz nun in einen breiten gesellschaftlichen und zugleich ortsbezogenen Diskurs einbetten.

S T A D T S E H E N Das interdisziplinär kuratierte Projekt war als ‚städtisch-theatrale Versuchsanordnung' konzipiert. Bewusst als ergebnisoffener Prozess ohne vorgefertigtes Konstrukt an Themen, Strukturen, Zeitlichkeiten oder Werkzeugen angelegt, wollte ‚Stadt sehen' das kontrollierte Refugium des Theaters verlassen, um neue Wege des Stadtmachens künstlerisch zu erforschen. ‚Stadt sehen' bediente sich während seiner zweijährigen Laufzeit vielfältiger Formate, angepasst an den jeweiligen Prozessstand: interpretative Kartierungen, thematische Salons mit ausgewählten Akteuren, Spaziergänge mit lokalen Experten und Künstlern, Koproduktionen und Kooperationen oder die Verortung einer mobilen ‚Stadt sehen'-Dependance an mehreren Orten im Stadtteil.

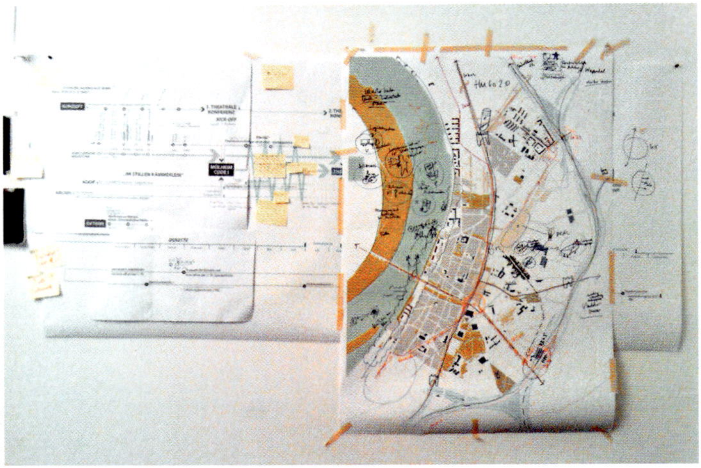

1 | Offener Prozess | Open process

sought to leave the controlled refuge of the theater behind to explore new ways of city making with artistic approaches. During its two-year process, 'Seeing the city' made use of a wide range of formats, adapted to the respective process status: interpretive mappings, thematic salons with selected protagonists, walks with local experts and artists, coproductions and cooperations, or the placement of a mobile 'Seeing the city' subsidiary in various locations in the neighborhood.

While the artistic and theatric practice played a significant role especially for the arrangement of the subprojects, the urban planning competences came into play in the strategic orientation of the complex process, in the spatial analysis and interpreting observation of the sphere of action of Mülheim and in the setting of central topics from current urban discourse, urban planning theory and its set of tools – for example promenadology, discursive city exploration or collective urban development.[2] The direction of the translation of the artistic themes onto the various levels of municipal administration and the feedback into one's own discipline were also significant. In addition, an important theoretical background was formed by the theatrical conference 'Thinking city and theater together' halfway through the project.

The central format emerged as a consequence of the kick-off event: the wish for a more intensive engagement with the district and the participation in artistic projects over a longer period of time prompted the development of the so-called 'complicities'. Gesa Ziemer frees the term from its negative connotation and penal meaning and reinterprets it as a "specific form of work that can turn a destructive into a constructive, exciting way of working", "that leads to alternative structures being developed that result in innovations".[3] Three 'Seeing the city' complicities intended to offer precisely that: an open and successively developing working structure and collective art

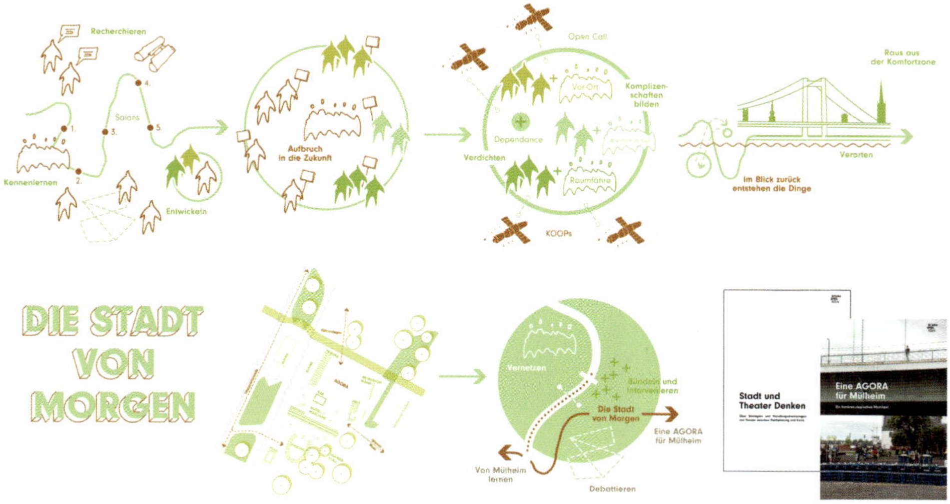

2 | Prozessstruktur | Process structure

Während die künstlerische und theatrale Praxis insbesondere bei der Ausgestaltung der Teilprojekte eine wesentliche Rolle gespielt hat, kamen die stadtplanerischen Kompetenzen in der strategischen Ausgestaltung des komplexen Prozesses, in der räumlich-analytischen und interpretierenden Betrachtung des Handlungsraumes Mülheim und in der Setzung zentraler Themen aus dem aktuellen Stadtdiskurs, der Stadtplanungstheorie und deren Instrumentarium – beispielsweise der Promenadologie, diskursiven Stadterkundung oder kollektiven Stadtentwicklung – zum Tragen. Ebenfalls bedeutend war die Übersetzungsleitung der künstlerischen Themen in die unterschiedlichen Ebenen der Stadtverwaltung und Rückkopplung in die eigene Disziplin. Einen wichtigen theoretischen Hintergrund bildete die Theatrale Konferenz ‚Stadt und Theater Denken' zur Halbzeit des Projektes.

Das zentrale Format kristallisierte sich als Konsequenz der Auftaktveranstaltung heraus: Der Wunsch nach einer intensiveren Auseinandersetzung mit dem Stadtteil und die Teilhabe an künstlerischen Projekten über einen längeren Zeitraum waren der Anlass für die Entwicklung der sogenannten ‚Komplizenschaften'. Der Begriff wird von Gesa Ziemer von seiner negativen Konnotation und strafrechtlichen Bedeutung befreit und neu interpretiert als „spezifische Arbeitsform, die von einer destruktiven in eine konstruktive, lustvolle Arbeitsweise umgedeutet werden kann" und „die dazu führt, dass alternative Strukturen entwickelt werden, die zu Innovationen führen". Drei ‚Stadt sehen'-Komplizenschaften sollten genau das bieten: eine offene und sich sukzessive entwickelnde Arbeitsstruktur und kollektive Kunstproduktion zwischen den Künstlerteams und interessierten Mitstreitern. Den roten Faden von ‚Stadt sehen' bildete die eklektische Erzählung, verbunden mit unterschiedlichen Maßstabsebenen und Zeitlichkeiten. Insbesondere auf kuratorischer Ebene hat sich sukzessive ein Erzählstrang herauskristallisiert, der sich in den insgesamt drei Theatralen Konferenzen und den dort angewandten Formaten klar ablesbar manifestierte.

3-5 | Formate | Formats

production between the artist teams and interested fellow campaigners. The guiding thread of 'Seeing the city' was formed by the eclectic narration, combined with various scale levels and time schedules. A narrative thread crystallized gradually especially on a curatorial level, which manifested itself clearly in the total of three theatrical conferences and the formats applied there.

The first conference 'Departure into the future' formulated the starting point and the departure into the public process, after six months of research and a concurrent development of a project structure. Ten workshops, conceived by ten partly interdisciplinary teams, had ten locations in the neighborhood at their disposal to regroup with their participants, to work and to negotiate their ideas and research results collectively.

Halfway through the project, the second theatrical conference cast a 'look back'[4] – to the building site of the opera and theater ensemble, where the first actual departure of the theater started with a lot of uncertainty in its baggage. For three different expeditions the journey was the destination, as well as representing a level of reflection. The triumphant return into the Mülheim 'city area' took place by Rhine ferry, disembarking next to the Mülheim bridge, under which the picture opera 'Trumpets of Jericho' by the theater collective subbotnik, proclaimed as a public rehearsal, held its premiere. Theatrically and atmospherically charged, worlds collided in a location that once represented the (economic) center and the cradle of the city of Mülheim, namely participants in the expeditions, youths from the 'hood', passers-by and neighbors. The visited locations – the interim venue in the Carlswerk, the former and at the same time future, still undescribed venue at Offenbachplatz and the Mülheim Bridge as a central 'void' situated in the urban context – exemplarily showed the significance of institutional places and their multilayered development potential. However, the latter emerged especially through its usage as the complex space, where the artistic works were designated to be consolidated conceptually in the ensuing process.

6-8 | Formate | Formats

Die erste Konferenz ‚Aufbruch in die Zukunft' formulierte nach sechsmonatiger Recherche und gleichzeitiger Entwicklung einer Projektstruktur den Startpunkt und besagten Aufbruch in den öffentlichen Arbeitsprozess. Zehn Workshops, konzipiert von zehn teilweise interdisziplinären Teams, hatten zehn Orte im Stadtteil zur Verfügung, um sich dort mit ihren Teilnehmenden zu formieren, zu arbeiten und ihre Ideen und Rechercheergebnisse kollektiv zu verhandeln.

Zur Halbzeit des Projektes warf die zweite Theatrale Konferenz den ‚Blick zurück' – zur Baustelle des Opern- und Schauspielensembles, wo der erste, eigentliche Aufbruch des Hauses mit vielen Ungewissheiten im Gepäck begann. Den Weg als Ziel, aber auch als Reflexionsebene hatten drei unterschiedliche Expeditionen. Der triumphale Wiedereinzug ins Mülheimer ‚Stadtgebiet' fand per Rheinfähre mit Ausstieg an der Mülheimer Brücke statt, unter der die als öffentliche Probe proklamierte Bilderoper ‚Trompeten von Jericho' des Theaterkollektivs Subbotnik uraufgeführt wurde. Theatral und atmosphärisch aufgeladen trafen Welten an dem Ort aufeinander, der einst das (ökonomische) Zentrum und die Wiege der Stadt Mülheim darstellte, namentlich Teilnehmende der Expeditionen, Jugendliche aus der ‚Hood', Spaziergänger und Nachbarn. Die besuchten Stationen – die als Pionier besetzte Interimsspielstätte im Carlswerk, der ehemalige und zugleich zukünftige, noch unbeschriebene Spielort am Offenbachplatz und die Mülheimer Brücke als zentrale, im Stadtkontext verortete ‚Void'– haben dabei exemplarisch die Bedeutung von institutionellen Orten und deren vielschichtige Entwicklungspotentiale aufgezeigt. Insbesondere aber hat sich letzterer durch das Bespielen als jener komplexe Raum herauskristallisiert, an dem sich die künstlerischen Arbeiten konzeptionell im darauffolgenden Prozess verdichten sollten.

Die dritte Theatrale Konferenz und damit das Grande Finale proklamierte ‚Die Stadt von Morgen' und installierte eben diese als physisch ausformuliertes Manifest unter der Mülheimer Brücke. Sie war also nicht nur Abschluss und Ausblick gleichermaßen, sondern

9 | Raumfähre | Space ferry

The third theatrical conference and therefore the grand finale was proclaimed 'The city of tomorrow', installed as a physical manifesto under the Mülheim Bridge. It was therefore not only both the conclusion and outlook, but also a crystallization point of the eclectic consolidation of the principle of an 'agora', of 'space' as a place and infrastructure of a potent urban society, of 'action' through collective and artistic practices, of 'time' and 'people' through the consolidation of atmospheres and the layering of history and stories. Artistic subprojects of the overall process made use in turn of the narration from different perspectives: abstracted and interpreted in the form of said picture opera, directly and tangible through the collecting, exhibiting and performative scene setting of individual stories and objects from the district[5], collectively experienced through the development of a "noodle machine as a social condenser"[6], or analyzing and intervening through the redesigning of café façades of different national origins[7].

If the stories were the determining anchors and the respective formats the moments of 'Seeing the city' that could be experienced, superordinate aspects can be derived from an urban planning perspective that go beyond the actual project and present central questions for the interface between city planning and city making, artistic and research-connected practice. In the following, these are elaborated on in the form of theses.

TRANSITIONS Transitional practices are essential for working on complex processes and generating new content. It is only through dialog and cooperation with other perspectives and knowledge that it is possible to identify synergies, which place the depths of one's own discipline horizontally in relation to each other and generate additional value from it. These practices can also be used situationally in different contexts and enable new accesses to those involved. This applies on the one hand to the question of the 'role' that one acts in or the 'language' that one makes use of.[8] On the other hand,

10 | Wunderkammer | Cabinet of wonder

auch Kristallisationspunkt der eklektischen Verdichtung des Prinzips einer ‚Agora', von ‚Raum' als Ort und Infrastruktur einer potenten Stadtgesellschaft, von ‚Handlung' durch kollektive und künstlerische Praxen, von ‚Zeit' und ‚Mensch' durch die Kristallisation von Atmosphären und Überlagerung von Geschichte(n). Künstlerische Teilbausteine des gesamten Projektes wiederum bedienten sich der Erzählung aus unterschiedlichen Blickwinkeln: abstrahiert und interpretiert in Form besagter Bilderoper, direkt und erfahrbar durch das Sammeln, Ausstellen und performativ In-Szene-Setzen individueller Geschichten und Gegenstände aus dem Stadtteil, kollektiv erlebbar durch den Aufbau einer „Nudelmaschine als Sozialverdichtungsapparat" oder analysierend und intervenierend über die Neugestaltung von Caféfassaden unterschiedlicher nationaler Herkünfte.

Waren die Erzählungen die bestimmende Klammer und die jeweiligen Formate die erlebbaren Momente von ‚Stadt sehen', können aus stadtplanerischer Perspektive übergeordnete Aspekte abgeleitet werden, die über das eigentliche Projekt hinausreichen und zentrale Fragestellungen für die Schnittstelle zwischen Stadtplanung und Stadtmachen, künstlerischer und forschender Praxis ausformulieren. Im Folgenden werden diese in Form von Thesen weiter ausgeführt.

GRENZGÄNGE Grenzgängerische Praktiken sind essenziell, um komplexe Prozesse zu bearbeiten und um neue Inhalte zu generieren. Erst im Dialog und in der Zusammenarbeit mit anderen Perspektiven und anderem Wissen ist es möglich, Synergien zu erkennen, welche die Tiefenbohrungen der eigenen Disziplin horizontal miteinander in Beziehung setzen und einen Mehrwert daraus generieren. Diese Praktiken können außerdem situativ in unterschiedlichen Kontexten angewendet werden und ermöglichen dadurch neue Zugänge zu Akteuren. Dies betrifft einerseits die Frage der ‚Rolle', in der man agiert oder der ‚Sprache', der man sich bedient. Andererseits erlaubten sie die

11-13 | Eklektische Erzählung | Eclectic narration

they allow the freedom to position oneself in terms of content between artistic freedom, provoking radicality and selective in-situ project work, as well as an urban planning practice obliged to the public, based on consensus and moderation.

PARTICIPATION Artistic-participative practices are not politically legitimized and cannot or do not necessarily want to integrate the wider population, achieve a consensus or mediate, as ideally envisaged in participation procedures accompanying urban planning proceedings. However, due to their often low-threshold participation access, including through e.g. non-verbal and non-frontal organized formats, they generate alternative content that is not bound to predetermined issues. Owing to their dynamic, they can pool those involved quite differently from urban planning practice, as well as activate new involved parties and population groups. They also contribute to specifying target knowledge for more specific planning.

TIME The understanding and presence of different time schedules influence processes in a very central manner – from the programming to communication and work on parallel interlinked result strands. In particular, time is evaluated and processed differently in various disciplines. For the theater, for example, a two-year project duration enables the extension and adjustment of the otherwise customary focus on the premiere and the run-up of just a few weeks by means of the applied principles of 'researching' and 'testing'. However, in order to be truly effective, this transition must occur on a strategic, artistic, but especially also institutional level. In city planning with a focus on sustainability and continuation, but also due to the often complex contexts and constellations of those involved, two years is most of the time just the first phase in which a project structure, networks, formats etc. are established, before embarking on the actual project and implementation stage. If this phase ends without reaching any further agreements,

14-16 | Zeitlichkeit | Temporality

Freiheit, sich inhaltlich zwischen künstlerischer Freiheit, provozierender Radikalität und selektiver In-situ-Projektarbeit und einer der Allgemeinheit verpflichteten, auf Konsens und Moderation basierenden Stadtplanungspraxis zu positionieren.

TEILHABE Künstlerisch-partizipative Praktiken sind nicht politisch legitimiert und können bzw. wollen auch gar nicht, wie in Partizipationsverfahren ideellerweise angedacht, die breite Bevölkerung integrieren, einen Konsens erzielen oder vermitteln. Jedoch erzeugen sie aufgrund ihres oft niedrigschwelligen Teilhabezugangs, unter anderem durch beispielsweise non-verbale und nicht-frontal organisierte Formate, alternative, nicht an vorformulierte Fragestellungen gebundene Inhalte. Sie können durch ihre Dynamik Akteure ganz anders als die Stadtplanungspraxis bündeln bzw. neue Akteure und Bevölkerungsgruppen aktivieren. Und sie tragen dazu bei, Zielwissen für konkretere Planungen zu spezifizieren.

ZEIT Das Verständnis und das Vorhandensein unterschiedlicher Zeitlichkeiten beeinflussen Prozesse auf ganz zentrale Art und Weise – von der Programmierung über die Kommunikation bis hin zur Arbeit an parallelen, miteinander verschränkten Ergebnissträngen. Insbesondere wird in den verschiedenen Disziplinen Zeit unterschiedlich bewertet und bearbeitet. Für das Theater beispielsweise ermöglicht eine zweijährige Projektlaufzeit, den sonst üblichen Fokus auf die Premiere und den Vorlauf von nur wenigen Wochen durch die angewandten Prinzipien des ‚Forschens' und ‚Testens' zu ergänzen und neu zu justieren. Um jedoch wirklich wirksam werden zu können, muss dieser Übergang sowohl auf strategischer, auf künstlerischer, aber insbesondere auch auf institutioneller Ebene erfolgen. In der Stadtplanung mit Fokus auf Nachhaltigkeit und Verstetigung, aber auch aufgrund der zumeist komplexen Kontexte und Akteurskonstellationen, sind zwei Jahre oft nur jene erste Phase, in der eine Projektstruktur, Netzwerke, Formate etc. etabliert werden, um dann in die eigentliche Projekt- beziehungsweise Umsetzungsphase einzustei-

17 | Trompeten von Jericho | Trumpets of Jericho

valuable knowledge is lost. It appears interesting in this context to use this stage zero as an experimental work and reflection process, to initiate a project and district development adapted to local requirements and that integrates the potency of the cultural players and institutions rooted there in a synergetic manner, which both sides benefit from.

OPENNESS Successively developing topics and processually designed results are problematic for the communication and mediation of projects. Especially for the wider public, for amateurs and non-specialists, abstract statements are reasons that hinder participation. New, more flexible forms of communication are therefore required between enabling maximum openness and offering reference points and participation. Strategic action therefore always requires a certain presence, a place or a structure, in which the simultaneity of non-simultaneous processes becomes visible and can be negotiated. This is a task that urban planning or architectural design, communication and visualization competences can contribute.

CONCRETION The manifestation of (participation) processes in specific results or places is central to socially anchor the dynamics set in motion and allow them to take effect. Embedding them into institutional structures, the placement in their spaces or the establishment of new places represent basic possibilities. However, it is also especially about creating informal reference points for participation and further developments. The project 'Spatial Agency' by the University of Sheffield, for example, describes a new way of developing buildings and spaces. Instead of placing the focus on the design and building structure, it shows possibilities in which architects and non-architects can take action collaboratively and thereby achieve a new way of making architecture.[9] In this respect, the creation of places and negotiation spaces is also about creating structural-spatial enabling architectures.

18 | Institution

gen. Endet diese Phase ohne weitere Verabredungen getroffen zu haben, geht wertvolles Wissen verloren. Interessant in diesem Zusammenhang erscheint, eben diese Vorbereitungsphase als experimentellen Arbeits- und Reflexionsprozess zu nutzen, um eine den lokalen Bedürfnissen angepasste Projekt- bzw. Quartiersentwicklung anzustoßen, die die Potenz der dort verankerten kulturellen Macher und Institutionen synergetisch integriert und von denen beide Seiten profitieren.

O F F E N H E I T Sich sukzessive entwickelnde Themen und prozesshaft angelegte Ergebnisse sind in der Kommunikation und Vermittlung von Projekten problematisch. Insbesondere für die breite Bürgerschaft, für Laien und Fachfremde sind abstrakte Aussagen Hinderungsgründe von Teilhabe. Es braucht daher neue, flexiblere Formen der Kommunikation zwischen dem Ermöglichen einer maximalen Offenheit und dem Angebot von Anknüpfungspunkten und Beteiligung. Strategisches Agieren braucht also immer eine gewisse Präsenz, einen Ort oder eine Struktur, in der die Gleichzeitigkeit ungleichzeitiger Prozessstränge sichtbar wird und verhandelt werden kann. Eine Aufgabe, zu der stadtplanerische bzw. architektonische Gestaltungs-, Kommunikations- und Visualisierungskompetenzen beitragen können.

K O N K R E T I O N Die Manifestation von (Partizipations-)Prozessen in konkreten Ergebnissen oder Orten ist zentral, um deren Relevanz, und die in Bewegung gesetzten Dynamiken gesellschaftlich zu verankern und wirksam werden zu lassen. Grundsätzliche Möglichkeiten stellen die Einbettung in institutionelle Strukturen, die Verortung in deren Räumen oder die Etablierung neuer Orte dar. Insbesondere geht es aber auch darum, informelle Anknüpfungspunkte für Teilhabe und für weitere Entwicklungen zu schaffen. Das Projekt ‚Spatial Agency' der Universität Sheffield beispielsweise beschreibt eine neue Art, Gebäude und Räume zu produzieren. Anstelle des Fokus auf die Gestalt und Bauweise zu legen, werden Möglichkeiten aufgezeigt, in denen Architekten und Nicht-Architekten

I N S T I T U T I O N Cultural institutions have a central social task – as an educational provider and conveyor, or in the anchoring of topics and programs. Their 'houses' as public venues are important motors of the physical city. In addition, owing to their institutionalization, they have continuous monetary and personnel resources at their disposal and are considered as legitimate, potent and reliable partners in the dialog and in working practice. However, to be able to assume their responsibility as collective and threshold-free spaces, it is not sufficient to develop project satellites within a limited time. Instead it requires a radical opening of their doors and their institutional 'reinvention', the introduction of a learning process of control delegation and cooperation, the institutional anchoring of processes and innovative organization structures with personnel and monetary resources, decision-making competences and time budgets, as well as the reconquering of a social relevance of institutions in the city discourse and daily life.

O U T L O O K The interface of artistic practice and city planning and their interaction in the palimpsest of the city is not simple. Differing systems and interpretations, methods and practices, protagonists and processes come face to face with each other. In addition, negotiation processes are rarely carried out objectively and along the actual lines of the core issues. Even so, with their immanent competences and energies they provide the opportunity to potentiate each other mutually. 'Seeing the city' was a central moment for sounding out possible topics through research, developing formats and testing these in situ. These results were consolidated, generating further interesting questions. The resulting synergies, which bring together the best of two 'worlds', are especially worth studying and examining regarding the applicability to planning practice. This means the simultaneity of strategy and tactic, of a bird's-eye and eye-level perspective, of analytical observation and atmospheric charging, of legitimate power potency and the development of unexpected contents through inter- and transdisciplinary cooperation, from the direction and continuation of the translation of everyday codes into the tools of city planning, as well as their scientific reflection.

kollaborativ tätig werden können und dadurch zu einer neuen Art des Architekturmachens kommen. In diesem Sinne geht es bei der Formulierung von Orten als Verhandlungsräumen auch darum, baulich-räumliche Ermöglichungsarchitekturen zu gestalten.

I N S T I T U T I O N   Kulturelle Institutionen haben eine zentrale gesellschaftliche Aufgabe – als Bildungsträger und -vermittler oder in der Verankerung von Themen und Programmen. Ihre ‚Häuser' sind als öffentliche Orte wichtige Motoren der physischen Stadt. Zudem verfügen sie aufgrund ihrer Institutionalisierung über kontinuierliche monetäre und personelle Ressourcen und gelten als legitimierte, potente und verlässliche Partner im Dialog und in der Handlungspraxis. Um aber ihre Verantwortung als kollektive und schwellenfreie Räume übernehmen zu können, reicht es nicht aus, zeitlich begrenzte Projektsatelliten zu entwickeln. Vielmehr bedarf es der radikalen Öffnung der Häuser und ihrer institutionellen ‚Neuerfindung', der Einleitung eines Lernprozesses der Kontrollabgabe und Zusammenarbeit, der institutionellen Verankerung von Prozessen und innovativen Organisationsstrukturen mit personellen und monetären Ressourcen, Entscheidungskompetenzen und Zeitbudgets sowie der Rückeroberung einer gesellschaftlichen Relevanz von Institutionen im Stadtdiskurs.

A U S B L I C K   Die Schnittstelle von künstlerischer Praxis und Stadtplanung und deren Zusammenwirken im Palimpsest Stadt ist keine einfache. Unterschiedliche Systeme und Selbstverständnisse, Methoden und Praxen, Akteure und Prozesse treffen aufeinander. Aushandlungsprozesse werden zudem nur selten sachlich und entlang der eigentlichen Kernfragestellungen geführt. Gleichwohl bieten sie mit den ihnen immanenten Kompetenzen und Energien die Chance, sich gegenseitig zu potenzieren. ‚Stadt sehen' war ein zentraler Moment, mögliche Themen forschend auszuloten, Formate zu entwickeln und diese in situ zu testen. Generiert wurde eine Verdichtungsleistung, aus der sich weiterführende spannende Fragen ergeben haben. Insbesondere untersuchenswert und auf Übertragbarkeit in die Planungspraxis zu prüfen erscheinen die sich daraus ergebenden Synergien, die das Beste aus zwei ‚Welten' vereinen: nämlich die Gleichzeitigkeit von Strategie und Taktik, von Vogel- und Eye-Level-Perspektive, von analytischer Betrachtung und atmosphärischer Aufladung, von legitimierter Machtpotenz und der Entwicklung unerwarteter Inhalte durch inter- und transdisziplinäre Zusammenarbeit, von der Übersetzungsleitung und Verstetigung alltäglicher Codes in das Instrumentarium der Stadtplanung sowie ihrer wissenschaftlichen Reflexion.

1 Vgl. | Cf. Uwe Schäfer: Strukturförderung bis 2016 verlängert, in: https://www.ksta.de/koeln/muelheim/-strukturfoerderung-muelheim-2020-bis-2016-verlaengert-192448/, 30.5.2018 **2** Vgl. | Cf. Universität Kassel, Promenadologie. Spaziergangswissenschaft, in: https://www.uni-kassel.de/fb6/person/burckhardt/promenadologie.html/, 30.5.2018; Helmut Holzapfel/Martin Schmitz, Lucius Burckhardts Promenadologie, in: Berlin: ARCH+ 183 (2007), 30-31 sowie | as well as Urban Catalyst Studio, http://www.urbancatalyst-studio.de/de/startseite/intro-wie-entsteht-stadt-gemeinsam.html, 30.5.2018 **3** Gesa Ziemer, Komplizenschaft. Neue Perspektiven auf Kollektivität, Bielefeld: Transcript 2013 **4** Der vollständige Titel lautet ‚Im Blick zurück entstehen die Dinge – Eine Expedition auf die andere Seite'. „Im Blick zurück entstehen die Dinge" ist dem Songtext von Tocotronic ‚In höchsten Höhen' entlehnt. | The full title is ‚In retrospect, things come into being - an expedition to the other side'. „In retrospect, things come into being" is borrowed from the lyrics of Tocotronic ‚In höchsten Höhen'. **5** Vgl. | Cf. Markus Ambach/Kay von Keitz, Komplizenschaft Mülheimer Wunderkammer, in: https://www.schauspiel.koeln/spielplan/vergangenes/stadt-sehen/komplizenschaften/k3-wunderkammer, 30.5.2018 **6** Einer Aussage des Künstlers Lukas Kopf, Studierender des Studiengangs space&designSTRATEGIES der Kunstuniversität Linz entnommen. | Taken from a statement by the artist Lukas Kopf, a student of the space&designSTRATEGIES course at Linz University of Art. **7** Vgl. | Cf. Anna Marijke Weber/Anne-Julchen Bernhardt mit Studierenden der | with students from the RWTH Aachen, Zwei Seiten einer Fassade, in: https://gbl.arch.rwth-aachen.de/ddb/?page_id=2, 30.5.2018 **8** Bei ‚Stadt sehen' konnten situativ und je nach Notwendigkeit die Rollen Stadtplanerin, Kuratorin, Theatermacherin oder Vertreterin der Institution eingenommen werden. | In ‚Stadt sehen' roles of the city planner, curator, theater maker or representative of the institution could be assumed depending on the situation and according to necessity. **9** Vgl.| Cf. University of Sheffield – School of Architecture, Spatial Agency, in: http://www.spatialagency.net/, 30.5.2018; Nishat Awan/Tatjana Schneider/Jeremy Till, Spatial Agency. Other Ways of Doing Architecture, Abingdon: Taylor & Francis 2011

APPENDIX

BIOGRAFIEN BIOGRAPHIES

GIORGIA AQUILAR ist Architektin und Postdoktorandin an der Technischen Universität München und Stipendiatin der Alexander von Humboldt-Stiftung. Zuvor war sie Postdoc-Stipendiatin der TUM Universitätsstiftung sowie Universität IUAV in Venedig sowie Lehrbeauftragte an der Universität Neapel Federico II. Sie erhielt Forschungsstipendien von nationalen und internationalen Institutionen. Sie war beteiligt an der Erstellung des europäischen Berichts in der UNESCO-Publikation Kultur: Urban Future – Globaler Kulturbericht für eine nachhaltige Stadtentwicklung. | Giorgia Aquilar is an architect and postdoctoral researcher at the Technical University of Munich, holding a fellowship awarded by the Alexander von Humboldt Foundation. Prior to that, she was postdoctoral fellow of the TUM University Foundation and at the University IUAV of Venice, and adjunct professor at the University of Naples Federico II. She has been awarded research grants by national and international institutions. She was involved in the drafting of the European report included in the UNESCO's publication Culture: Urban Future – Global Report on Culture for Sustainable Urban Development. | Ausgewählte Publikationen | selected publications: Giorgia Aquilar, The Ideal of the Broken-down: Porous States of Disrepair, in: Sophie Wolfrum (ed.), Porous City, Basel: Birkhäuser 2018; Giorgia Aquilar, Heritage vs. Patrimoine: Again and Beyond, in: Sara Marini (ed.), Heritage. Orchestra Rehearsal, Venice: Bruno 2017, 58-75; Giorgia Aquilar, La città imperfetta. Architetture di sovvertimento urbano, PhD Thesis in Urban Design, Università degli Studi di Napoli Federico II, 2013.

T O M A V E R M A E T E ist Professor für Geschichte und Theorie des Städtebaus am Institut für Geschichte und Theorie der Architektur (gta) der ETH Zürich. Seine Forschung konzentriert sich auf die sich verändernden Rollen, Ansätze und Werkzeuge von Architekten und Stadtplanern aus einer interkulturellen Perspektive. | Tom Avermaete is Professor for the History and Theory of Urban Design at the Institute for the History and Theory of Architecture (gta) of the ETH Zurich. His research focuses on the changing roles, approaches and tools of architects and urban designers from a cross-cultural perspective. | Ausgewählte Publikationen | selected publications: Tom Avermaete/Rajesh Heynickx, Making a New World, Leuven University Press 2012; Tom Avermaete/Mark Swenarton/Dirk Van Den Heuvel (eds.), Architecture of the Welfare State, New York: Routhledge 2014; Tom Avermaete/Maristella Casciato, Casablanca - Chandigarh: A Report on Modernization, Zürich: Park Books 2014

K A T J A B E N F E R ist Professorin für Darstellung in der Landschaftsarchitektur am Institut für Landschaftsarchitektur der Fakultät für Architektur und Landschaft Hannover. Studium der Landschaftsarchitektur an der Universität Kassel. Lehrtätigkeit an der TU Berlin und der Universität Kassel. Seit 2003 eigenes Büro in Partnerschaft mit Prof. Ulrike Böhm und Dr. Cyrus Zahiri. | Katja Benfer is Professor of Landscape Architecture at the Institute of Landscape Architecture of the Faculty of Architecture and Landscape Hannover. Studied landscape architecture at the University of Kassel. Teaching at the TU Berlin and the University of Kassel. Since 2003 own office in partnership with Prof. Ulrike Böhm and Dr. Cyrus Zahiri.
C Y R U S Z A H I R I ist Dr.-Ing. Architekt. Studium der Architektur an der TU Berlin. 2012 Promotion zum Phänomen der Unschärfe im städtebaulichen Entwurf. Von 2013 bis 2015 Vertretungsprofessor für Städtebau an der Universität Kassel. Seit 2003 eigenes Büro in Partnerschaft mit Prof. Ulrike Böhm und Prof. Katja Benfer. | Cyrus Zahiri is Dr.-Ing. Architect. Studied architecture at the TU Berlin. Doctorate on the phenomenon of fuzziness in urban design in 2012. Professor of Urban Design at the University of Kassel from 2013 to 2015. Since 2003 office in partnership with Ulrike Böhm and Katja Benfer. Numerous lectures at symposia on architecture and landscape as well as design. | Ausgewählte Publikationen | selected publications: Katja Benfer/Ulrike Böhm/Cyrus Zahiri, Von Grau zu Grün. Grüne Infrastruktur, Lemgo: Dorothea Rohn 2017; Katja Benfer/Ulrike Böhm/Cyrus Zahiri, DIY Beijing. Fluid Spaces, Lemgo: Dorothea Rohn 2017; Katja Benfer/Ulrike Böhm/Cyrus Zahiri, The Design Process. Between imagination, implementation and evaluation, in: Amsterdam European League of Institutes of the Arts: Designing Design Education. Proceedings part 1, Designtrain congress, Amsterdam: 2008, 42-56

M A R G I T T A B U C H E R T Leibniz Universität Hannover, ist Professorin für Architektur und Kunst 20./21. Jahrhundert am Institut für Geschichte und Theorie der Architektur an der Fakultät für Architektur und Landschaft. Lehrinhalte fokussieren Architekturtheorie, Entwurfstheorie, Grundlagen der Gestaltung sowie Spannweiten der Moderne. Forschungsschwerpunkte bilden ‚Reflexives Entwerfen', ‚Urbane Architektur' sowie Ästhetik und Kontextualität von Architektur, Kunst, Stadt und Natur. | Margitta Buchert, Leibniz Universität Hannover, is professor in Architecture and Art 20th/21st Centuries at the Institute of History and Theory of Architecture in the Faculty of Architecture and Landscape Sciences. Contents focus on architectural theory, design theory, and design principles. The primary fields of research are 'reflexive design', 'urban architecture', as well as the aesthetics and contextuality of architecture, art, cities, and nature. | Auswahl an Publikationen | selected publications: Bigness and Porosity, in: Sophie Wolfrum et al. (ed.), Porous City. From Metaphor to Urban Agenda, Berlin u.a.: Birkhäuser 2018, 84-88; Margitta Buchert (ed.), Praktiken reflexiven Entwerfens, Berlin: Jovis 2016; Margitta Buchert (ed.), Reflexives Entwerfen. Reflexive Design, Berlin: Jovis 2014; Margitta Buchert/Laura Kienbaum (eds.), Einfach Entwerfen. Simply Design, Berlin: Jovis 2013; Formen der Relation. Entwerfen und Forschen in der Architektur, in: Ute Frank et al. (eds.), EKLAT, Berlin: Universitätsverlag 2011, 76-86; Mobile und Stabile, in: Anett Zinsmeister (ed.), Gestalt der Bewegung. Figure of motion, Berlin: Jovis 2011, 50-73; Margitta Buchert/Carl Zillich (eds.), Performativ? Architektur und Kunst, Berlin: Jovis 2007.

I S A B E L M A R I A F I N K E N B E R G E R ist Freie Stadtplanerin AKBW und Dipl.-Ing. Architektur. Nach Stationen in Hamburg, Berlin, London, Stuttgart und Sydney bearbeitet sie seit 2009 mit ihrem Kölner Büro STUDIO if+ Projekte an der Schnittstelle von Planung, Forschung, künstlerischer Praxis und Lehre. Von 2015-2017 leitete sie mit der Regisseurin Eva-Maria Baumeister das Pilotprojekt der Nationalen Stadtentwicklungspolitik des Bundes ‚Die Stadt von der anderen Seite sehen' am Schauspiel Köln. Seit 2018 ist sie Prof.-Vertr. an der Hochschule Ostwestfalen-Lippe am Lehrgebiet Städtebau, Stadt- und Regionalentwicklung. | Isabel Maria Finkenberger is an urban planner and architect. After stops in Hamburg, Berlin, London, Stuttgart and Sydney she is working with her Cologne based office STUDIO if+ on projects between urban planning, research, artistic practice and teaching. 2015-2017 she curated, together with the theatre director Eva-Maria Baumeister, the pilot project of the German programme 'National Urban Development Policy' 'Die Stadt von der anderen Seite sehen' at the Schauspiel Köln. Since 2018 she is visiting professor for Urban Planning, Urban and Regional Development at the University of Applied Sciences Ostwestfalen-Lippe. | Auswahl Publikationen | selected publications: Isabel Finkenberger/Eva-Maria Baumeister, Working in between: Die Stadt

von der anderen Seite sehen. Where Urban Planning Meets Artistic Practice, in: Hilke Marit Berger/Gesa Ziemer (eds.), New Stakeholders of Urban Change, Hamburg: Jovis 2017 119-129; Isabel Finkenberger/Christoph Schlaich, Mehr als Wohnen. Vom Zusammenleben in integrierten Nachbarschaften, in: Bonn: APuZ 20-21 Wohnen (2014) 46-52; BU Wuppertal (Hrsg.), Nospolis. Räume gemeinsamer Zukünfte. Dokumentation, Wuppertal 2014

OLE W. FISCHER ist Theoretiker, Historiker, Kurator und Architekt. Seit 2011 berufen an der School of Architecture der University of Utah, Salt Lake City, für Geschichte und Theorie der Architektur, zuerst als Assistant Professor, seit 2017 als Associate Professor. Gastprofessor im Herbst 2009 an RISD, im Frühjahr 2010 an MIT und im Sommer 2015 an der TU Wien, im Frühjahr 2018 Gastwissenschaftler an der FU und TU Berlin (sabbatical). 2002–08 wissenschaftlicher Mitarbeiter am Institut für Geschichte und Theorie der Architektur der ETH Zürich, 2008 Dissertation über die programmatische Übertragung der Philosophie Friedrich Nietzsches in Theorie und Werk Henry van de Veldes. | Ole W. Fischer is a theorist, historian, curator and architect. Since 2011 appointed to the School of Architecture at the University of Utah, Salt Lake City, for History and Theory of Architecture, first as Assistant Professor, since 2017 as Associate Professor. Visiting professor at RISD in autumn 2009, at MIT in spring 2010, and at the TU Vienna in summer 2015, guest re-searcher at the FU and TU Berlin in spring 2018 (sabbatical). 2002-08 research assistant at the Institute for History and Theory of Architecture at ETH Zurich, 2008 dissertation on the programmatic transfer of Friedrich Nietzsche's philosophy into the theory and work of Henry van de Velde. | Auswahl an Publikationen | selected publications: Ole W. Fischer (ed.), peer-reviewed Journals Dialectic VI: Craft, San Francisco: Oro Editions 2018; Ole W. Fischer, Nietzsches Schatten, Berlin: Gebr. Mann 2012; Cordula Rau/Eberhard Tröger/Ole W. Fischer (eds.), Sehnsucht - The Book of Architectural Longings, Wien: Springer 2010; Ole W. Fischer/Àkos Moravánszky (ed.), Precisions - Architecture between Sciences and the Arts, Berlin: Jovis 2008.

HILDE LÉON gründete 1987 mit Konrad Wohlhage (†2007) das Büro léonwohlhage Architekten. Seit 2000 ist sie Professorin am Institut für Entwerfen und Gebäudelehre der Leibniz Universität Hannover. 2002 war sie Generalkommissarin des Deutschen Pavillons der Architekturbiennale in Venedig und von 2008 bis 2010 Mitglied im Hochschulrat der Hafencity Universität (HCU) in Hamburg, deren Neugründung sie begleitete. Mitglied in den Gestaltungsbeiräten der Städte Salzburg und Berlin sowie der Akademie der Künste Berlin. Von 2008 bis 2012 beriet Hilde Léon die Bausenatorin Regula Lüscher im Berliner Baukollegium. | Hilde Léon and founded the office léonwohlhage Architekten with Konrad

Wohlhage (†2007) in 1987. Since 2000 she is professor at the Institute of Design and Building Theory at Leibniz Universität Hannover. In 2002 she was General Commissioner of the German Pavilion at the Architecture Biennale in Venice and from 2008 to 2010 she was a member of the University Council of Hafencity University (HCU) in Hamburg. She is also a member of the design advisory boards of the cities of Salzburg and Berlin and the Berlin Academy of the Arts. From 2008 to 2012 Hilde Léon advised the building senator Regula Lüscher in the Berliner Baukollegium. | Auswahl Publikationen | selected publications: Hilde Léon/Marc-Philip Reichwald/Peter-Karsten Schultz (eds.), Der kontrollierte Größenwahn. Über die Ambivalenz beim Entwerfen, Ostfildern: Hatje Cantz 2011; Hilde Léon (ed.), NEXTliegend, at hand, in-mediato, Ausstellungskatalog der Biennale Venedig, 8. Internationale Architekturausstellung, Berlin: Gebr. Mann 2002; Kristin Feireiss (ed.), Hilde Léon und Konrad Wohlhage. Berliner Projekte. Ausstellungskatalog, Galerie Aedes, Berlin 1992

ANDREAS NÜTTEN ist Architekt und Dozent für Kulturlandschaft an der FHNW in Basel. 2001-2006 wissenschaftliche Mitarbeit am Institut Landschaft und Garten an der TH Karlsruhe. Selbstständige praktische und beratende Tätigkeit im Bereich landschaftsbasierter Städtebau. 2008-2012 Zusammenarbeit mit yellow z Zürich Urbanism Architecture. Seit 2012 Dozent für Kulturlandschaft an der FHNW in Basel. Laufende Dissertation ‚Landschaftsmetropole' an der TU München bei Prof. Dr. Udo Weilacher. Seit 2017 Lehrbeauftragter an der TU München innerhalb des internationalen Doktorandenkollegs ‚Forschungslabor Raum'. | Andreas Nütten is an architect and lecturer in cultural landscape at the Institute of Architecture at the University of applied sciences of Northern Switzerland (FHNW) in Basel. 2001–2006 scientific assistant at the Institute of Landscape and Garden at TH Karlsruhe. Practitioner in the field of landscape-based urban design. 2008-2012 cooperation with yellow z Urbanism Architecture in Zurich. Since 2012 lecturer in cultural landscape at the FHNW in Basel. Ongoing PhD Project 'Landscape Metropolis' at the TU Munich with Prof. Dr. Udo Weilacher. Since 2017 teaching at TU Munich within the international doctoral college 'Spatial Research Lab'. | Ausgewählte Publikationen | selected publications: Andreas Nütten/Dominique Salathé, Mehrwert Landschaft, Muttenz: Fachhochschule Nordwestschweiz (FHNW), Hochschule für Architektur, Bau und Geomatik, Institut Architektur 2016; Andreas Nütten, Kunstquartier als Impulsgeber, in: Garten + Landschaft 09/2016, 30-33 München: Callwey 2016; Oliver Bormann/Martin Diekmann/Andreas Nütten/Julian Petrin/Christian Scheler/Guido Spars, Team Zwischenstadt: Die Gartenstadt als ganzheitliches Nachhaltigkeitskonzept, in: BBSR (ed.), Gartenstadt 21 Grün – Urban – Vernetzt, Band 2, Bonn: BBSR 2017

C A R O L I N E V O E T ist Mitbegründerin des preisgekrönten Architekturbüros Voet en De Brabandere in Antwerpen, Belgien. Ihre Schwerpunkte liegen in der Rekonstruktion und Gestaltung von Kulturbauten, öffentlichen Innenräumen, Szenografie und Möbeln. Sie ist Assistenzprofessorin an der KU Leuven, Fakultät für Architektur, Campus St-Lucas Gent und Brüssel, wo sie 2013 über die Arbeit von Dom Hans van der Laan promovierte. Ihr Forschungs- und Lehrschwerpunkt liegt im Bereich der räumlichen Systematik und Architekturmethodik und wurde u.a. in ARQ und Interiors Routledge veröffentlicht. | Caroline Voet is co-founder of the award winning architectural practice Voet en De Brabandere in Antwerp, Belgium. She focuses on reconversions and the design of cultural buildings, public interiors, scenography and furniture. She is assistant professor at the KU Leuven, Faculty of Architecture, Campus St-Lucas Ghent and Brussels, where she received her Ph.D. in 2013 on the work of Dom Hans van der Laan. Her research and teaching focus is on spatial systematic and architectural methodology and has been published in for example ARQ and Interiors Routledge. | Ausgewählte Publikationen | selected publications: Sofie De Caigny/Lara Schrijver/Katrien Vandermarliere/Carolin Voet (eds.), Autonomous Architecture in Flanders, Leuven University Press 2017; Caroline Voet, Dom Hans van der Laan. A House for the Mind, Antwerpen: VAI 2017; Caroline Voet, Dom Hans van der Laan. Tomelilla, Amsterdam: Architectura & Natura 2016

S A R A H W E H M E Y E R studierte Architektur an der Leibniz Universität Hannover und arbeitete in Architekturbüros in Münster, Winterthur und Hannover. Nach dem Master 2015 Mitarbeit bei Römeth BDA . Wagener Architekten in Hannover sowie wissenschaftliche Mitarbeit in der Abteilung a_ku (Architektur und Kunst 20./21. Jahrhundert), IGTA, der Fakultät für Architektur und Landschaft Hannover. Laufendes Promotionsvorhaben zum Thema ‚Die Collage als Praktik des forschenden Entwerfens' bei Prof. Margitta Buchert. | Sarah Wehmeyer studied architecture at Leibniz University Hannover and worked in architectural offices in Münster, Winterthur and Hannover. After the master's degree 2015 cooperation with Römeth BDA . Wagener Architects in Hanover and scientific assistance in the department a_ku (Architecture and Art 20th/21st century), IGTA, the Faculty of Architecture and Landscape Hannover. Current dissertation on 'Collage as a practice of research-oriented design' with Prof. Margitta Buchert.

„Denn Erkennen ist weder passive Kontemplation noch Erwerb einzig möglicher Einsicht im fertig Gegebenen. Es ist tätiges, lebendiges Beziehungeingehen, ein Umformen und Umgeformtwerden, kurz ein Schaffen." | 'For cognition is neither passive contemplation nor the acquisition of the only possible insight from a finished work. It is an active, vital forming of relationships, transforming and being transformed, in short: a creation.'

Ludwik Fleck

ZITATE CITATIONS

TREIBENDE KRÄFTE DRIVING FORCES: Michel Serres, Vorwort | Preface, in: Elemente einer Geschichte der Wissenschaften, Frankfurt/Main: Suhrkamp 1994, 11-36, 35 VERSCHRÄNKUNGEN ENTANGLEMENTS: Bryan Lawson, What Designers Know, Amsterdam et al.: Elsevier/Architectural Press 2004, 3 TRANSFORMATION TRANSFORMATION: Rem Koolhaas, in: Brett Steele (ed.), Supercritical. Peter Eisenman & Rem Koolhaas, London 2010, 13 APPENDIX: Ludwik Fleck, Zur Krise der ‚Wirklichkeit', in: Die Naturwissenschaften 17 (1929) 425-430, 425

ABBILDUNGENS LIST OF ILLUSTRATIONS

LÉON: **1-2** Stephan Huber **3-4** Dani Karavan, Duisburg, Fotos | photos: Margitta Buchert **5** Qin Yufen, Schwartzsche Villa Berlin, Foto | photo: Hilde Léon **6** Qin Yufen, Staatsgalerie Stuttgart **7** Gerda Steiner & Jörg Lenzlinger, Chiesa San Staë, Biennale Venedig **8** Fotos | photos: Hilde Léon BENFER: **1-21** bbzl böhm benfer zahiri VOET: **1-3** Caroline Voet **4-11** Voet en De Brabandere **12** Foto | photo: Ans Brys FISCHER: **1** Eisenman Architects New York, NY, USA **2-9** Preston Scott Cohen Inc., Cambridge, MA, USA WEHMEYER: **1-5** OFFICE Kersten Geers David Van Severen **6-7** DOGMA **8** OFFICE Kersten Geers David Van Severen NÜTTEN: **1-14** Andreas Nütten AVERMAETE: **1** Phototheque Ecole Nationales d'Architecture de Rabat **2** GAMMA: Groupe d'Architectes Modernes Marocains; Phototheque Ecole Nationales d'Architecture de Rabat **3** Het Nieuwe Instituut Rotterdam **4-7** Phototheque Ecole Nationales d'Architecture de Rabat AQUILAR: **1** Nieder-Österreichische Landes-, Heil- und Pflegeanstalt für Geistes- und Nervenkranke ‚Am Steinhof' in Wien **2** Niederösterreichisches Landesarchiv, Box F5, Landes-Registratur 1973-1904, 1.2/n. no. 66813 **3-11** Giorgia Aquilar FINKENBERGER: **1-2** Isabel Maria Finkenberger **3-8** Martin Miseré, Mirko Plengemeyer, Ana Lukenda, Dana Kurz **9-10** Ana Lukenda **11-13** Martin Miseré, Mirko Plengemeyer, Ana Lukenda **14-16** Ana Lukenda **17** Mirko Plengemeyer **18** Vera Lisakowski

Impressum

Herausgeberin Editor: Margitta Buchert,
Architektur und Kunst 20./21. Jahrhundert Architecture and Art 20th/21st Centuries,
Leibniz Universität Hannover Leibniz University Hanover,
www.igt-arch.uni-hannover.de/a_ku

Übersetzungen Translations: Lynne Kolar-Thompson, Steffen Bösenberg
Gestaltung Design: Margitta Buchert, Julian Benny Hung, Hannover
Satz Setting: Julian Benny Hung, Hannover
Lithographie Lithography: Bild1Druck, Berlin
Druck und Bindung Printing and Binding: GRASPO CZ, a.s., Zlín

Bibliographische Information der Deutschen Bibliothek
Bibliographic information published by Deutsche Nationalbibliothek:
Die Deutsche Nationalbibliothek verzeichnet diese Publikation in der Deutschen Nationalbibliographie; detaillierte bibliographische Daten sind im Internet über http://dnb.ddb.de abrufbar.
The Deutsche Nationalbibliothek lists this publication in Deutsche Nationalbibliografie; detailed bibliographic data are available on the Internet at http//dnb.d-nb.de.

jovis Verlag
Kurfürstenstraße 15/16
10785 Berlin

www.jovis.de

ISBN 978-3-86859-558-1